Our Brother's Keeper

Our Brother's Keeper

The Life of Sam Israel

Richard S. Hobbs

FOREWORD
by Rabbi Rob Toren

When the Samis Foundation Board of Trustees began its work shortly after Samuel Israel passed in 1994, they decided they were content to continue Sam's understated image. Sam's legacy in the real estate community was complicated, and he did not seek recognition for his philanthropy during his lifetime, and neither did the foundation, at first.

In 2010, the board and staff leadership began to ask themselves whether the Samis Foundation should be more proactive in communicating its work and, if so, to what end. The board gradually moved in the direction of greater visibility, to encourage or inspire others of means to become donors, to enlist funding partners for its causes, and ultimately, to inspire others with Samis's missions and vision.

As part of this visibility discussion, the Samis leadership revisited the topic of Sam Israel's personal story and legacy and discussed writing a biography of Sam. Stories were out there, but how many of them were true? To many, Sam Israel was a complicated and reclusive real estate mogul; to others, he was an outgoing and generous philanthropist. Given that no biography can ever be all-inclusive, on what would this biography focus? Were we writing this biography for a specific reason and audience in mind?

FOREWORD

Samis Board of Trustees, 2006. From top left, Irwin Treiger, Barry Ernstoff, Al Maimon, Ernie Sherman, Jerome O. Cohen, Eli Almo, Eli Genauer, Victor Alhadeff; front row, Mike Israel, David Friedenberg, Dave Azose, Lucy Pruzan, Eddie Hasson, Rabbi William H. Greenberg, and Dr. Alex Sytman. Missing from photo Morris Piha and Martin Selig. Photo © Rick Dahms.

An important and entirely practical impetus to moving ahead with this project was the fact that many who knew Sam had either recently passed or were approaching an age at which this was increasingly likely. Memories of Sam would disappear and with them the roots of the Samis Foundation. As you will read in the pages that follow, Sam appointed a group of sixteen trustees for lifetime terms, exceedingly rare in the philanthropy world. Five of those original trustees have died. The board has appointed new ones to take their place, not for lifetime terms, which is limited to the original sixteen. Most of the original sixteen knew Sam, but few of the recently appointed ones did. How important is it for trustees to know something of Sam, his story, how he amassed his wealth, and the reasons for his passionate commitment to the

Jewish people and the State of Israel? How important is it to understand the foundation's roots and Sam Israel's personal values and wishes?

These questions in turn relate to the age-old philosophical debate regarding the study of the past. The conventional reason given for studying the past is that it helps us understand our present, which is, at best, partially true. To cut oneself off from the past, or to purge that past of unpleasantness, is to rob oneself of the richness and complexity of human life. The concept in Judaism of *zakhor* (זכור, or "remember") is one of the most powerful and ubiquitous in our tradition. Not only are the sources for remembering and retelling the past innumerable, but their ubiquity is only exceeded by the importance attached to remembering and telling of this past.

I suggest that there are additional purposes for this undertaking:

1. To convey to new trustees the Samis roots. Who was Sam Israel? Why did he become a philanthropist? What were some of his most cherished beliefs? How has the foundation carried on his wishes and, in some instances, departed from or enriched them?
2. To once again demonstrate the paradigmatic American immigrant success story. The success of this great nation is inseparable from the immigrant experience.
3. To appreciate, if not embrace, the fascinating connections between an eccentric but hardworking, opinionated individualist and his passionate devotion to his people and their traditions. You will read how Sam had inscribed on his headstone the words of a psalm, for the simple reason that he loved the Sephardic melody when it was sung on Passover Seder night.
4. To learn the lesson of Jewish Sephardic pride. Sam's immense pride led to his deepening appreciation for the value of Jewish education, which he did not receive as a youngster growing up in impoverished early twentieth-century Rhodes.

Doubtless readers of this biography will add to the reasons why this record is important. With nearly $100 million in philanthropy since the formation of the Samis Foundation, Sam's legacy continues to be a blessing for Jewish communities of Washington State and the State of Israel. May this book inspire others to follow Sam Israel's lead in ensuring the continuity of the Jewish community.

PREFACE

Without memory, there is no culture.
Without memory, there would be no civilization,
no society, no future.

—Elie Wiesel

NIZKOR, "LET US REMEMBER"

Samuel Israel, or "Sam," as he liked to be called, had an amazing memory. He could recite by heart numerous poems. He could remember details of buildings on Seattle streets decades after he moved away from the city. He loved history and archaeology, and he especially loved to *talk* about history—his personal stories, as well as Jewish history and, later in life, Israel and its history. He was widely known for his love of his family; his love for acquiring property; his love for photography, hunting, and hiking; and his love for the natural world. He valued education, though he himself had little formal schooling.

As Sam aged, he became more conscious of the fact that he had no children, no heirs, and he wanted what he loved and valued to thrive and to be remembered. He started the Samis Foundation to realize his lifelong ambitions to enhance the quality of Jewish life and to ensure the continuity of the Jewish people. The foundation represented, in effect, the repository for his memory and a way to carry on his dreams.

History, as a special form of remembering, offers a curious collage of our collective pasts, an unending, constantly shifting panorama. Like a great

Sam and Boy Scouts at his 90th birthday celebration, February 12, 1989.

flowing river, an individual's history begins with a single day, and every day after collects into a small trickle that, over months and years, joins the streams of many others, eventually becoming a river so massive that all of the rivulets and streams lose their individuality as they merge into one. Sam Israel's life grew into a mighty river, a unique history well worth remembering.

Author Lesli Koppelman Ross notes, "It is memory that has allowed us to last through thousands of years of history. Our religion and our people are founded on the collective memory of revelation at Sinai. Scripture throughout commands us to remember." That instruction is important for honoring the memory of individual victims of the Holocaust, as well as its larger cultural context, and also indicates a broader, practical value of remembering—it must function as a positive force, or, as Ross notes, a "positive context for purposeful living."[1]

Sam lived his Sephardic Jewish identity and Rhodesli history, honoring the generations that preceded him. In doing so, he created his own positive context for purposeful living, preserving the past and laying a strong foundation for the generations that followed him.

PREFACE

ABOUT WORDS AND SOURCES

While this book centers on the life of Sam Israel, the reader will find a number of other prominent individuals in the story who left bright marks along their way. The focus is driven by one central factor: the limited available archival sources. We have the stories—the memories—of living family members, friends, and colleagues, plus a modest trove of documents and photographs, that provide landmarks on the course of Sam's river over the last century. The surviving historical documents that reveal his traits, temperament, thoughts on issues, faith, and philosophy are relatively few. One of the largest resources is newspaper articles. Sam did not seek, nor did he mind, publicity. His first notice in the print media appeared when he joined a YMCA climbing group that scaled Mount Rainier in 1925. Thanks to Sam's combative attitude toward government taxation and overzealous bureaucrats, his dislike of being told what to do by anyone, and his substantial property holdings, we have newspaper articles with facts about and quotes from Sam scattered across five decades, until his death in 1994. Several journalists wrote short profiles of Sam toward the end of his life (when Sam was in his mid-eighties), and one television journalist managed to interview Sam in the course of reporting on housing issues in Seattle.

We also have a handful of Sam's letters, both outgoing and incoming. These contain important event documentation, as well as glimpses of Sam's unique and colorful ways of expressing himself, like the time he wrote to a physician and apologized for involving the man "in this SKATA (that's Greek for shit)." Sam's nephew Eddie Hasson was instrumental in securing some three dozen letters written to Sam by friends, girlfriends, and cousins between 1937 and 1942. The correspondence provides wonderful windows into the lives of Sam and the letter writers, like the young woman who asked, "Are you still swimming in your icy cold lake? . . . Are you still seeing your nice fat Swedish girl?"

Sam Israel was not particularly a keeper of documents, but he did retain (probably with the aid of several secretaries over the years) legal and financial files, as well as property-related records generated by Samis Land Company. Among the litigation files, one of Sam's court depositions contains brief but valuable comments on his youth in Rhodes and early real estate ventures. While archival records relating to Sam's personal life are few, fortunately, there is a wealth of oral history interviews in the Samis Foundation's archives—video interviews by Stephen Sadis of some members of Sam's family, colleagues, and foundation trustees, plus more than a dozen interviews I conducted with Eddie Hasson. Their testimonies are

Watercolor painting of Cascade Market c. 1970s by Leatrice "Lucy" Sytman. Her father, Nissim, was a partner in the store.

wonderfully revealing, providing insights that help us understand the choices and actions that Sam took over the years.

The historical materials retained by Sam, then by his nephews and other family members, and finally by the Samis Foundation represent a small treasure trove of records dating roughly from the early 1900s to the early 1990s—business records, correspondence, scrapbooks, newspaper clippings, Sam's home movies (dating roughly from the 1930s to the 1960s), and photographs. (The photographs of Sam's early years are relatively few, yet they provide fascinating views into Sam's life and times.) The narrative here provides a general historical flow of events in Sam's life and the threads that connect the various episodes and stories. The book may be seen as an impressionist painting; we have to step back to gain a broader perspective, to see the splay of colors coalesce and reveal a clearer view of the person and his movements, interactions, failures, and triumphs. Hopefully, the result is a better understanding of and appreciation for the breadth and complexity of Sam's personality and his unique sojourn on the planet.

The Samis Foundation's dedication to and affection for Sam Israel's memory, their sense of Jewish identity, and their commitment to the Jewish community have made this book possible. While not every piece of historical data about Sam Israel has found a place in this short history, each remains a sacred trust in the legacy he and his family passed to the foundation and to younger generations.

ACKNOWLEDGMENTS

Sam Israel lived more than nine decades, and in the course of his amazing journey, he touched many lives. Weaving the multitude of colorful threads that tell his story into a coherent pattern is a work that proceeds only with the help of a host of people. I extend my sincere appreciation to all who supported this project in large and small ways.

First among those who graciously offered time and information is Eddie Hasson, one of Sam's nephews. He has been a constant inspiration, guiding spirit, and enthusiastic contributor to the research and the words found in these pages. Sharing this project with Eddie has been the brightest highlight among my many memorable experiences while developing Sam's story.

Rabbi Rob Toren, during his tenure as executive director of the Samis Foundation, was a thoughtful and wise steward of the enterprise. I am indebted to him for his insights, probing questions, and encouragement, all of which improved the quality of the manuscript.

My colleague and friend Howard Droker has been an exemplary and supportive critic. He is an exceptional man, an earnest and skilled historian, and a rock in any storm.

ACKNOWLEDGMENTS

Sam, c. 1985.

Staff at the Samis Foundation deserve a mighty nod of appreciation. First in those ranks is Peggy Longeway, who endured my endless emails and queries, always responding with a smile and can-do effort that measurably improved the information gathering. My special thanks to Adam Hasson, director of real estate at the foundation, for taking time to review the manuscript and to answer a barrage of inquiries, thereby enhancing the research and earning my heartfelt gratitude. Connie Kanter, chief executive officer, offered a sharp editorial eye and kind voice of encouragement as the manuscript evolved through several drafts.

Others who contributed their time, experience, and expertise, and whom I'm pleased to acknowledge, include Marilyn Hasson Henry (one of Sam's nieces); Dr. Devin Naar, chair of the Sephardic Studies Program at the University of Washington and associate professor of history and Jewish studies; Jack Hamann, award-winning journalist and producer at no little things Productions; Dr. Eugene Normand; author Karen Treiger; Greg Kucera of the Greg Kucera Gallery; John Bolcer, university archivist at the University of Washington Libraries' Special Collections; Brigid Clift, archivist at the Washington State Archives' Central Regional Branch; Isaac "Ike" Azose, president of the Sephardic Traditions Foundation; the reference

ACKNOWLEDGMENTS

staff at the Seattle Public Library; Ashley Mead at the Seattle Art Museum; Theresa Bennett Scheib at Patrick Real Estate in Ephrata, Washington; Bonnie Holt Morehouse of Soap Lake; Kim Jorgensen and other staff at the *Grant County Journal*; and finally, Penny Miller, Kim Erickson, and Canan Bolel, who provided technical assistance.

I have benefitted enormously from the work of a small but significant cadre of committed scholars, including Aron Hasson, Dr. Devin Naar, and Rabbi Marc D. Angel, who have published works that are growing our body of

Documents and letters from Sam's personal files.

knowledge about the history of Sephardic Jews and Rhodes. I offer special thanks to Aron Hasson, founder of the nonprofit Rhodes Jewish Historical Foundation in Los Angeles, who graciously contributed photos and his expertise to this project. His work in preserving the history of the Jews of Rhodes is of extraordinary value for Sephardic communities everywhere and for all who appreciate their contributions to world culture.

It is a pleasure to acknowledge my debt to members of the Samis Foundation Board of Trustees for their willingness to undertake this venture. Their support and insightful review of early versions of the manuscript substantially improved the breadth and accuracy of the narrative. In particular, I wish to thank those who contributed stories and critiques of this work: Victor Alhadeff, Eli Almo, David Azose, Dana Behar, Jerome O. Cohen, Barry Ernstoff, Eli Genauer, Eddie Hasson, Al Maimon, Lucy Pruzan, Greg Roer, Ernie Sherman, Dr. Alex Sytman, and former board member Martin Selig.

Dr. Yossi Leshem, professor of zoology on the faculty of life sciences at Tel Aviv University and founder and director of the International Center for the Study of Bird Migration in Latrun, Israel, deserves special recognition for contributing a story about Sam Israel and the Samis Foundation, without which this narrative would not have been complete—thank you, Dr. Leshem.

Finally, and most of all, I wish to thank Sam Israel, whose memory serves as a daily blessing. The role of author in leading this enterprise of remembering Sam's stories is an honor.

INTRODUCTION

Opposite: Sam, c. 1980.

Haz bien, y no mires con quien.
(Do good, and don't care about with whom.)

—Sephardic proverb[1]

FROM SHOEMAKER TO MILLIONAIRE

Sam Israel is one of the most original, controversial, and little-known immigrants ever to land in Seattle. Despite his importance in regional and state history, few have heard of him. He wanted it that way. To his family and friends, he was the revered "Uncle Sam," but to most others, he remained a mystery. He never married and, after the age of sixty-one, lived alone in a humble shack. Yet his reputation as an ill-tempered recluse and wealthy absentee landlord who left his buildings in dilapidated condition earned him various tags, including "the Howard Hughes of Washington State" and "the ultimate eccentric." At the time of his death in 1994, he owned more than five hundred properties, including dozens of buildings in Seattle and thousands of acres of land in western and eastern Washington valued at more than $40 million. Scorned by developers and admired by preservationists, he was credited for protecting much of Seattle's historic architecture.

The story of Sam Israel's rise from immigrant shoemaker to multimillionaire is as uncommon as it is fascinating, and yet, in many ways, it is the quintessentially American tale of the immigrant who arrives with no

English, applies himself to a trade, and in the course of his years, amasses a sizable fortune. Born into a Sephardic Jewish family in Rhodes in 1899, Sam emigrated to the United States at the age of twenty. He came from a cultural universe—a small Sephardic family and community with centuries-old roots in Rhodes, perched on the edge of the decaying Ottoman Empire, a world circumscribed by family, friends, and synagogue—vastly different from the one he found in Seattle in 1919. As a young and ambitious immigrant, Sam knew four languages but not a word of English. He learned quickly, and in the years from the end of World War I to the end of World War II, he enjoyed a heady range of successes, establishing a shoe repair business that yielded profits enough to invest in local real estate. At the beginning of World War II, he landed a contract with the US Army to repair boots, and by 1946, he had acquired more than two dozen properties in Seattle, many of which later became historic landmarks in downtown and Pioneer Square.

Sam; the photo appears on his "Declaration of Alien About to Depart for the United States," September 25, 1919.

Sam's most productive mature years, 1946 to 1973, were marked by his move to Soap Lake in 1961 and a substantial accumulation of properties on both sides of the Cascades that made him the largest private property owner in Washington State. He came to the attention of the press, thanks to fiery bouts with bureaucrats and court cases that provided a public arena for him to exercise the full force of his opinions and wealth.

Although marriage eluded Sam, he was a family man. He was devoted to his parents and his siblings, nephews, and nieces, and he found ways to care for young people and affect the lives of thousands. Sam's vision of himself as a caretaker led him to create the Samis Foundation in 1979, which would serve to carry on his lifelong ambition of building an asset to be used on behalf of the Jewish people of Washington State and Israel, to fund archaeology and wildlife projects in Israel, and to provide assistance to victims of natural disasters around the world. To this day, the Samis Foundation trustees are guided by Sam's vibrant spirit and his commitment to Jewish education and sound business.

A MAN OF MANY NAMES

In the course of his nine decades, Sam Israel garnered a host of nicknames and appellations. He was a deeply patriotic American, as many immigrants are, and he was equally passionate about the Promised Land, Israel. He fully embraced his identity as a Jew and took great nourishment from his Sephardic roots and Jewish culture. Sam, like other Sephardim, considered his beliefs, traditions, and customs as the original and standard way of fulfilling a commandment. Thus, he described himself as Orthodox, meaning, in essence, his worldview was that of a Sephardic Jew, shaped by his family, community, and the culture of late nineteenth- to early twentieth-century Rhodes. At the same time, he was "never one to go to synagogue," in the words of his nephew Eddie Hasson, and in other ways not rigorously observant. He felt strongly about and followed some Sephardic traditions and was comfortable ignoring others, like the time he celebrated Passover a week early because favorite family members happened to be with him at his farm.

Some descriptions of Sam were flattering, while others were not, sometimes bordering on anti-Semitic. He was a bold, forceful personality with strong opinions. At times, he was confrontational, controlling, and controversial. He embodied a directness and honesty that endeared him to many, though he could be impatient and brusque in a way that put off many, including family members. He was also a private man at heart, and few outside of his family and a handful of friends knew him well. Some of Sam's neighbors in Soap Lake and Ephrata admired, appreciated, and befriended him, while a handful called him crazy or a kook.

Many names for Sam were associated with his property business: the prince of parcels, the collector, real estate tycoon, land mogul, low-rent Sam, slumlord, miserly landlord, the bane of neighborhood developers, and the Howard Hughes of Washington State. Even adversaries in the real estate business conceded, however, that Sam was always a man of his word. Colleagues, business associates, zealous journalists, and others wrote him off as an oddball, a colorful loner, a recluse, or a perplexing mix of craftiness and eccentricity. He was a genuine character, which sometimes obscured the elemental goodness of his heart; his temper often masked the breadth of his generosity and the depth of his compassion for fellow humans.

In part because he preferred to keep to himself, most people's notions about Sam Israel were of a one-dimensional caricature. Sam's description of himself is telling: "I am a simple man. I do not need luxuries." In fact, two key features of his personality are etched on his headstone: "A Shoemaker" and "For We Are Our Brother's Keeper."

A MAN OF CHARACTER

During the seventy-five years Sam lived in America, he remained grounded in the simple life he knew as a Jew in Rhodes. His values of honesty and diligence, pride in his Jewish heritage, and love of Israel were at the core of his being. He expressed this in various ways during his lifetime, from playing in a Jewish folk band to providing financial support to the Jewish community. Yet Sam, like other Jews, led a life of "delicate balance," as some have termed it, on the one hand maintaining the unique system of beliefs and traditions passed down through generations, and at the same time participating as a citizen of the larger society, even playing a significant role in Washington State, mainly Seattle, Puget Sound, and Grant County.

Sam's personality displayed an array of qualities not often found in a single individual. He was at once humble and determined to have his way. He trusted few people, and as time went by, his distrust verged toward paranoia that he might be kidnapped or killed for his money or possessions. Sam was emotional and could be impatient and quick to anger, sometimes blasting a brother, a nephew, or a stranger with a brutally harsh outburst. He could be capricious and distractible, launching projects with great enthusiasm, then dropping them after a few days or weeks. Yet he also possessed enormous persistence, especially when it came to things that mattered to him, such as lawsuits and philanthropic ventures, and he had both the resources and determination to shape circumstances more favorably for himself, his family and friends, and any person, group, or cause he deemed worthy.

In most ways Sam was frugal, choosing a lifestyle more befitting a shoemaker than a millionaire, though he didn't hesitate to spend money on "luxuries" meaningful to him: mainly, cameras and guns. After he moved to eastern Washington, he gave little thought to his appearance, dressing casually and comfortably around his farm, although for a photo opportunity or any public appearance, he took care to don a dapper hat, slacks, a turtleneck sweater, and a sport coat, usually wearing a prominent Star of David pendant. In Eddie Hasson's words, "He didn't care about clothing. But he had the best camera equipment in the world."[2]

A MAN OF COMMITMENT

One unvarying thread through Sam's life was his sincere dedication to the welfare of others—family members, other Jews, the Jewish homeland, young people, and the destitute. To some, Sam was warm hearted and gentle, but for those whom he greeted at his farm with a loaded shotgun and a howling pack of dogs, his inconspicuous generosity might have been surprising.

For decades, Sam contributed generously to his family and to numerous Jewish and general community organizations. The establishment of his Samis Foundation in 1979 was a culmination of his years of informal philanthropy. In the 1980s, Sam went so far as to abandon some of his reclusive habits to step out into his adopted home of Grant County—Soap Lake and Ephrata in particular—as he donated or loaned property and gave money to environmental causes and outdoor recreation. He celebrated his ninetieth birthday by giving cash to the Boy and Girl Scouts and a lecture on the biggest lesson of his life—learn to save money.

Seattle Times, Pacific Northwest Magazine, "Immigrant's Dream," April 11, 1999.

Though Sam eschewed the trappings of most wealthy Americans, he lived what can only be called an epic life by committing to something bigger than himself. As Eddie Hasson says, "He was for the common man." Indeed, Sam Israel left an indelible mark on the world by being his brother's keeper, a legacy that is powerfully embodied in the properties and works he shaped into the Samis Foundation. He brought his faith in God, his Jewish identity, and a sense of personal responsibility for Jews and non-Jews to the community and the world, and it is his generosity we recall most clearly. Connie Kanter, chief executive officer of the Samis Foundation, asks the same question of us that Sam freely lived: "When we consider life and mortality—don't we want to leave the world a better place?"[3]

CHAPTER 1
The Crucible: A Sephardic Family in Rhodes, 1899–1919

Opposite: Israel family portrait, 1911. Left to right: Nissim, Sam, Sarah (holding Bona), John, Isaac, Morris.

Quien hijo cria, ora hila.
(To beget a son is to spin gold.)

Quien no tiene hija, no tiene amiga.
(To not have a daughter is to not have a friend.)

In September 1919, young Sam Israel stood on a dock in Mandraki Harbor, the main port of the island of Rhodes for more than two thousand years. The weather was warm and sunny. Beside him were friends, the Rahamin Capouya family. Other families and friends crowded around them, anxious to board a steamship bound for Naples, Italy, the first leg on their journey to the United States. They carried luggage holding their most prized and portable family possessions, as well as money and immigration documents. They also carried a wealth of Sephardic heritage, traditions, and memories. Their paperwork was in order, but an uncertain reception awaited Jews emigrating from Rhodes. More uncertain was the future if they remained.

The journey their Sephardic ancestors made centuries earlier from Spain to Rhodes had been both successful and full of the persecutions and traumas that Jews have faced since ancient times. To leave extended family, friends, the Jewish quarter, and the island home the Israel family had known for generations was a daunting prospect. Yet Sam had the example of his older brothers, David and Jack, who had emigrated to America a decade earlier and then returned on the eve of World War I for David to be married. In 1914, David and his bride Marie, along with Jack and their

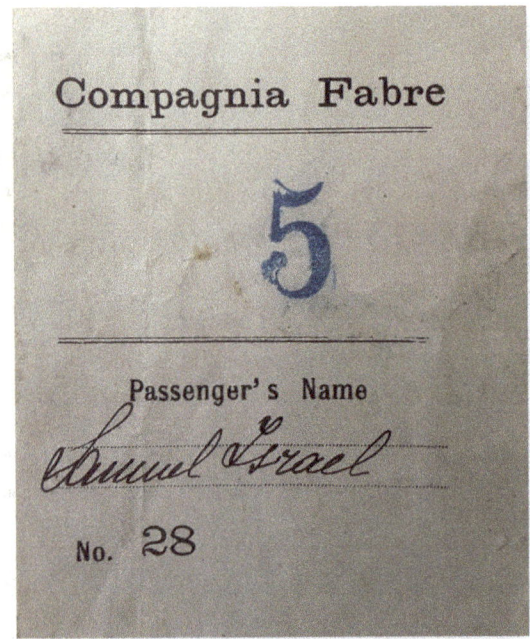

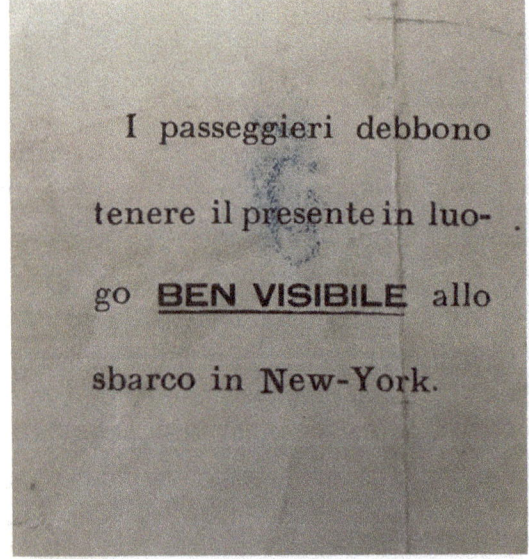

Luggage tag (front and back).

brother Morris, returned to the US. By the end of 1919, the Israel parents, Yitzhak and Sarota; brothers Nissim and Asher; and eight-year-old sister, Bona, would follow. In America, there was opportunity and hope for a better life. Sam was ready.

BEGINNINGS: RHODES SEPHARDIM—RHODESLIS

In the eastern Mediterranean, Rhodes is one of the numerous small islands in the Dodecanese group that lie amid the blue waters of the Aegean Sea. The island, now part of Greece, is known as Rodos (Greek and Turkish), Rodi (Italian), and Rodi or Rodes in Ladino (Judeo-Spanish). Despite its small size—some forty-five miles long and twenty miles wide—Rhodes has a history of singular importance in the story of Sephardic Jews. Lying a mere twelve miles southwest of the Turkish coast, Rhodes is within easy sailing distance of Greece, Egypt, and Crete. Its accessible location prompted early European travelers to visit and later extoll the island's strategic maritime military position; fine climate; forested mountains; sparkling streams; fertile farmland that produced tobacco, wheat, barley, vegetables, figs, olives, and other fruits; and how the fragrance of lemon trees, almond trees, and roses filled the air. One seventeenth-century visitor concluded, "In a word, this place is a kind of paradise."[1]

Thanks to its geography, for centuries Rhodes served as a popular stop for merchants, pilgrims, and international traders. The island, with its five harbors—three in the city of Rhodes—was a regional center of commerce in both the ancient and modern worlds. Accordingly, a cosmopolitan local population developed in the port villages, notably the city of Rhodes itself, founded in 408 BCE. The little island of farmers, fishermen, and merchants also found itself invaded and dominated by one regional power after the next. The eras of Greek rule (408 BCE–164 BCE) and Roman rule (164 BCE–395 CE) were followed by Byzantine Empire rule (395–1204), then two centuries of rule by the Knights of the St. John Hospitallers (1309–1522), crusaders who captured Rhodes as they retreated from the Holy Land. The Knights built a massive castle-fort and thick walls that enclosed what became known as the Old City.

The Ottoman Empire under Sultan Suleiman, "the Magnificent," conquered Rhodes in 1522, and the Ottomans reigned until 1912. There had been a Jewish presence in Rhodes since at least the second century BCE, and by the end of the sixteenth century, an estimated five hundred Jews lived on the island. The Ottoman ruler encouraged settlement in Rhodes by Sephardic Jews, those who had been expelled from Spain (*Sepharad* in Hebrew) in 1492 and Portugal in 1497 and had settled in the eastern Mediterranean. Gradually, the island became a significant Sephardic center, and many Jews modestly prospered. At one time there were six synagogues and prayer halls, and several rabbinical schools. Commerce flourished, and Jewish merchants did as well, trading in textiles, tobacco, vegetables, fruits, and other products. The "Rhodeslis" developed a vibrant, small, relatively coherent, and close-knit community. Among the most prominent chief rabbis were those of the Israel family (no relation to Sam's family), who, after thirteen generations and two hundred years, represented the longest unbroken line of rabbis in Jewish history at the turn of the twentieth century. The family, synagogue, and community circles formed a kind of crucible, a series of interacting influences that developed Sam's fundamental values and world outlook throughout his boyhood.

FAMILY AND GROWING UP IN RHODES

Under the four-century rule of the Ottoman Turks, the Jewish population of Rhodes lived in circumscribed but relatively stable peace. At the turn of the twentieth century, their numbers were about one-third of the island's total (the majority were Greek), and the population peaked in the 1920s at around 4,500. The Rhodeslis embodied a complex religious and ethnic cultural heritage. "The Rhodian Jews," notes one writer, "served as significant carriers of the long-lasting Sephardic heritage since they did not only preserve but also contributed in the perpetuation of the Sephardic tradition."[2]

Jewish merchant shops at the beginning of Arriva del Kadi (now Socratous Street), c. 1915.

Sam and his family lived in the Jewish quarter, the densely populated area located in the eastern section of the walled Old City built by the Knights of St. John and known as *la Juderia*. It remained a virtual medieval town, noted for its intricate labyrinth of narrow and winding cobblestone streets and alleys, overhanging balconies, and tents and canopies that shaded commercial areas where merchants showed their wares. Among this network were traditional fountains, Byzantine and medieval Gothic churches, mosques, picturesque shops, homes, and other buildings decorated with oriental motifs. Most dwellings, including the Israel family home, were whitewashed mud-brick structures. A few relatively wealthy Jews owned large stone houses that, by contrast, seemed almost palatial. Typically, an extended family lived under one roof. Courtyards between houses were alive with neighborly gossip and female voices singing traditional Ladino songs.

Jews and Turks shared the living space inside the old, walled part of town. For the most part, Jews on the island had coexisted in relative peace with their Ottoman rulers, but at times they experienced anti-Semitism and persecution by the majority Orthodox Christian Greeks, often suffering beatings, bullying, shunning, and other torments. However, there were many who got along with their Greek neighbors; they had, after all, coexisted, collaborated, and traded with one another for centuries. Jews, Greeks, and Turks frequented some of the same taverns in *la Juderia*, perhaps growing friendlier after a glass or two of wine. Also, around the turn of the century, the quarter was so densely populated that "Jews began to take up residence outside the walls, in the Greek town." Sam—and presumably his father—apparently had positive dealings with some Greeks.[3]

Sam grew up in a family that was an integral part of their community, distinguished by Sephardic religious practices, traditions, customs, and language. Their culture—an ancient and rich tapestry unique to the island, developed over the centuries after the 1492 Sephardic diaspora—was an intrinsic part of daily life, passed down from parents to children as it had been for generations. The language of the Israel home and other Rhodeslis was Ladino, the Judeo-Spanish language rooted in a fifteenth-century Castilian dialect and flavored with multiple cultural influences from the eastern Mediterranean, sprinkled with Hebrew, Portuguese, Greek, Arabic, Italian, and Turkish words and expressions. In the cosmopolitan community of Rhodes, Sam Israel became fluent in four languages—his native Ladino, as well as Italian, Greek, and Turkish—and he even learned a little French.

The center of the family's life was the Kahal Kadosh Shalom Synagogue (the Holy Congregation of Peace, or Kahal Shalom Synagogue for short), where they regularly attended services. The synagogue, founded in 1577 (5338 in the Hebrew calendar), was a place of prayer, celebration, and joy for the congregation. Because of their island isolation, the Sephardim of Rhodes developed numerous cultural differences from other Sephardim, from pronunciations of words to daily prayer practices, blessings, Shabbat and holiday liturgy and music, the coming-of-age ritual of bar mitzvah, and wedding traditions, to name a few. Sephardic music and songs added another rich texture to the sounds of life in *la Juderia*. There were special foods for Shabbat and holidays, especially for the Pesach (Passover) Seder and Rosh Hashanah (Jewish New Year). Cooks in Rhodesli kitchens followed kosher requirements while employing the distinctive flavors and aromas of local cuisine, distinguished by (among other things) herbs and spices, desserts, beverages (such as Turkish coffee served with cardamom in tiny cups), pickles, and condiments.

The Israel family lived among many relatives in the Jewish quarter. "Our community was mostly interrelated by marriage, many being first and second cousins," explains Sylvia Hasson-Berro, former resident and Holocaust survivor. Hasson-Berro, a sister of Bona's husband, Albert Hasson, published a memoir of her life on Rhodes and her Holocaust experience. She paints a colorful portrait of her childhood home: "Lindos, the Valley of the Butterflies on Rhodes, is the habitat of hundreds of exquisite butterflies. We enjoyed these nature's delights on the last day of Pesach, Passover, as we wandered over the rolling hills towards the local villages to have our spring picnics. Sometimes we would hire a bus with up to twenty-five relatives and go off on our picnic to admire the pink and white blossoms of the orchards. We would also see deer, which was a symbol of the island."[4]

In the *Calle Ancha*; view of the main market square in *la Juderia*, 1920.

At the social center of *la Juderia* was *la Calle Ancha*, "the wide street," where small shops offering vegetables, fruits, textiles, housewares, and a host of commodities from local farms and the eastern Mediterranean crowded one another around a central fountain that offered a source of water for all. Sam Israel later told the story of how as a boy he carried bucket after bucket of water from the fountain to the family home. We may guess that in Sam's youth he walked the hills and mountains of Rhodes, for Sam became an avid hiker after coming to the US. His family may also have visited the medicinal springs in the small village of Kallithea, a short distance south of the city of Rhodes, which had been a spa in use since Roman times, as they later often visited the healing waters of Soap Lake, Washington.

We know relatively little about Sam's boyhood home. We can, however, make a basic assumption that it was rather like the majority of Sephardic homes in *la Juderia*. Men worked in shops or small craftsmen's stores; women provided for family life, cooking, cleaning, and raising children. Sam's father, Yitzhak Israel, was one of the many Sephardic merchants on Rhodes but more successful than most. He became what Sam later called "well-to-do" as the sole wholesale distributor of olive oil, charcoal, and cigarette paper on Rhodes. Yitzhak made occasional trips to Turkey, where he purchased reams of cigarette paper; back home, he then cut it into cigarette-size strips for local sale. He also owned a cigarette-making machine. He may have imported Fatima brand cigarettes for resale. The brand, launched in the 1870s, with an exotic image conjured by a Turkish woman's name and Turkish tobaccos, was one of the first to be made on machines. In the early 1900s, Fatima cigarettes gained a large share of the market and became a top-selling brand in Europe and America. Sam's father made a good income, and they lived frugally, putting most of the earnings in the bank, which, after Italy gained control of Rhodes in May 1912, meant Italian lire. Because Yitzhak traveled to Turkey for business, and probably also traded with Greeks, it is likely that he spoke both

> *Sam's father, Yitzhak Israel, was one of the many Sephardic merchants on Rhodes but more successful than most.*

Turkish and Greek (besides his native Ladino). As a traveling merchant, Sam's father had more exposure to other groups and Western ways than most Sephardim in *la Juderia*.[5]

As for Sam's family and extended family, we know only a handful of elementary facts of the Israel genealogy (see figure 1). Samuel Israel was born—probably—on February 13, 1904, the birth date entered on Sam's Preliminary Form for Petition for Naturalization filed in the King County Superior Court in 1923. Sam claimed the date March 4, 1899, as his birthday, and that date is cited on the US Social Security Death Index. Curiously, other records indicate his birth date as "3/4/1899," European style for April 3, 1899. Among the small trove of documents that Sam carried from Rhodes to America was an Ottoman citizen identification paper, issued on January 13, 1904, which listed his birth year as 1897/98 and his name in Hebrew, Shemuel. Sam's chosen birth date made him older than his brother Morris, who was born in 1900. Morris, throughout his life, disputed Sam's claim. Furthermore, several early documents, as well as family photographs in 1911

14 THE CRUCIBLE

and 1915, appear to confirm that Morris was older than Sam. Nonetheless, generally for this book we will use Sam's preferred date.[6]

Sam's father, Yitzhak ben (son of) David Israel, was born in 1852. His father's mother we know only by her first and married name, Bulisa Israel. Sam's mother was Sarota Biton, born probably in 1857, the daughter of Jacob Biton (also spelled Beaton) and Mazaltov Capuano. Israel, Biton, and Capuano were all old family names in Sephardic Rhodes.

Over the course of twenty-one years, Yitzhak and Sarota Israel were blessed with seven children, six boys and a girl. At the time of the first child's birth, Sam's father was thirty-eight years old, and his mother thirty-three years old—a rather late entry into parenthood compared to others in the Sephardic community. In keeping with Sephardic custom, they named their children after living relatives, beginning with the children's grandparents. The first son and the first daughter were named after the paternal grandparents, and the mother's parents were next in line as namesakes. After that, Yitzhak and Sarota could choose names freely without familial obligation.

Firstborn was David ben Yitzhak on March 15, 1890. Two years later, Jacob "Jack" ben Yitzhak Israel was born on February 2, 1892. Sarota gave birth to the couple's third son, Yecoutiel (he later took the name "Morris") ben Yitzhak Israel on May 10, 1900. Unless he was born in 1899 as claimed, next came Samuel ben Yitzhak Israel, probably on February 13, 1904. The fifth child, Nissim ben Yitzhak Israel, was born April 15, 1906, and four years later, the couple's sixth and final son arrived, Asher (later "John" and "Johnny") ben Yitzhak Israel on September 7, 1910. The seventh and last child born to the Israel home was Bulisa (later "Buena" and then "Bona") Israel on August 10, 1911. By this time, Sam was seven years old (twelve years old using the 1899 birth year), his father was fifty-nine, and his mother fifty-four.

Opposite, top: Israel family portrait, 1911. Opposite, bottom: Israel family portrait, 1915. Left to right: back row: Nissim, Sarah, Sam, Isaac, Morris; front row: John, Bona. The family's clothing reflects a fascinating mixture of Ottoman and unmistakable modern influences. In the 1911 portrait, Sam and his brother Morris follow their father's example in wearing the fez ("tarboosh" in Turkish), preferred by many Jews and other non-Muslim men, as well as younger Turks; only Isaac wears the fez in 1915. Sarah's dress is more conservative in the 1911 photo, and more modern in the 1915 image. The children's clothes reflect Western styles in both portraits, but more so in the 1915 photo.

The Sephardim of Rhodes were a deeply religious and traditional community. For centuries and generations, rabbis and the cheder (elementary religious schools) controlled education of the young. It was not until the late nineteenth century that secular educators began to introduce some Turkish language study. French influence, especially in secular education, spread across the Ottoman Empire in the late nineteenth and early twentieth centuries. On Rhodes, by the beginning of the twentieth century, a growing number of families were embracing Western-style education. By

Alliance Israélite Universelle School, c. 1915.

the time Sam Israel attended school, the island had French Catholic and French Jewish schools, as well as an Italian school for girls run by nuns.

Sam's education probably began at home and the synagogue. It is likely that he attended a local cheder, where he would have received the traditional instruction on reading and writing in Ladino and Hebrew and the basics of Judaism—for boys only, ages five to thirteen typically. One document in Sam's handwriting survives, showing that his education included Soletreo, the cursive script of Ladino that uses the letters of the Hebrew alphabet. At some point, perhaps around age eight, his family enrolled him in the Alliance Israélite Universelle school for boys, which opened in Rhodes in 1901. The Alliance school offered a secular education and an egalitarian environment. Jewish children played alongside (and sometimes with) Turks, Greeks, and others. Sam attended the school up to the time of his bar mitzvah, age thirteen.

The Alliance Israélite Universelle was a philanthropic organization established in Paris in 1860 to benefit Jews, safeguard their rights, and create examples of what was termed "the citizen-Jew" primarily through education and vocational skills development. The founders, inspired by the motto of the 1789 French Revolution, "Liberté, égalité, fraternité," aspired to carry the notions of emancipation and religious freedom to oppressed Jewish communities everywhere. In a larger context, the efforts of the Alliance Israélite Universelle represented one facet of French colonial power initiatives to "civilize" the oppressed and underdeveloped peoples of Africa and the Middle East.[7]

During the late nineteenth and early twentieth centuries, the Alliance's influence spread throughout the countries bordering the Mediterranean, part of a general wave of secular French culture and education that shifted cultural perspectives in many parts of the aging Ottoman Empire. By the time Sam Israel attended school in Rhodes, the organization had established more than one hundred schools in the Middle East and North Africa, mainly in Turkey, Tunisia, and Morocco. In Rhodes, as elsewhere, there were separate schools for boys (1901) and girls (1902)—typical for the Jewish, Muslim, and other traditional cultures of the region—that provided Jewish children from poor families with basic elementary school and vocational education. Instruction focused on French language, history, literature, and culture; after 1914, classes in Hebrew were offered.

The motto of the Alliance organization—Sam's school included—was the Talmudic maxim "Kol yisrael arevim ze baze" (All Jews bear responsibility for one another). The family and home environment, the synagogue and rabbinical teachings, the Alliance school's ethos and curriculum, and the multicultural milieu of Rhodes that Sam grew up in imbued the young Jewish boy with a deep respect for all people and an appreciation for diverse cultures. Many years later, he recalled the annual Greek festival that was part of island life: "On the Island of Rhodos where I was born and raised, the majority of the citizens were Greeks. They had a festival once a year in a village quite a distance from the city of Rhodos. It was a great festival—I do not know how many days the festival lasted. Greeks from all the other villages used to come through the city of Rhodos, and the citizens of the city of Rhodos used to go to that village for the festival."[8]

In 1912 (using the 1899 birth year), Sam reached the age of bar mitzvah and by tradition became a full-fledged member of the community and responsible for his actions. He already had been apprenticed for two or three years to a Greek shoemaker who worked in what was, according to Sam, the "best shoe shop" in Rhodes, owned by a Rhodesli. Here, Sam learned the trade of custom shoemaking. He and two other boys worked under the "Greek Master" without pay, sitting on small stools for long ten- and twelve-hour days. After five years, he became a "full-fledged shoemaker." Many

SS *Patria*, c. 1914.

years later, Sam recalled the experience: "He was the finest shoemaker in all of Rhodes. When I think of that man, I bless him. He only whipped me once." Sam also told his nephew Victor Hasson that during the apprenticeship, he went to the shoemaker and asked for "a little bit of money, and the shoemaker threw him out."⁹

Sam's youth on Rhodes was a time in which gradually increasing European "modern" influences overlapped with age-old traditions, preserved by rabbis who directed the religious, social, and intellectual life of the Sephardic community. During Sam's final year at the Alliance school, the Italo-Turkish War raged, from September 1911 to October 1912. In the end, Italy captured various parts of the Ottoman Empire, notably several provinces in what later became Italian Libya and the Dodecanese Islands, including the Island of Rhodes. Under Italian rule, Rhodes began shifting from the staid ways of the Ottoman world to the newer attitudes and social conventions brought by global influences.

Soon, cars and buses mingled with horse-drawn carts and pack animals. The first cinema arrived almost immediately, showing Italian films outdoors, and not long afterward, an indoor theater opened its doors to moviegoers in *la Juderia*. One former resident recalled, "On Saturday and Sunday nights, Jews, Greeks, Turks, and Italians would gather to stroll along the promenade [the quay in Mandraki Harbor] and to sit at the outdoor cafes while listening to the military bands that performed at the nearby plaza." Young Rhodeslis could meander down *la Calle Ancha* or walk the harbor quay on weekends and get the chance to see or speak to a prospective spouse—a level of liberty unknown to the older generation. Young people, no longer compelled by traditional matchmaking by parents, gravitated to the modern style of meeting a mate.[10]

The new Italian immigrants on Rhodes were not as hospitable toward the island's Jews as the Turks had been. Hundreds of Italians immigrated to Rhodes and took up work in roadbuilding, construction, and tourism, bringing about a dramatic change to the farming, fishing, and regional trading economy, notably to Jewish merchants such as Yitzhak Israel, who operated out of the old bazaar and had long-standing trade relationships with Ottomans. It became harder to feed a family, and at the same time, the influence of European education and Western ways made young men more restless and motivated to leave their old, closed, and static world.[11]

LEAVING HOME

The number of Rhodesli émigrés was relatively small in the 1890s but grew rapidly between 1900 and the outbreak of World War I in 1914. In the United States after the war, another surge followed in the 1920s, until Congress curtailed immigration in 1924.

Initially, émigrés, usually men age eighteen to thirty-five, intended to earn money and then return home to establish a family, or to send money to their families to help those who remained in Rhodes. As time passed, however, many began to establish homes and to provide funds to help their families emigrate and join them.

Major destinations included America, the Congo, Rhodesia (now Zimbabwe), and several other locations in Africa. Most Rhodesli émigrés went to the US, especially New York, Seattle, Los Angeles, and Atlanta. Parents were heartbroken to see their children head off to a distant land, another life. One scholar notes, "In time it became part of the Rhodian experience to wave farewell to dear ones, bound for other continents." Once

Above: Identification document for Ottoman citizens, issued to Shemuel Israel; father's name Isak Israel; mother's name Sarota; born in 1897/1898 in Rodos; Jewish; unmarried. The second part of the document states that Rodos is a sancak of the vilayet of Cezayir-i Bahr-i Sefid. Şhemuel lived in the Jewish mahalle (neighborhood) and at the Yahudi Sokağı (Jewish street). The last part of the document states that Şamuel İsrael is an Ottoman national (Osmanlı tebaası/ Osmanlı tabiiyeti). The document was signed with the seal of the Ministry of Foreign Affairs on January 13, 1904. Opposite, above: "Comune di Rodi," September 10, 1919; official city government document from the Commissioner of Rhodes declaring that Sam Israel, born in Rhodes in 1899, is a person of "good conduct." Opposite, below: "Certificato Penale," official document certifying that Samuel Israel has no criminal record, September 10, 1919.

a brother or cousin left and established himself, for those who followed, stepping onto a boat bound for America shifted from a great unknown to a manageable overseas challenge.[12]

When Sam was still a child, his two older brothers had boarded ships for the US, creating dramatic change in the home. In 1906, sixteen-year-old David left Rhodes, and when Jacob (Jack—his name probably was Anglicized after he arrived) was sixteen in 1908, he followed in David's footsteps. We don't know what motivated this move, but at the time, conditions on the island drove a host of young Rhodeslis to emigrate. Many in their late teens abruptly emigrated to avoid compulsory military service in the Ottoman army. By the early twentieth century, families living in the confines of *la Juderia* faced growing economic hardships and poverty that resulted from overpopulation and underemployment. Some young men, tired of the lack of opportunities, sought the boundless economic possibilities rumored to lie waiting in America. Some émigrés may have sought political freedom or relief from religious persecution.

David and Jack settled in Vancouver, British Columbia, where they found jobs doing menial work shining shoes and waxing floors at a shoe company for about five years. On the eve of World War I, they returned to Rhodes. David, now twenty-four, sought a wife. He found a lovely mate in seventeen-year-old Marie Franco. In Rhodesli society, marriages were arranged by parents, despite the growing trend toward modern dating in mainstream Rhodes culture. The preferences of Rhodesli children or notions of love played no role. However, David and Marie's pairing was nontraditional. Their daughter Rita Israel Calderon tells the family story: "My mother was born on the Island of Rhodes and my father had gone there to get a bride, which was arranged by his mother. They picked somebody else, but my father saw my mother at the fountain, which is still there in the *Calle Ancha* on Rhodes. And he says, 'No, I want that one.' So, she [his mother] talked to her parents and arranged that marriage."¹³

At the age of fourteen, Sam's brother Morris joined Jack, David, and Marie on their journey back to the New World. The trip became part of family folklore. Morris's daughter Daisy Israel recalls the story: "Grandpa Isaac put them on the boat, never knowing if he'd ever see them again. I mean, this was a new world." They arrived at Ellis Island, then went directly to Vancouver. (We don't know the connection, but typically immigrants followed family or friends.) The town proved not as welcoming as Marie had hoped. She found the place cold and damp, and there were no Sephardic families in the area. Rita Israel Calderon tells the story she heard from her parents: "My mother was in tears the whole time because there was nobody Jewish, nobody Sephardic, in Vancouver. My mother didn't speak English, so she was afraid to leave the house." Before long, they moved to Seattle, where a small but vibrant Sephardic community had been forming.¹⁴

In late 1919, Sam prepared to follow his older brothers. The reason, he later recalled, was simple: "Opportunity. It looked a little bit dull at that time for the younger person." He possessed the Ottoman citizen's identification document that certified his age as "at least 19." He knew—probably from his brothers or other Rhodeslis who had emigrated—that immigration restrictions in the US were growing tighter, and if he traveled as a fifteen-year-old unaccompanied by an adult parent or guardian, he faced certain exclusion and deportation as a "likely public charge." The fraudulent Ottoman identification card was a common device used by thousands of hopeful Sephardim in the early years of the twentieth century to bypass US

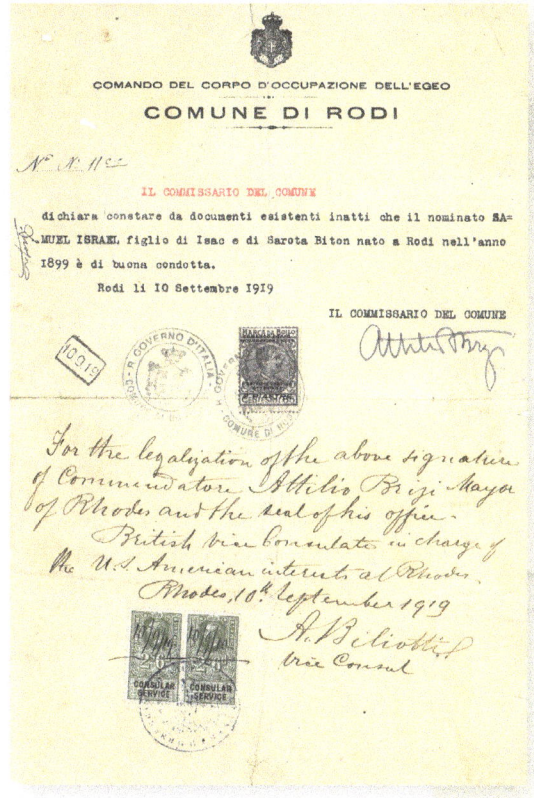

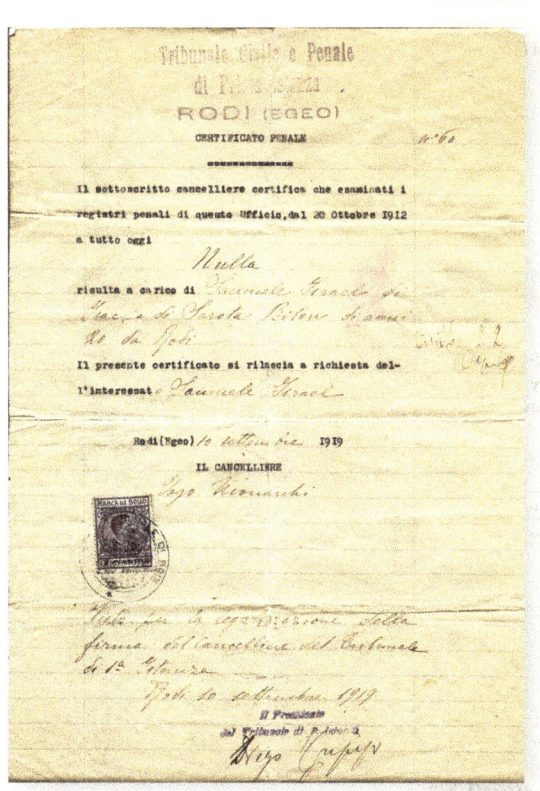

immigration regulations and enter the country. Perhaps this was the reason he tinkered with his birth date. Why he continued the charade long past its usefulness is unknown.[15]

On September 10, 1919, Sam received his first official immigration papers, a certificate from Il Commissario del Comme de Rodi and a certificate of good conduct—Certificato Penale indicating "nulla," that is, no criminal record—a prerequisite to obtaining permission to emigrate to the United States. Sam's passport, no. 3926, issued on September 12, 1919, identified him as an Italian citizen, born in Rhodes (then part of Italy) on "3/4/1899" (April 3, 1899), occupation "Calzolaio" (shoemaker). On September 18, Sam said goodbye to his parents and younger siblings and boarded a ship bound for Naples. The boat stopped at Perea, Greece, where Sam went ashore briefly with seventeen Italian soldiers. They stopped again at Patras, Greece, then sailed to Brindisi on the east coast of Italy before heading to Naples. After a week, Sam reached Naples, and on September 25, 1919, he completed the Declaration of Alien About to Depart for the United States form at the US Consulate General in Naples.[16]

On October 3, the SS *Patria* of the Fabre Line left the dock in Naples loaded with passengers bound for America, including Sam and family friends the Rahamin Capouyas. After two weeks on the stormy Atlantic, the ship docked at Ellis Island in New York. Sam would not return to Rhodes for more than fifty years.

Top: "Declaration of Alien About to Depart for the United States," September 25, 1919 (front). Bottom: Sam's trip log: Travel itinerary, from departure from Rhodes on September 17/18 to October 28 arrival in Seattle. The document is written in Soletreo, the written alphabet of Ladino, which uses the letters of the Hebrew alphabet. Opposite: "Declaration of Alien About to Depart for the United States" (back).

7. I expect to go to the United States for _____
   Desidero andare negli Stati Uniti   Object of visit. |Motivo del viaggio|

   as shown by   cert of good conduct, Rhodes
   come risulta da   Documents or other proofs of object |Documenti ossia altre prove del motivo|

   to reside at _____ _____ for a period of _____
   per domiciliarmi a   City, street, and number.   *per un periodo di tempo di*
   |Città strada e numero|

8. I have informed myself of the provisions of section 3. Immigration Act of February 5, 1917
   Ho preso conoscenza delle disposizioni di Sezione 3. dell'atto sull'immigrazione del 5 Febbraio 1917 e sono convinto di poter es-

   and am convincend that I am eligible for admission into the United States thereunder.
   sere ammesso negli Stati Uniti in conformità alle dette disposizioni:

9. (a) I realize that if I am one of a class prohibited by law from admission into the United States
   (a) Io mi rendo conto che se risulta che appartengo ad una delle classi alle quali la legge proibisce l'ingresso negli Stati Uniti,

   I will be deported or detained in confinement in the United States ; and (b) I am prepa-
   sarò soggetto a deportazione o detenzione negli Stati Uniti e (b) sono pronto ad assumere il rischio della deportazione e di

   red to assume the risk of deportation and of a compulsory return trip in case of my rejection
   un viaggio di ritorno compulsorio conseguente sul mio respingimento da un porto Americano.

   at an American port,

   Samuel Israël
   Signature of declarant. |Firma del dichiarante|

   Subscribed and sworn to before me this _____ day of _____
   |Data| Month and year. |Mese e anno|

   Official signature |Firma d'ufficio|

N. B. — The taking of this declaration and visaing of the bearer's passport give no assurance that the
N. B. — L'accettazione della presente dichiarazione ed il visto del passaporto del latore non costituiscono qualsiasi assicurazione

bearer is not excludible from the United States under section 3 of the Immigration Act of February 5, 1917.
che il latore non sia da escludere dagli Stati Uniti in conformità e Sezione 3 dell'Atto sull'immigrazione del 5 febbraio 1917.

The decision in each case must be made by the immigration authorities in the United States.
La decisione dovrà essere fatta in ciascun caso dall'autorità per l'immigrazione agli Stati Uniti.

Remarks by official taking declaration:
Osservazione del funzionario al quale è presentata la dichiarazione

Napoli R. Stab. Tipografico Francesco Giannini & Figli

Figure 1

The Family of Sam Israel

Yitzhak (Isaac) ben (son of) David Israel (b. 1852; d. July 19, 1944)
    Father: David Israel
    Mother: Bulisa Israel

Sarota (Sarah) Biton (b. 1857; d. May 8, 1947)
    Father: Jacob Biton
    Mother: Mazaltov Capuano

CHILDREN:

David (David) ben Yitzhak (March 15, 1890–November 3, 1977)
    m. (1914) Marie Franco (b. 1897; d. January 2, 1955)
    Isaac
    Sarah
    Rita
    Jack
    Grace
    Rachel
    m. (1958) Esther Bensussen (1898–1970)

Jack (Jacob) ben Yitzhak (February 2, 1892–March 22, 1962)
    m. (February 1, 1920) Reina Galante (March 10, 1900–February 1, 1984)
    Raye
    Sarah
    Solomon
    Emily

Samuel (Shemuel) ben Yitzhak (March 4, 1899–June 11, 1994)

Morris (Yecoutiel) ben Yitzhak (May 10, 1900–October 21, 1980)
m. (September 7, 1924) Gentil Levy (May 25, 1905–August 1, 2001)
Leon
Daisy
Beverly
Yitzhak

Nissim (Nissim) ben Yitzhak (April 15, 1906–March 1978)
m. (August 12, 1934) Violet Hasson (April 6, 1912–January 10, 2005)
Sallie
Lucille
Robert

Asher (Asher) ben Yitzhak aka John (September 7, 1910–February 5, 1985)
m. (January 23, 1938) Juliette Levy (1918–2010)
Irving
Shirley
Rose Lee

Bona (Bulisa, Buena) bat Sarah
(August 10, 1911–October 4, 2001)
m. (August 9, 1931) Albert Hasson (April 2, 1904–December 1978)
Robert
Eddie
David
Victor
Marilyn

CHAPTER 2

A Shoemaker in Seattle, 1919–1940

Opposite: Wingfoot Shoe Repair opened by Sam in 1930. John Israel on the left.

Aboltar cazal, aboltar mazal.
(A change of scene, a change of fortune.)

OLD FAMILIES IN A NEW COMMUNITY

We have conflicting stories about Sam's arrival in Seattle. One family member says he was twelve years old and came with David and his wife Marie. Others report that Sam came with brothers David and Jack and sister-in-law Marie. However, we know from US Census records that David, Marie, Jack, and Morris arrived in 1914 and remained in Seattle afterward. Sam's immigration papers indicate he arrived in October 1919 and had traveled with family friends. At least two family members, Eddie Hasson and Daisy Israel, tell the version that coincides with the official documentation. "Uncle Sam came all by himself," Daisy says. Eddie Hasson recalls, "He came by himself, that's what he told me." And, in a court deposition in 1980, Sam declared that he had traveled alone.[1]

The SS *Patria* steamed into New York harbor on October 17, 1919, after a two-week journey from Naples. Sam and the Rahamin Capouya family, along with the other immigrants, disembarked at Ellis Island and began the process of officially entering the United States. After a week, Sam and his group secured passage on a train heading west to Chicago, and there changed to the Northern Pacific line, arriving in Seattle on October 28. He was heartily welcomed by Morris, Jack, David, and Marie.[2]

In December 1919, three months after Sam left his home in Rhodes, the rest of the family—Sam's parents; brothers Nissim and John; and sister, Bona—followed. They boarded the SS *Pesaro* in Naples and arrived in the US on December 7, 1919, then made their way to Seattle a couple of weeks later. With the family reunited, the Israels settled in the Central Area (commonly called the Central District) neighborhood, the heart of Seattle's Sephardic Jewish community.

In Seattle, a small but thriving Sephardic community had been established some years earlier. Sephardic Jews began the third wave of Jews immigrating to Washington with the arrival in 1902 of two young men, Solomon Calvo and Jacob Policar, from the Turkish island of Marmara. These Sephardim and those who followed spoke Ladino, in contrast to the earlier Ashkenazic pioneers, who spoke Yiddish and German. By 1904, the first settler from Rhodes, Nessim Alhadeff, had arrived in Seattle. Within a decade, as life for Jews in the troubled Ottoman Empire became harsher, a wave of Rhodeslis and Sephardim from Turkey and other parts of the eastern Mediterranean followed the same path to Seattle. By 1913, well before Sam Israel and his family arrived, the city had developed an "astonishingly large Sephardic community" of six hundred, representing the largest Sephardic urban group in the US, outside of New York. Many from the Alhadeff family came, and other prominent surnames among more than forty others included Israel, Adatto, Calvo, Cohen, Policar, Benezra, Levy, Piha, Eskenazy, and Hazan.[3]

Many early arrivals had few English skills and worked for Greeks (whose language they knew) who had established themselves. While some could find only manual labor jobs, many Sephardic and Ashkenazic immigrants managed to open their own businesses, operating produce carts, grocery stalls, fish markets, tailor shops, and shoeshine and shoe repair shops. Pike Place Market became a focal point for shopping and socializing at Sephardic fruit and vegetable stands, or Solomon Calvo's Waterfront Fish and Oyster Co., or the Alhadeffs' City Fish Market.

A wave of Sephardic immigrants from Turkey, Rhodes, Greece, and Syria numbering in the hundreds arrived following the end of World War I and the demise of the Ottoman Empire. By the time the US changed its immigration policies in 1924, virtually ending arrivals from eastern Europe, southern Europe, and the Mediterranean, Seattle's Sephardic community counted more than two thousand souls, less than 1 percent of Seattle's population of 315,000. Economically, the first-generation immigrants did not thrive, and although a handful became successful, the great majority "lacked the skills or resources to achieve more than a bare subsistence."[4]

Initially, in January 1920, Yitzhak and Sarota (now Americanized to "Isaac" and "Sarah") and their children Nissim, John, and Bona moved in with David and Marie, whose house at 167 Twentieth Avenue included their first two children, Isaac and Sarah, named in accord with tradition in honor of David's parents. In 1921, Sam and his family—except for David, Jack, and their wives and children—moved briefly to a house at 1907 East Spruce Street. As of 1922, David and Jack and their families remained at the home on Twentieth Avenue, while Sam and his parents, plus Nissim, John, and Bona, moved to a nearby house at 1924 East Fir Street. A year later (1923), while Jack and David remained at the Twentieth Avenue house, the others moved to a home they purchased at 1805 East Spruce Street, less than two blocks away.[5]

Daisy Israel recalls, "They bought the home on 18th and Spruce, . . . and that house became the center of our family."[6] Years later, Sam recalled the turning-point events:

Sam soon after arrival in Seattle, c. 1921. Note the stylish sport coat and shirt with stick-pin collar.

> *After the First World War, the Italian lira was worth four lira to one dollar. And then it was devalued to eight to one dollar after 1921, '22. And my father at that time thought the war was over, Italy won the war, and they would normalize and go back to four to a dollar, but it didn't. It kept on going the other way, it was depreciating ever continuously. And then my father suggested to buy a house; to sell the money, get rid of it; salvage as much as he can; pick up the pieces and see if he can buy a house with the money earned from the old country. So, we sold the Italian liras that he had. And we bought a house, 1805 East Spruce, money paid by my father, 1923 or '24. We paid cash.*

> *This was my father's house. His entire fortune went into this one house. That was all there was left of the earnings, including the $1,500 for the shop because we paid them in one year's time. So, that's about all he could salvage.*[7]

At the time, home ownership in Seattle was attainable not only for middle-class workers but also for tradesmen and the average working-class family. The Israels, like other Sephardim in the city, sought to live in a community that brought the familiarity of extended family members and friends with similar language and culture. Eastern European Jews as well as Sephardim concentrated in the area described as the Yesler Way–Cherry Street neighborhood, located between Yesler Way on the south, Cherry Street on the north, Twelfth Avenue on the west, and Twentieth Avenue on the east. It was not a homogenous neighborhood in the classic sense but a concentration of several groups that included Jews, African Americans, Asians, and Scandinavians. The Israel homes were close to one of the two Sephardic synagogues, Congregation Ezra Bessaroth, where the family worshipped. The congregation, which had been incorporated in 1914 by Jews from Rhodes, dedicated the first new Sephardic synagogue building in 1918, located at Fifteenth Avenue and East Fir Street.[8]

Sam, Ike Levy, unknown, in San Francisco, September 1938.

The Central Area was a positive environment for Sam, his parents, his siblings, and their growing children. There were many Jewish businesses, including kosher grocery stores, butcher shops, and coffeehouses. It felt like a Jewish neighborhood, though Jews composed less than 40 percent of the population. Historians affirm the importance of the area: "The presence of a large number of Sephardim relative to the whole Jewish population lent a richness and diversity to Seattle Jewry. The Sephardim formed a critical mass that allowed them to maintain their traditions, customs, and language to an extent not seen outside of New York."[9]

A SHOEMAKER IN SEATTLE

When Sam Israel arrived in Seattle, his brothers David and Morris (who had worked as a rivet heater in a shipyard during World War I) were unemployed. For a time, however, Jack had a job at Baxter Shoe Company shining shoes and waxing floors. Unlike many immigrants who arrived without a trade and searched for manual labor jobs, Sam knew the shoemaking trade as a *calzolaio*, a skilled shoemaker. He also arrived with $600 in his pocket, a substantial amount of money at the time. He later told his nephew Eddie Hasson, "Eddie, you could buy a house for $600 when I came to this country." He was an ambitious, hardworking young man with money, which gave him a head start over many kinsmen who arrived in Seattle just after the end of World War I.[10]

Though Sam knew no English, he soon (probably around November 1919) found a job with a shoemaker at a shop on First Avenue and Yesler Way that made boots for loggers and repaired shoes. Sam was put to work repairing cork-soled logger's boots. Years later, Sam recalled the experience: "Boy, that was terrible," he told a reporter, "but that was the only job available." Sam labored nine hours a day, six days a week, and earned the shoemaker's standard salary of $15 per week. He knew how to make boots but not repair them. Worse, because he spoke no English, he could not read the work orders and so immediately began to make mistakes. He lasted one week. "Saturday came along and the boss told me he could not use me anymore until I learned to read. No objections to the work." Sam felt so miserable that he was ready to write to his father, who was still in Rhodes, that he wanted to return. Meanwhile, Sam and his brothers received a letter from their mother, who wrote that she was deeply missing her children and that the rest of the family might move to Seattle. Some days later, Sarota's next letter brought the news that she and their father had decided to come to America and join their sons.[11]

Before long, Sam—perhaps because he spoke Greek—found a job with a Greek shoemaker in a shop at Third Avenue and Pine Street. The man did custom work, including making boots for lumberjacks and repairing shoes. Sam learned to repair shoes and earned an extra $15 a week on top of the standard rate. Eddie Hasson recalls how Sam told the story: "He always stated that he immediately made a lot of money. He was making the sum of $30 a week, which was a lot of money then." Sam's nephew Robert Hasson heard the story from Sam with one additional detail. He told Robert, "They fired me because I work too slow. I do a good job. I do an excellent job and they fire me. Figure that one out."[12]

The job lasted until March 1920. The firing proved a turning point for Sam and his brothers. Now with skills either to make or repair shoes, in early 1920, Sam, David, and Jack opened their own shop, Israel Brothers Shoe Repair, at 224 Madison Street. Years later, Sam recounted how they began:

> *In 1920, there was a shoe repair shop for sale on Madison Street between Second and Third where the Rosaia Florist was. And they wanted $1,500 for it. And nobody had the $1,500 except my father. My brother David insisted that I ask my father if he would buy the shop. And then there was a shoeshine stand in there so he would be shining shoes, and I would repair the shoes, and my brother Jack would be there collecting. And then my father was going to put up the $1,500 and buy the shop to teach my brothers the shoemaking trade, because you can always make money on shoes. To me he said, "You go up there and teach your brothers to repair shoes. When they learn to repair shoes, they can take care of themselves and you can go on yourself. You must go there and help your brothers. We are our brother's keeper."*[13]

They bought the shop, including its shoe repairing machinery, from George Burgett. "In less than a year," Sam proudly noted, "we paid back the $1,500 to my father and we were doing well."[14]

Under Sam's direction, the Israel brothers' business prospered. The year 1925 marked the next milestone. Their business name changed to Rotary Shoe Repair, and Morris, financed by Sam, opened his own shop, Orpheum Shoe Repair, located a block away from Rotary, at 910 Third Avenue. The same year, Nissim, now nineteen years old, took a job as a clerk for Benjamin Zoberblatt, a Russian Jew and local fruit merchant. Two years later, in 1927, Sam opened a second Rotary Shoe Repair shop at 215 Madison Street, with Jack as manager.

Sam's success in the shoe repair business enabled him to help his brothers in the trade, as well as to begin making the investments that would become the hallmark of his career. Eddie Hasson recounts this story he heard from Sam: "He lived at home with his parents. He walked from 18th and Spruce to where his shop was every day. He wasn't a big spender. So, he started buying properties, and he told me that the reason why he bought properties was because of the experience of his parents, who lost pretty much all their savings when they left the Isle of Rhodes."[15]

The lesson lasted a lifetime. In 1980, Sam reflected, "For that reason, I didn't keep any money, didn't believe in keeping any money, has no value. And bought real estate, the most secure thing that I could think of. I own no stocks; no partnerships with anybody but my brothers; no share of stocks of any kind; no savings accounts." He counseled his nephew Eddie, "The last thing you should keep is money. But property and land will always be valuable."[16]

Sam's interest in property got a huge boost from Henry R. Audley, a real estate salesman and mortgage loan manager for William A. Eastman & Company Realty. The two men met around 1920, when Sam first opened Israel Brothers Shoe Repair on Madison Street. The shop, by good fortune, was located in an area with a number of real estate brokers. Sam recalled, "And the real estate brokers, they used to come to the shop almost every day, because they used to go and see a piece of property and their shoes used to get muddy all the time. So, sometimes they used to come twice to get their shoes cleaned up, and my brother used to say, 'How much did you make today?' 'No good. We show the property, no sale.'" Over the next two decades, some 90 percent of Sam's property purchases came through Audley and his associate at Eastman, John Dane. Audley, said Sam, was "a very honorable man." When a good deal came along, Audley gave Sam first option to make the purchase.[17]

The Israel Brothers Shoe Repair shop brought Sam into another fortuitous relationship. The space was owned by a notable realtor-entrepreneur in Seattle, Henry Broderick (1880–1975), who had become a highly visible and active member of the Seattle business world in the years following his arrival in the city in 1901. By 1908, Broderick had founded the company that bore his name, and he turned Henry Broderick Inc. into Seattle's largest real estate and property management firm.

The shop space rental began Sam's long association with "HB," as he was known about town. Their business relationship later yielded significant results as Sam started acquiring his own properties. By the late 1930s, Sam began using Henry Broderick almost exclusively for real estate transactions. Sam held Broderick in high regard. "Mr. HB took an interest in me, and he knew every transaction on every piece of property that I bought or dealt with," Sam later wrote. "He was the most humanitarian person I have ever met. He was a monument to the City of Seattle."[18]

Broderick earned Sam Israel's respect for good reason: he refused to join colleagues in real estate covenants that excluded Jews. Though Broderick was a Roman Catholic, his business ethics attracted many of Seattle's Jews as clients. (Sam remained with Broderick and one of his agents, James

Horrigan, until 1982, more than a decade after the firm was acquired by Coldwell Banker.) Eddie Hasson recalls Sam's stories about the relationship with Broderick: "He said that they were colleagues and friends, and that he had an office at Henry Broderick's. He was an investor and Broderick gave him a desk and managed all his properties. Broderick was getting 10 percent or whatever the percentage for managing; they would do the leasing for him."[19]

In 1927, the same year that Rotary Shoe Repair expanded to two locations, Sam purchased four properties: (1) a waterfront lot on the north end of Mercer Island at Faben Point (roughly eighty feet by three hundred feet) for $995; (2) a waterfront lot on Mercer Island's south end; (3) a house at 1910 Spruce Street for $4,000; and (4) a wood-frame store building for $1,400. In 1931, Sam remodeled the house at 1910–1912 Spruce Street, turning it into a duplex, one part of which became the residence of Bona and Albert Hasson after their 1931 marriage.

The shoe repair business grew rapidly, and 1929 was a pivotal year. On December 15, Sam signed a rental agreement with the United Shoe Repairing Machines Company of Boston to rent equipment at $8.50 a month. It was a bold step, coming just weeks after the Black Thursday stock market crash on October 24, 1929. But Sam knew that regardless of dire straits on Wall Street in New York, the outlook for his business was rosy—he was at the beginning of his decade-and-a-half relationship with the US Army, bringing in shoes for repair from army bases at Fort Lawton in Seattle and Fort Lewis in Tacoma.

In 1930, Sam opened another shop called Wingfoot Shoe Repair. The family shoe business now counted four locations: Orpheum Shoe Repair Shop at 910 Third Avenue, operated by Morris; Rotary Shoe Repair at 224 Madison, operated by David; Rotary Shoe Repair at 215 Madison, operated by Jack; and Wingfoot Shoe Repair at 1609 Third Avenue, operated by Sam with the youngest Israel brother, John, as clerk.[20]

Sam's careful stewardship of the family shoe repair shops brought steady growth despite the fact that Seattle and the rest of the country had entered the economic crisis of the Great Depression. Large numbers of building owners suffered bankruptcy, and properties could be bought for astonishingly low prices, often for only the back taxes owed. While buildings were selling for a song, Sam's financial savvy was showing itself as he purchased more and more properties as the 1930s progressed. In the six years between 1933 and 1939, he acquired sixteen properties for sums ranging from $600 to $42,577. Among the most notable were the Austin A. Bell Building at 2324–2328 First Avenue, the Douglas Hotel at 2300–2308 First Avenue, and the Paramount Building at First Avenue and Battery Street. The Paramount Building was the only commercial structure that Sam built for a client. The two-story reinforced concrete building, completed in November 1937, was home to Paramount Pictures Distributing Company for more than a decade, until it became the focus of litigation associated with the Alaskan Way Viaduct construction project. (See figure 2.)

Sam built another commercial building, but this time for a family business. Sam's mother, echoing his father, often urged him, "You need to help your brothers." He had set up David, Jack, Morris, and John in the shoe repair business, but Nissim had little interest in the trade. In 1930, Nissim had his own fruit market, Victory Fruit Company, but in the hard times that gripped Seattle in the early years of the Depression, the business suffered and finally closed. Nissim went to work in the P.O. Fruit Market in 1932. Soon, Sam acquired enough capital to give Nissim another opportunity. In October 1933, Sam began buying residences and properties in the 1900 block of Aurora Avenue North. At the time, there were few businesses in the area, and a curbside fruit market sounded like a good idea. In 1935, a new building for Cascade Market at 1922 Aurora Avenue North was completed, and the new proprietors, Nissim Israel and Albert Hasson, proudly opened for business.[21]

Top: Austin A. Bell Building, built 1890. Bottom: Paramount Building, built 1937. Sketch by Norman E. Fox, 1937.

Eddie Hasson recalls the story of the beginnings of Cascade Market: "My grandmother said that you have to help your brother Nissim, because Uncle Nissim couldn't do shoes, I guess. So, Sam said, 'Okay, we'll start a grocery store.' He went and found a property on Aurora Avenue, 1922 Aurora Avenue. He hired an architect, and he built the store for my uncle and my father and they opened up the Cascade Market. He charged $50 a month rent, only charged $50 a month for 40 years, never raised the rent, $50 a month."[22]

The pattern repeated with John. At age nineteen in 1929, he had begun working with Sam and David in the Rotary Shoe Repair shop; then, in 1930 and for the next six years, he worked as clerk in his brother's Wingfoot Shoe Repair shop. In March 1936, Sam purchased a store at Ninetieth and Aurora Avenue North for $12,500 and proceeded to set up John in the grocery business. It lasted for several years, and when it closed, John again went to work for Sam in the shoe business.[23]

FAMILY AND RELATIONS

Sam's nephews and nieces portray similar images of his father and mother—their grandfather and grandmother. "Sam's father was the meekest, most gentle, nicest man," recalls Eddie Hasson. "I don't ever remember hearing him talk. I never heard him say anything." Daisy Israel describes him as "a very quiet man; nobody remembers his voice." Victor Hasson says, "He was blind in one eye and never worked a day once he came to the United States." He wore a short, grizzled beard and donned a hat, even indoors; rolled his own cigarettes; and would amble around the neighborhood with hands clasped behind his back. Sarah was altogether another story. Short in stature, even "tiny," according to family members, she was chatty and always carried the conversation. "Sarah was the chief of the house," says Daisy Israel. Others called her "the commander."[24]

At home, the family spoke Ladino. The youngest children, John and Bona, were mainly schooled in Seattle, and their English was excellent, but Sam and his brothers spoke English with a heavy accent, and their grammar fell short of the younger siblings'. (After all, English was Sam's fifth language.) Eddie Hasson says, "They did keep the old ways." Bona would sing Ladino songs all the time, and Sam loved to listen to Ladino music. "I think they thought of the Isle of Rhodes," says Eddie.[25]

Like many first-generation immigrants, Sam's parents learned little English. There was no need. They were elderly and stayed mainly at home or

Left: Sarah Israel, c. 1938. Right: Isaac Israel, with his usual hand-rolled cigarette, c. 1938.

in the neighborhood. Even the stores in that era on Twenty-Fourth Avenue were Sephardic, and the shopkeepers spoke Ladino. Eddie Hasson recalls, "In the area that we lived, they were all Spanish-speaking people, so they didn't need to speak English—grandmother never went downtown or anything like that. It was a close, close world to them. And when the kids came home, they spoke to her in Ladino not English. That's how it was."

Albert Hasson brought a similar experience to the family. Albert had left Rhodes in the 1920s and landed in New York not knowing a word of English. His daughter, Marilyn Hasson Henry, tells the story she heard from her father: "Before he left for America, he had heard about a delicacy called 'apple pie,' in Ladino 'pastel di manzana.' He was told that America was a great place. It had apple pie! On the train, not knowing English, he ordered 'pie of apple.' The waiter misunderstood and brought him a bowl of canned pineapple, which he thought disgusting. It wasn't until much later he discovered the true 'apple pie,' which he loved, and mama made for us as one of the few 'American' desserts we had growing up."[26]

Sarah Israel was a keeper of the old ways in another respect. Eddie Hasson explains: "My grandmother was a really powerful woman. She was also a healer. If somebody had a fever, she would have herbs and things. There was a lot of that in the Sephardic community, and they had a name for those people, *curandera*. She would do chants and put her hands on the head. She was like a community person; she had a reputation as a woman healer. Anyway, she was a pretty tough bird."[27]

Sam's relationship with his brothers was framed partly by their individual personalities and partly by the controlling role Sam played in their social and business activities. He didn't have a particularly close bond with them, choosing other family members for closer relationships, notably his sister, Bona; his niece Sarah (David and Marie's daughter); and nephews Jack (David and Marie's son) and Robert Hasson. Eddie says Sam was "very hard to get along with, because it was his way or the highway. But he had such a tender spot for real humanitarian things, and I think he was close to his nephews and nieces, and much later, his brothers." Sam also loved dogs and often brought along a German shepherd he named Mariuch (Italian for "little Mary") for visits.[28]

Eddie Hasson recalls his other uncles: "Uncle David was almost like a grandfather, because he was the oldest. Sam, Uncle Jack—all of them—were very hard workers. Uncle Nissim was also a hardworking man. He and my father both worked six and a half days a week, alternating the store opening on Sundays. The only day they ever closed was Yom Kippur."[29]

Daisy Israel describes Sam's relationship with his brothers as "really interesting." When the family gathered for Sunday dinners or the holidays, she says, "You would think they were arguing, because their voices would raise and raise and raise, and they would argue." They argued about the economy and President Roosevelt or events in Europe. "And then one of the aunties would say, 'Okay, everybody, coffee's on,' and we would all step down."[30]

Sam's nephew Robert Hasson adds another valuable perspective on Sam and his brothers: "Well, Sam was the only one who was really successful in his business dealings. He set all of his brothers up in business, and they all were successful. So, he was the big guy of the family. Everybody turned to him and he would support everybody. . . . He held up the family. Very interesting how one person can have that much influence in the family."[31]

Daisy Israel offers another view of the family's relationships and Sam's role in the dynamics: "The biggest holiday we always had together forever was Passover. I mean, that was the entire family. I look at the house now. It doesn't look that big, but we must have been 60 people in the house, or 50 people in the house, and there always room for more. The door was open. . . . And Uncle Sam was just one, but he was unusual, because he was the bachelor. So, he was a step apart, and yet part of the unit."[32]

Sam and his family were typical of many Sephardic Jews of the time—they were religious and kept a kosher house, though they were not strictly observant in daily practice. Though Sam and his brothers worked on Shabbat, they were serious about the holidays, especially Rosh Hashanah (Jewish New Year), Yom Kippur (the Day of Atonement), and Pesach (Passover). They enjoyed celebrating together, usually at one house or another, and most often at the home on 1805 Spruce Street. "Uncle Morris," recalls Eddie Hasson, "was probably the most religious of all of them, but even he usually worked on Saturday, the busiest day in retail." Moreover, while Sam, as typical of Sephardic Jews, embraced the totality of the Jewish people, he considered his belief system to be the only "true" Jewish religion.[33]

Dana Behar, Sam's great-nephew (grandson of his brother David), recalls how patriotic the family was, like the rest of their generation that came from Rhodes: "They could eat meat if they wanted to, and most were homeowners; they were so full of gratitude." The better life they found in Seattle made them very patriotic. Behar explains: "They thought when they came to America they had hit the lottery. Their lives here, even the poor ones, were so much more comfortable, they didn't see themselves as having a barest existence. They were incredibly patriotic. My grandfather David

> *Sam's relationship with his brothers was framed partly by their individual personalities and partly by the controlling role Sam played in their social and business activities.*

Israel, and this is common, always had the American flag hanging on his house, always wanted to celebrate the 4th of July, and all the holidays. He was so proud to be able to send his kids to serve in the U.S. military; he had a Victory Garden; he would always say how America was the greatest country."[34]

A MAN ABOUT TOWN

For Sam, the 1920s and 1930s were exciting decades, full of both business success and personal achievements. In 1923, the same year that Sam and most of his family moved to 1805 Spruce Street, he submitted his Preliminary Form for Petition for Naturalization to the government, hoping to become a naturalized citizen of the US.

Young Sam Israel was "a man about town; a bon vivant in those days," in the words of Eddie Hasson. Sam was nice-looking, of average size, standing five feet, six-and-a-half inches tall, with a light complexion, brown hair, bright blue eyes with a hint of hazel, and an athletic, well-muscled physique. Sam enjoyed fine clothes (custom-made shoes and tailored suits, pants, and shirts), cigar smoking, whiskey drinking, and celebrating Thanksgiving. His nephew David Hasson says, "Sam was very generous, and when he'd come over, he was very dapper. He was a very well-dressed man. Always had a fancy car, not necessarily a big car, but this was prior to World War II. He would show up always with a big smile."[35]

Sam fully enjoyed a busy social life and loved going to dances with various women. Later, he wrote about the local scene: "When I came to this country in 1919, there was a great influx of other foreigners that came to this country, and during the summer months on every Sunday, there were picnics going on from various ethnic groups at Fortuna Park on Mercer Island and at Peoples Park in Renton Junction.... Both places had big dance halls. There was dancing, games and concerts. It was very entertaining, and it was sponsored by each group on Sundays throughout the summer."[36]

The energy that Sam devoted to his shoe shops was duplicated in his hobbies—hiking, skiing, bodybuilding, fishing, and photography. In September 1924, Sam's brother Morris (age twenty-four) married Gentil Levy (age nineteen) at Congregation Ezra Bessaroth. By this time, Sam had become an avid—and talented—amateur photographer. "All of our family pictures, all of our wonderful pictures that we all have, they're all from Sam," recalls Morris and Gentil's daughter Daisy Israel. "He always had an eye for photography, for balance, for the buildings. It wasn't just a casual snapping of the camera, it was very methodical. Every picture that he took was not just a snap; it was a composition."[37]

Sam's photograph of the wedding party on the steps of the synagogue later became widely circulated (including on various websites and in the Ellis Island National Museum of Immigration, the Rhodes Jewish Museum, and the University of Washington), although he has never been credited. The occasion became a family story, as Daisy Israel recalls: "It was a very hot September day. And Sam had the wedding party posed on the steps of the building, and he kept moving his equipment, moving, and moving, and moving his equipment. And finally, our grandmother and grandfather said, 'We have to go home and get ready for company.' They left, so they're not in the picture. Sam wanted the whole building. And it's a beautiful picture, and now it's archival. It's everywhere."[38]

Above: Family gathering on the occasion of Morris and Gentil's engagement, 1924. Left to right: back row: Sam, John, Jack (holding Sara), Isaac, David, Nissim, Morris, Gentil; front row: Marie, Robert, Sara, Bona, Sarah, Rita, Raye, Reina. Far Left: Gentil Levy in vintage 15th century Turkish dress with gold embroidery; about the time of her wedding to Morris Israel, c. 1924. Right: Morris Israel (age 24) and Gentil Levy (age 19), about the time of their marriage, September 1924.

Morris and Gentil Israel's wedding, September 7, 1924, on steps of Congregation Ezra Bessaroth. Left to right: Mr. & Mrs. Sam Benezra with infant Joe Benezra, Isaac Levy (sitting), Sarah Levy and Bona Israel (bridesmaids), Morris and Gentil Israel, Hortense Levy, unknown, unknown, Violet Hasson (by tree), Nissim Israel (straw hat).

Sam was equally enthusiastic about developing himself physically. He joined the YMCA, where he found companionship as well as a place to lift weights and train his body. He loved hiking (perhaps from his youth in Rhodes). Sam's nephews recall his stories about hiking around Mercer Island and climbing Mount Rainier. His first adventure on the iconic mountain came in September 1925, the same year he opened Rotary Shoe Repair. Sam was one of a group of fifteen YMCA hikers who climbed to the summit and a couple of days later found their feat pictured in the *Seattle Daily Times*. Sam's second ascent of Mount Rainier came three years later. On July 15, 1928, he and friends from the Mountaineers, an alpine club, scaled the summit. A year later, on July 7, 1929, Sam climbed Pinnacle Peak near Mount Rainier, again with friends from the Mountaineers. Eddie Hasson recalls hearing Sam tell of the events: "I said, 'Uncle, what did you bring to eat? Did you have sandwiches or anything?' He said, 'Nope, I had chicken legs.' He said he'd have four or five chicken legs in a bag—protein."[39]

Sam's love for the outdoors spanned all seasons. In springtime, he went fishing. He swam and fished in Lake Washington during summers and autumns. In the winter months, Sam took up skiing, and by the mid- to late 1930s, he was a member of the Sahalie Ski Club, with which he enjoyed outings to Snoqualmie Pass. He became good friends with Sam Warshal, owner of Warshal's Sporting Goods, and the two often skied together.

Sam heartily enjoyed music as well. He played the oud (a stringed instrument with a short neck and pear-shaped body common throughout the Middle East). Sam's nephew Robert Hasson recalls, "He called it a 'takatookie,' and I remember him playing, strumming." For a time, Sam played in a band that performed Sephardic folk songs (and perhaps Turkish ones as well), appearing once onstage at the Orpheum Theatre. To share his love for music, he bought a violin for his sister, Bona, and paid for her to take lessons. It was an investment that proved worth the expense. Rita Israel Calderon recalls, "Oh, my aunt Bona was a wonderful violinist, she was an excellent violinist. She used to play the violin at the theaters."[40]

"On The Icy Slope..." newspaper clipping in Sam's scrapbook, 1927. Sam is fourth from right.

Other family milestones in the two decades before World War II were cause for celebration. On March 5, 1927, Sam received his Certificate of Naturalization (at age twenty-three, according to the document). In 1931, on August 9, Sam's sister, Bona (age nineteen, one day before her twentieth birthday), married Albert Hasson (age twenty-seven). In keeping with customs from Rhodes, Sephardic parents continued to arrange their children's marriages in Seattle. Eddie Hasson tells the story: "When my mother met my father, my grandmother forced my mother to marry him. He wasn't her first choice. She was a young, gorgeous girl of nineteen. She already was a very accomplished violinist, giving concerts and such. And this guy worked in a produce stand. It was kind of a letdown. She was thinking something else. But that's it. The parents had control over the children's destiny. That was the era. It wouldn't happen today, but that was the era then."[41] The couple soon moved to the duplex owned by Sam at 1910–1912 Spruce Street, where they lived for ten years, until 1941.

In 1932, Sam's brother Morris initiated the first family visit to Soap Lake, a resort town and lake in rural central Washington with "medicinal"

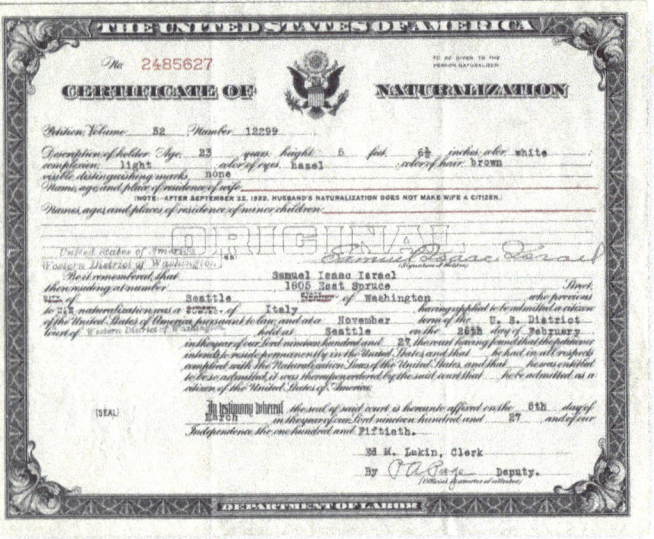

Above: Sam's "Certificate of Naturalization," 1927. Below: Albert and Bona Israel Hasson with Sam, about the time of their marriage, 1931.

healing properties that became a favorite gathering place for Jews, Italians, Greeks, and Russians from Seattle as well as other areas of the Northwest. Mother Sarah suffered from rheumatism, and they quickly discovered that soaks in Soap Lake brought her much-needed relief. Thus, the trek to the sunny resort community became an annual event. Daisy Israel recalls:

> *I was probably two years old, and our grandmother, who had some arthritis or something, came to my father and said, "Ziegman the butcher said I should go to a place called Soap Lake. They won't heal me, but I'll be more comfortable." So, he packed up the car with the pots and pans, because you had to take kosher meat and you couldn't use their pots and pans. And we drove to Soap Lake, which probably took 10 hours. From that point on, we went every year. That was the first time that I know of that anybody in our community ever went to Soap Lake.*[42]

A couple of years after the family's first visit to Soap Lake, on August 12, 1934, Sam's brother Nissim (age twenty-eight) married Violet Hasson (age twenty-two) at Congregation Ezra Bessaroth with Reverend David J. Behar officiating. The family's second generation would have one more marriage, this time near the end of the decade. On January 23, 1938, John (age twenty-seven) married Juliette Levy (age twenty). John became the last of Isaac and Sarah Israel's children to marry.

SAM'S MERCER ISLAND HOUSE

In 1927, on one of Sam's hikes around Mercer Island, he'd spotted a sign advertising an auction of waterfront lots at Faben Point on the west shore of Mercer Island. On October 25, he purchased a lot that measured sixty to eighty feet along Lake Washington and roughly three hundred feet deep for $995. Around the same time, he also bought a waterfront parcel on the south end of the island but chose to focus on the Faben Point lot because it was more accessible by ferry from Seattle at Leschi Point, where he began keeping a small boat to make the trip across the lake to the property. Over the years that followed, Sam added adjoining parcels, giving him a total three hundred contiguous feet of waterfront. The lots, like most of Mercer Island, originally had been forested, but after logging they were covered with heavy brush and brambles, and the waterfront held beautiful views of Lake Washington and Seattle to the west.

Sam's house on Mercer Island, view from beach, c. 1938.

Sam made plans to build a house with a big yard, but first he undertook the seemingly endless chore of clearing brush and tree limbs. Sam continued to work at the shoe shop six days a week, and on Sundays he brought his nephews Robert and Eddie out to the island to help him. A well was dug, and in the mid-1930s, Sam hired a contractor to build a beautiful brick house, probably finishing the basic structure in 1937. There was a small turret over the kitchen and a fireplace in the living room. Sam also had a small cabin built, where he and his nephews often slept in the summer.

Over time, the Mercer Island property came to resemble a mini farm. Sam had a tractor, as well as a riding mower with which he cut the huge grass lawn. He kept dozens of chickens, a donkey, and of course, a dog or two. Eddie Hasson recalls, "When he built the house, there was no bridge. He would park his boat at Leschi, and then he'd take the boat over to Mercer Island. I remember going on the boat and him telling me 'Keep your

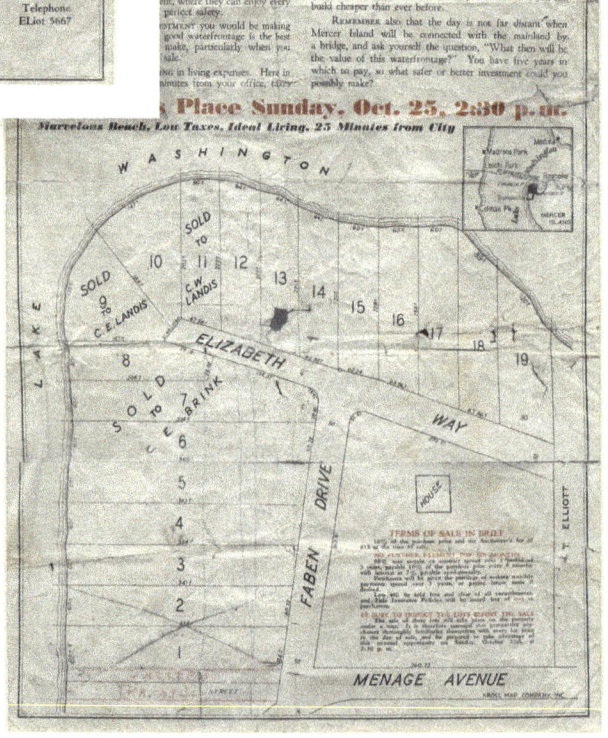

Poster for lots on Mercer Island's Faben Point auction sale, October 25, 1927 (front and back). Sam purchased lots 3, 4, and 5.

head down! Keep your head down!' He didn't want anybody to fall out." Completion of the Lake Washington Floating Bridge in July 1940, with its first Mercer Island exit only a hundred yards from Sam's property, made travel to the house far easier, and it became a favorite weekend getaway for many of Sam's family and friends for more than two decades.[43]

LOVE LOST, WORK FOUND

Sam's heavy work schedule and fast-paced personal life left him with little time to pursue a wife. Yet he was prosperous when many men were struggling, and he made numerous efforts to attract a woman for marriage. The limited documentation we have—a handful of home movies and a couple dozen letters from girlfriends and nieces—suggests there were plenty of women interested. Some were in Seattle, some in San Francisco, and some in Los Angeles. But only one captured Sam's heart: Julia Hanan.

Julia Hanan was born in 1917 in Seattle to Morris and Matilda Hanan.

> *Before the US entered the war in December 1941, Sam also had geared up for the conflict and its domestic repercussions.*

Her parents, like Sam's, had come from the Sephardic community of Rhodes. Morris had found successful employment in the fruit and vegetable trade, and by 1930, he owned his own home. Julia excelled at school, and her father earned enough money to put her through the University of Washington. She graduated in June 1936 with a bachelor of arts in French, then received a University Five-Year Normal Diploma in June 1937 and a master of arts in Spanish in June 1937.[44]

Julia was not only smart and educated, she was pretty, and Sam fell in love with her. "He was crazy about that girl," says Eddie Hasson. Sam

Sam enjoying sun at Soap Lake, c. 1940.

took home movies of Julia, her mother, and her younger sister, Leatrice, on a visit to Sam's Mercer Island house, probably around 1938, showing the three Hanan women smiling and enjoying their time with Sam. The relationship never went further. Julia was twenty-one, and Sam was more than a dozen years older, but age was not the issue.

Sam's nieces and nephews later learned why Sam failed to secure marriage to the woman he loved. One story is recalled by his niece Rita Israel Calderon, who says, "Julia's father said Sam couldn't come around because he didn't have a college education. Sam always felt bad and he felt that it was important to get a good education after that."[45]

Eddie Hasson adds other details: "You ask the father's permission. That was absolutely what you did in the '20s and '30s. Doing proper procedures, he approached Mr. Hanan—who was very, very old country, and he says he wants to marry the daughter, and her father says, 'No. My daughter is only going to marry a professional person. You have an accent and you're a shoemaker.' The answer was no, and that was it."[46]

Sam did attend school, four nights a week, probably at Broadway High School, where he took classes in English and math. During the 1930s, Broadway High School and its neighbor the Edison Technical School, located on Broadway and East Pine Street and today the home of Seattle Central College, offered a number of courses for young men and women to learn skills that would help them make it through the Great Depression. We don't know the results of Sam's studies, nor whether they preceded or followed the conversation with Morris Hanan, but he clearly gained a deep appreciation for the importance of education. His niece Sarah Israel and his nephew Robert graduated from the University of Washington. Sarah majored in sociology and graduated with a bachelor of arts degree and cum laude honors in June 1938. She also attended as a graduate student from autumn 1938 through spring 1939 but did not receive any additional degrees. Sam was proud and "thrilled," says Rita Israel Calderon, and he took movie footage of Sarah's graduation ceremony.[47]

Sam's nephews and nieces have fond memories of Sam's affection. In the summer of 1940, Rita Israel, David and Marie's daughter, married Jack Calderon. She recalls her wedding and Sam's contribution: "When I first got married, all my wedding gifts were from the Kress 5 & 10 Cent Store, except the wedding gift I got from Uncle Sam. He gave me a chest of stainless steel, service for 12, kitchenware. That was the biggest gift I had ever received from anybody."[48]

After Sam's failure to win Julia's hand, he pursued other women, at least into the early 1940s, including "nice, fat Swedish girls," as one friend said. He courted them with gifts of nuts or chocolate. He took them on hikes or road trips to Mount Rainier. He asked several different women to marry him, but

Julia Hanan, c. 1939.

no lasting relationship developed. Increasingly, work became the focus of Sam's life. By December 1940, he had another government contract to repair boots for the US Army. With war in Europe and the Pacific underway, it was only a matter of time before America would become involved. Preparedness included drafting, training, and clothing troops for the impending conflict, from heads to boots. Before the US entered the war in December 1941, Sam also had geared up for the conflict and its domestic repercussions. The workload demanded virtually all of his time, leaving few spare moments to pursue the active social life he once enjoyed. His nephews and nieces ever after would think of him as their "bachelor uncle."[49]

Figure 2

Properties Acquired by Sam Israel, 1919–1940

NAME	DATE PURCHASED	PAID
Duplex, 1910–1912 Spruce Street	1927	$4,000
Mercer Island, Faben Point lot	1927	$995
Mercer Island, south end lot	1927	unknown
Frame Store Building	1927	$1,400
Frame Store Building (for Cascade Market, 1935–1960; later Aurora Rex Building)	10/15/1933	$1,500
Frame Dwelling	12/28/1934	$600
Hotel Building	1/1/1935	$12,933
Frame Building	4/1/1935	$1,500
Woodland Park Store, Ninetieth Street and Aurora Avenue	3/3/1936	$12,500
Austin A. Bell Building*	6/18/1936	$2,500
Douglas Hotel	1937	$12,933
Paramount Building	11/25/1937	$42,577
Rooming House	11/25/1938	$4,000
Stoneway Garage	4/1/1939	$1,500

NAME	DATE PURCHASED	PAID
Old Garage Building	4/10/1939	$1,000
Residence, 1805 Spruce Street	4/10/1939	$700
Leary Way House	4/10/1939	$700
Old Factory Building	4/10/1939	$1,000
Stoneway Building	4/15/1939	$1,500
Leary Way Studio Building	4/15/1939	$3,000
Total		$106,838

TOTAL: 20 properties
***Seattle historic landmark**

CHAPTER 3
Shoes in War, Properties in Peace, 1941–1960

Opposite: Yesler Building, built 1890.

Quien no risica, no rosica.
(Whoever doesn't laugh, doesn't bloom.)

Sam Israel entered his fourth decade in high style. For him these were years of a robust middle age, and the success of his work surpassed his expectations. Sam's personal life was filled with family, interesting friends, several girlfriends, fun hobbies, and outdoor adventures. As Europe and the Pacific plunged into war, Sam's work occupied increasing amounts of his time. It was hard on those around him, though he apparently only took notice occasionally. He marshaled his nephews to help clean up his Mercer Island house and property, and girlfriends chided him for "not writing more often."

In the late 1930s, as the world moved closer to war, President Franklin D. Roosevelt had pushed Congress to pass legislation to boost the nation's defense industries and rapidly improve the infrastructure—roads, tunnels, and bridges—to facilitate movement of troops, supplies, and equipment. Congress also enacted the first national peacetime draft in September 1940. The declaration of war following the Japanese attack on Pearl Harbor in December 1941 and the worldwide conflict that raged through 1945 heavily impacted the people and economy of Washington State. In the greater Seattle area, contracts let by the War Production Board brought an infusion of funds to various industries. Unemployment lines that had marked the city during the Great Depression vanished as job opportunities soared, especially in the shipbuilding and aircraft manufacturing industries. The Boeing Company, Todd Shipyards, and other businesses attracted a host of workers, many from rural towns and the South. The Puget Sound population soared to more than a million residents.

Of course, the men and women who supported the US wartime effort on the home front all wore shoes, and it was cheaper to repair old footwear than to buy new ones. While the local economy gradually moved out of stagnation, the shoe repair business boomed.

> *As the US geared up for war, so did Sam. He had been doing work for the government, and a new request for bids prompted a crafty move by the shoemaker.*

THE ARMY SHOE BUSINESS

In late 1939, many believed that it was "a question of time, there's going to be a war," as Sam said. In the late 1920s, Fort Lawton had been home to some three hundred army soldiers and officers, a number that swelled in 1933, when the Civilian Conservation Corps, one of President Roosevelt's New Deal programs, put Americans to work. At nearby Fort Lewis, the years 1927 to 1939 witnessed major construction of permanent facilities. By 1938, some five thousand troops were stationed at the fort; by the end of December 1940, the number grew to twenty-six thousand; a year later, thirty-seven thousand soldiers were stationed at Fort Lewis.

As war clouds loomed over Europe, preparedness for facilities and training for soldiers intensified, and the newly populated army base at Fort Lewis issued a request for bids to repair shoes and boots. Sam had been doing work for the government, and a new request for bids prompted a crafty move by the shoemaker. All of Sam's competitors bid over $1.50 per pair, and his bid of $1.25 won the contract. "I wanted to help the war as much

Army Building, built 1923.

as possible, not be profiteering," he recollected later. "The idea is how reasonable you can make it and still make a profit—not what you can get away with." He planned to renegotiate his army shoe contract to reduce the amount he was paid by fifteen cents per shoe with the provision that the money go toward the war effort.[1]

Business was brisk and profits soared. Sam's operation needed more space, and fast. To meet the demand, in April 1942, just five months after the US entered World War II, Sam purchased a building next door to Wingfoot Shoe Repair at 2107–2111 Third Avenue (on Third and Lenora) and named it the Army Building. He set about installing equipment and systems for mass production. Since they worked on only one style of footwear—the army boot—they needed only one type of machine, and operations could be streamlined. He later told the story of how events unfolded:

> *I designed a few other little things to make it a mass production. And then I check on the time, the seconds, how long it takes each operation. It was 24 operations to repair a pair of shoes from the beginning, to be tied up, to be shipped away. Each move was timed. Then to be sure, I done the work myself to be sure. . . . And then when I found out just exactly what it cost, the next bid that came along, I bid sixty-five cents instead of a dollar and a quarter. I didn't care what anybody else was going to bid. My idea was to make it just as reasonable as I can and get them out right. And that's it. I got all the contracts.*[2]

Sam employed up to thirty people during the day and a couple dozen most evenings, including carpenters (who knew how to drive a nail straight) and women, along with a dozen or more cobblers, many of whom worked at their own shops during the day and moonlighted at Sam's assembly lines. The Army Building hummed fourteen hours a day, seven days a week. Shifts ran from 8:00 a.m. to 6:00 p.m., then from 6:00 p.m. until 10:00 p.m. The work was intensive, and Sam rarely took a break. His niece Sarah Israel wrote to him from San Francisco on December 28, 1940, "I hope those government contracts are not getting you down."[3]

One facet of the operation had Sam's unique stamp—quality control. He would not sacrifice the superior quality of his company's shoe repair simply for money. He later told the story to a journalist, who reported Sam's tale: "[Sam] hired a woman whose only job was to run her hand through each finished boot and set aside those that didn't feel right. Sam said if the boot didn't feel right to a woman's hand it wouldn't feel right on a soldier's foot, and all of the rejected boots would be put on a shelf and Sam would come in at night and fix them himself."[4]

Wartime economics also brought challenges. A *Seattle Post-Intelligencer* article highlighted the issue after interviewing Sam:

> *Samuel Israel, in whose large plant at 2107 Third Avenue, hundreds of thousands of pairs of Army boots and shoes are being repaired and reconditioned on contract said yesterday he is no longer able to employ cobblers at regular union wages and must pay a premium considerably above scale.*

Scrapbook clipping, Sam's donation of surplus rubber to aid the war effort, "Four Tons of Rubber Heels," *Seattle Star*, June 16, 1942.

"I'd gladly pay a man $60 a week here. And the next thing I know he's working somewhere else for $80 or $100 a week. What is the result? The result is that in order to make a profit on $80 and $100 a week cobblers' buyers have to charge the public a good deal more than the ceiling price allows. They charge more and they add the cost of a lot of little unnecessary services." So, they charge for unnecessary services to make up.[5]

In June 1942, Sam's contributions to the war effort made the newspaper. He had been saving the discarded rubber soles and heels from boots for at least two years, and rubber was in short supply. When a campaign started to donate old rubber to be recycled, Sam was ready. A June 17 article in the *Seattle Post-Intelligencer*—complete with a photograph of a large mound of soles and heels being shoveled into boxes and loaded onto a truck—highlighted Sam's Wingfoot Shoe Repair shop's donation of several tons of shoe soles to aid the war effort in Seattle during the salvage rubber soles campaign. (The *Seattle Star* reported the total as four tons; the *Seattle Post-Intelligencer* reported six tons.) For his contribution, Sam received a check from Richfield Oil Company, which he donated to the Red Cross.[6]

Over the course of the war, the operation's production of a reported 2,500 pairs a day at a profit of ten cents each (he later told a reporter) gradually accrued a huge profit. Expenses were relatively high too, but the net income was significant. Robert Hasson recalls a memorable experience with Sam from this time:

> *He used to bring to Mercer Island suitcases of money, cash, banded $20 bills. He would be sitting at one end of the table, and I would be sitting at the other end of the table, and he would take the band off and he would count it because he didn't trust anybody. Then he would give it to me, and he said, "You count it," and I would count it.*
>
> *One time, he slipped a $20 bill away from it and he had me count it. Of course, I wasn't counting them all. I was nine, ten, eleven, twelve years old. I got tired of counting. So, I said, "It's all there." He says, "No it's not," and he held up the $20 bill. He says, "You're not counting it. Now you count it." I said, "Okay, Uncle. I'll count it."*[7]

Though all those suitcases of cash might have given an impression of easy money, the government paid many invoices late and sometimes not at all. Sam continued to submit invoices to the army and kept working but had to borrow money from a bank to keep the payroll going. Eventually, the delayed payment turned into a windfall. "He never did get paid until after the war," says Eddie Hasson. "I understand it was like several million dollars that he had earned all those years." However, none of the financial records from this period in Sam's life have survived to confirm the story. We do know that in the 1940s Sam's income came from two streams: the shoe repair business and rents from his properties. Most suggestive of the significant boost to his net worth are his property purchases.[8]

SAMIS LAND COMPANY

Between 1941 and 1947, Sam acquired fourteen properties valued at $653,500, and his growing real estate portfolio demanded more and more time. Many of Sam's buildings held special meaning for him, and in later years he passed on the stories to his nephews. One example is the Drexel Hotel. Eddie Hasson recalls:

> *That's the era that Sam had his office at Henry Broderick's. He bought the Drexel Hotel in 1944, because he obviously thought the price was right. The tenant was a Greek. There was a tavern. There was a Greek guy that Sam right away befriended because Sam spoke perfect Greek. The guy wanted a lease extension, something like that. Sam said, "No, I can't give you an extension. I'll give you a new lease. Because your lease has a percentage in it." In other words, the lease had where you'd have to pay a percentage of your gross. He says, "A Jewish person should never make a person a liar. Therefore, I'm going to just give you a flat rent"—$75 a month or whatever it is—"but I would never have somebody tell me what their sales are because I know they're lying." That was his quote.*[9]

Top: Scientific Building, built 1920. Bottom: US Rubber Building, built 1902.

Sam often renamed a building, as in the case of the Army Building, based on his purpose for it, or sometimes after a former occupant. The Scientific Building (purchased in 1946), for example, was formerly the Blumenthal Building, which Sam renamed in honor of the previous owner McKesson, a science and technical instruments supply company. The US Rubber Building (purchased in 1945), was named for the first tenant, US Rubber Company, from which Sam inherited a basement full of tires.[10] One acquisition was reported in the newspaper, his purchase in January 1947 of the Webster-Brinkley assembly plant on Airport Way. The property, located in the industrial area south of downtown Seattle, was composed of three separate parcels totaling seven acres, valued at $250,000 and acquired by Sam at the bargain price of $114,700. Today, ten of the fourteen buildings he purchased between 1941 and 1947 are either designated Seattle historic landmark buildings or are listed in the Pioneer Square Historic District (see figure 3).[11]

Sam's successful wartime and immediate postwar investing could be attributed, in part, to fortuitous timing. After the war, the local economy sagged, prices for consumer goods and services fell off, and the real estate market slowed down. Sam began to concentrate on real estate and gradually let go of the shoe repair business.

As one of a handful of investors with plenty of cash, Sam could purchase buildings and land at below market value, a tactic that fit perfectly with his real estate philosophy. And a little luck helped. "He had good deals and he had bad deals," reflects David Hasson. "He did have the ability to get very, very lucky. More than normal. There were things that should not have gone his way and went his way."[12]

After more than two decades in the real estate business, Sam had learned much from his association with Henry Broderick and had developed his personal approach, sprinkled with plenty of savvy. "He worked on instinct," says David Hasson. Sam viewed Seattle in terms of its growth potential, and to him that meant a north-south expansion. Accordingly, he focused on the areas that he thought the city was going to develop—downtown, Pioneer Square, and south into the SoDo district. At the time, Pioneer Square was better known as Skid Road, a run-down neighborhood marked by empty and dilapidated buildings, shabby hotels, and cheap taverns, populated mainly by the poor and destitute, vagrants, and alcoholics. Here, properties were much easier to acquire. Moreover, notes Adam Hasson, Sam's great-nephew, "He always focused on acquiring corners; control the corner and you control the whole block. And, he was always trying to assemble adjacent properties."[13]

By mid-1946, Sam's real estate holdings were substantial and needed full-time management. To facilitate the transition from shoemaking to property investing, Sam formed a corporation with a name derived from his own, Samis Land Company. The incorporation papers filed on July 1, 1946, tell an interesting story. Sam named three stockholders: himself, his brother John, and his niece Sarah Israel. Capital stock in the company was to be 500 shares; Sam owned 498 shares, and John and Sarah were minority shareholders, each owning one share. The reason for incorporation, Sam declared in the document, was "for purposes of financial prestige, deeding and accepting deeds to real property, and for other and sundry advantages." Most all of Sam's holdings were turned over to the Samis Land Company, except for the Paramount Building, which was under litigation, and Cascade Market, which was owned equally by Sam and Nissim.[14]

Assets of the company (buildings, furnishings, etc.) totaled $458,443. At the end of its first year of operation in July 1947, Samis Land Company reported rents of $101,848 and expenses of $57,968, with a net income of $44,480. Over the course of the next decade, as Sam's land and building values increased, the rental income and expenses remained roughly proportionate, and net annual income for the company averaged about $65,000. Sam also continued to buy property as an individual. Eddie Hasson explains, "And then after that, the corporation would buy a piece or he would. It would depend on whichever checking account had the most money. There was no rhyme or reason to it."[15]

By the early 1950s, Sam's transition from shoemaking to real estate had gained considerable momentum. Since 1946, he had been acquiring properties in Soap Lake, and as his interests there grew, he recognized it was time to plan his departure from the shoe business, and eventually from Seattle. In January 1954, Sam gave Wingfoot Shoe Repair to his brother John and transferred to him the contract for the shoe repair equipment that he had rented at $8.50 a month for twenty-three years from United Shoe Repairing Machines Company in Boston. It was a turning point for Sam. While he remained a simple shoemaker at heart, he was now officially, in the words of Eddie Hasson, "an accumulator of buildings and property."[16]

FAMILY IN WAR AND PEACE

While Sam's contract to repair boots for the army produced a good income, augmented by rents from his properties, his personal life revolved around family and friends. He continued to live with his parents in the house at 1805 Spruce Street, and he supported them in their final years. His siblings and their spouses had growing families, and soon his nieces and nephews were moving from childhood into their teens, then early adulthood. Fortunately, many of their recollections of the family have been recorded in a series of oral history interviews. Their insights draw a fascinating portrait of the 1940s and 1950s.

Bona and Sam maintained a strong sister-brother bond and remained connected as Bona's life took a new path after marriage to Albert Hasson. She and Albert rented half of the duplex owned by Sam at 1910–1912

Spruce Street for four years, and their first sons, Robert, Eddie, and David, were born there. It was while living there that Bona applied for US citizenship, filing her Declaration of Intention in 1936. (She used the name Buena, although the 1930 US Census lists her as Bona, as does the 1940 Census.) In 1941, they moved a dozen blocks east, purchasing a home at 317 Temple Place, where their next children, Victor and Marilyn, were born.

Sam's nephews and nieces recall their grandfather Isaac in his last years. To Eddie Hasson, a seven-year-old in 1943, he seemed to be "100 years old." Eddie recalls, "My only memory of him was in a rocking chair." One of the movies Sam took of his father shows him with a short white beard, wearing

> *By the early 1950s, Sam's transition from shoemaking to real estate had gained considerable momentum. . . . It was time to plan his departure from the shoe business.*

a hat, an open-collar shirt, a dark vest, and trousers, and smoking a hand-rolled cigarette, then walking along the neighborhood sidewalk with his hands behind his back. Sometime in 1943, Isaac fell and broke a hip. He never got out of bed. The end came almost a year later.[17]

Yitzhak (Isaac) David Israel died at the age of ninety-two on July 19, 1944. It was the first death in the family since coming to the US. Robert Hasson says, "Sam was really devastated." So was his widowed mother. She no longer wanted to live in the house on Spruce Street. "She took it very hard," Sam recalled. "She said, 'Take me away from here. I don't want to stay here anymore.'" They sold the home, and Sam's mother stayed at her children's homes for three months at a stretch, beginning with Bona and Albert's house on Temple Place.[18]

For several years, Bona gave violin lessons in her home. Eddie Hasson recalls one of her students was Jack Benaroya, who later became a major benefactor of the Seattle Symphony and other civic organizations. She also taught her oldest son, Robert, to play the violin starting at age five, and he became concert master of the Seattle Youth Symphony Orchestra. However, Bona had little time after more babies were born in the late 1930s and early 1940s. "She gave up after Robert," says Eddie. "She never taught me any instrument. I always felt cheated that I didn't learn an instrument. But my mother said, 'Eddie, I started you on the cello, but you didn't want to do it.'"[19]

The Hasson home continued many Rhodesli traditions. Eddie remembers his father trotting out old proverbs and sometimes cursing in Ladino and Turkish. "There would be a customer at the Cascade Market. The customer's giving him a bad time, so my dad would say, 'Okay, good to see you, such and such, and such and such.' It was a curse word in Turkish! Sometimes, he would say in Ladino, '*avlastino*,' which means 'he talks too much,' or he would say, '*martek*,' which is 'hammer' or 'hard head.'" Religion and education also were an integral part of the home. "We celebrated all the holidays," recalls Eddie Hasson. "My dad and mom made sure that all three of us went to synagogue on Saturday whether we wanted to or not."[20]

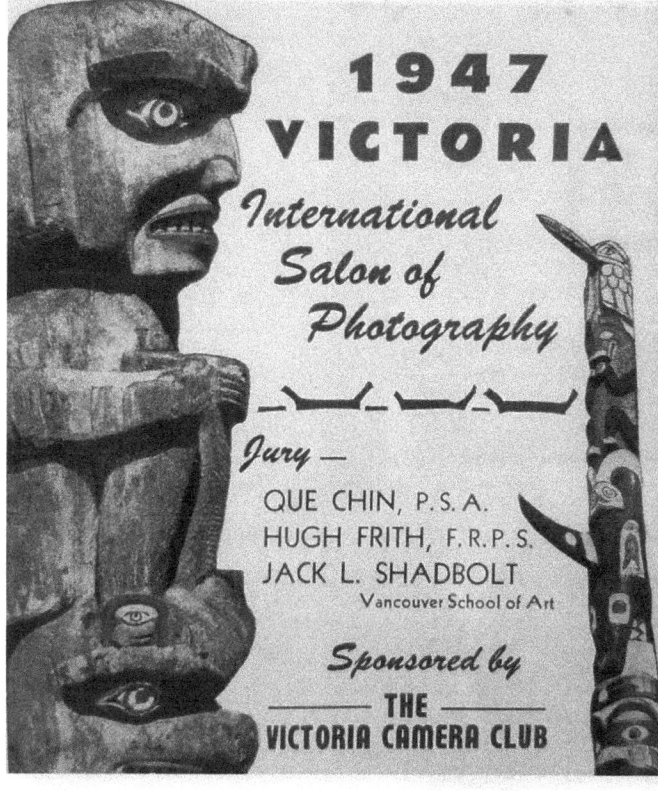

Sam's exhibitor card for the Victoria International Salon of Photography, 1947.

During World War II, Bona joined many Jewish women in the community in actively supporting the US war effort. "My mother was really Americanized; she was a modern mother," says Eddie Hasson. Bona worked with the local Community Chest, raising money and selling war bonds, and she served for a time as president of the Ladies Auxiliary at Congregation Ezra Bessaroth.[21]

Sam often enjoyed home life at the Hassons'. Eddie Hasson recalls, "I remember him coming to our house for dinner. My mother used to make Shabbat dinners for him. He'd come by, pick them up on his way home, and so we saw my uncle quite a bit. I think that, because he was close to my mother, so we saw him growing up. As I got older, we would go to his Mercer Island house and hang out, swim, and sunbathe on his dock."[22]

Sam's love of music was another bond with Bona. Robert Hasson tells the story: "Sam liked the idea that I had the violin, and he made me bring it with me when I used to come. He liked me to play for him. So, I played the violin for him. He liked me to sing to him. I would sing all these tunes that you learn at the synagogue. I knew them, and he just enjoyed them and liked me to sing. He said, 'Sing this song. Sing this song.'"[23]

Sam's favorite melody then, and apparently for the rest of his life, was from the Haggadah, when the family celebrated the Pesach Seder, the line in translation beginning "When Israel went out of Egypt . . ." (We might well wonder if Sam felt partial to the line because of the double meaning of the word *Israel*.) Though not strictly observant, Sam deeply enjoyed traditional holiday celebrations, particularly Pesach. In this, too, he asserted the force of his personality. Though Sam had no children, he took in a generic way the *mitzvah* to "tell your son" the story of the Jews' liberation from slavery in Egypt. "Sam had these cards printed up with the order of the Seder service for Passover; it was in Ladino," says Eddie Hasson. "He was the expert. He handed out copies so everyone would do it his way." The Israel and Hasson families enjoyed the traditional wine, Sephardic foods from Rhodes such as *yaprakis*, reading and stories, as well as music and the songs that Sam loved.[24]

RHODES, THE HOLOCAUST, AND DEATH IN THE FAMILY

For the extended Israel family, the death of Isaac in 1944 was only one tragedy that year. The other played out in their homeland. Rhodes had been taken over by Fascist Italy in December 1936. In September 1938, the regime enacted severe anti-Jewish regulations, prompting some two thousand Jews to flee the island. For a time, those who stayed felt hopeful, even after Benito Mussolini was removed from power in July 1943. British leaders tried to persuade the Italian forces on Rhodes to change allegiance to the Allies, but the German Army invaded and seized the island after the brief Battle of Rhodes, and the Nazis occupied the island starting in September 1943.

On July 19, 1944, the Nazi command issued orders that brought an end to six centuries of Jewish life on Rhodes. All valuables were confiscated, and Nazi soldiers forced 1,674 men, women, and children—nearly all of the island's 1,800 Jews—onto boats and shipped them to Auschwitz and other concentration camps where most were murdered. Only 151 deportees survived, 120 of them women. The Turkish consul, risking his own life and the lives of his family, managed to save 42 Jewish families, about 200 persons in total, who could document Turkish citizenship or were family members of Turkish citizens.[25]

The Israel extended families, as well as those of the Hassons and other in-laws, the Galantes, Francos, Alhadeffs, and Levys, were wiped out, along with the friends Sam and his family had grown up with. (After the war, the family would learn that one member had survived the Holocaust, Albert Hasson's sister, Sylvia, who had been in Auschwitz.) It was a bitter and tragic

> *Though not strictly observant, Sam deeply enjoyed traditional holiday celebrations, particularly Pesach. In this, too, he asserted the force of his personality.*

end to the community and a way of life for generations. In the terse words of historian Rabbi Marc Angel, "The Sephardic community in Rhodes was born as a result of the expulsion of the Jews from Spain. It died in the ashes of the German concentration camps."[26]

Sam's nieces and nephews never heard him speak of the impact of the Holocaust on Rhodes. Certainly, he and the Israel family felt the horror of their loss and the grief that came in its wake as deeply as other Jewish families. But Sam told few stories about his youth and family in Rhodes. Robert Hasson recalls, "He never talked, even my father never talked, about the fact that his family was still in the Island of Rhodes until they were killed. You never talked about that and neither did Sam. I never heard him talk about the Island of Rhodes."[27]

In 1947, Sylvia Hasson traveled to Seattle and spent a year with the family. The sudden appearance of Auntie Sylvia surprised Eddie:

> *There are no relatives left, everybody, every Jew, was taken away by the Germans in 1944, everyone. And my aunt was one of the survivors, my Aunt Sylvia. My dad kept his mouth shut, I had no idea when I was a kid, of course I was only a kid, 11 years old, I had no idea that my dad had a sister. My dad had a mother, a father, and five siblings. One of the*

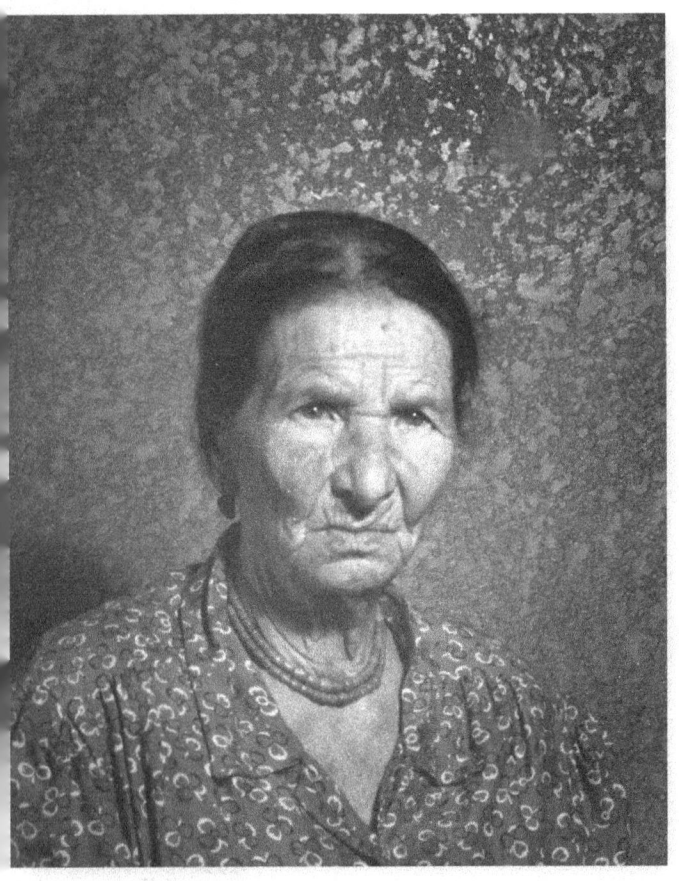

Sarah Israel, c. 1945.

siblings was married and had two children, and they all had lived in Rhodes. Then, one day my father got a letter from my Auntie Sylvia, that she is alive, and she's in Italy in a camp, and to help her come to Seattle. And my dad did everything he could to get her here. She was in Auschwitz, and she was the only one of my dad's entire family that survived. Everyone else was killed.[28]

Sam's mother, then in her mid-eighties, remained the matriarch. On weekends, Sam would work on his Mercer Island house, but during the week after work, he would stay with his mother. "All the brothers would meet there after work, but they all lived within an eight-block radius, and they would come and stop, say hello to their mother," recalls Robert Hasson. "On Friday nights, Nissim would bring a carton of cigarettes—Sarah and most of her family smoked—and they would bring food."[29]

Rita Israel Calderon recalls a special memory of Grandmother Sarah from one of the family trips to Soap Lake: "I went with my Aunt Gentil and my Uncle Morris, I went as a babysitter. I had to sleep with my grandmother in this little tin cabin and it poured rain that night and it had a tin roof. I thought we were going to die, because my grandmother was saying the *Shema* all night."[30]

In early 1947, the world lost another Rhodesli, Sam's mother. Sarah fell gravely ill, suffering from a gangrene infection associated with her diabetes. Sarota (Sarah) Biton Israel died at the age of eighty-nine on May 8, 1947. The loss deeply affected Sam. "He was very close to his mother," says Eddie Hasson. "According to my mother, he treated her like a god. She wielded over him. He did what she told him was right." Robert Hasson recalls that the day Sarah died, Sam was moving boxes out of the house. When Sam finished, Robert found him sitting at the top of the stairs, "bawling his eyes out, and there was no consoling him."[31]

PASTIMES: ART AND THE GREAT OUTDOORS

With both of his parents gone, Sam's Mercer Island house, which became much more easily accessible after completion of the floating bridge in 1940, became the hub of his personal and social life. Here, he enjoyed entertaining family, friends, and girlfriends. "He loved to talk, and he was always talking about his girlfriends," recalls Robert Hasson. Some stories were funny, some simply odd, and not all of them had a happy ending. In one story, a girlfriend asked Sam to drive her to Portland, Oregon. "When they arrived," says Robert Hasson, "and the door opened, she introduced him to her fiancé."[32]

Sam enjoyed amusing his guests by singing a favorite tune, "Oh My Darling, Clementine." He also loved poetry and amazed friends and family by reciting long verses from memory. His favorite poems were by Robert W. Service. Among those, none stood higher in the pantheon than "The Cremation of Sam McGee." Eddie Hasson tells an interesting story about this part of Sam's life: "He bought more than a dozen books—he gave me a book, Robert a book, David a book, *The Poems of Robert Service*. He would read 'The Shooting of Dan McGrew' and other Alaska ones. He knew 'Bessie's Boil' by heart. When we were in his house on Mercer Island, he would be reciting the poems to us, and we would be following him. Eventually I was able to do this entire poem by heart as a kid. He loved Robert Service."[33]

Sam prepared copies of the lyrics to the old favorite, "Clementine," to hand out at parties.

THE HOBBIES MATURE: PHOTOGRAPHY, FISHING, AND HUNTING

Among Sam's hobbies, the one he undertook with the most energy, ambition, and talent was photography. In one of his downtown properties, the Telephone Building, Sam organized a photography studio, stored

"WESTERN," by Samuel Israel, 1106 Third Ave., was made in a photographic class conducted by Que Chin, well-known camera artist.

Scrapbook clipping of Sam's photo, *Western*, featured in the fifth annual Seattle International Exhibition of Photography, 1948.

professional-quality equipment, and installed a full dark room, where he printed many of the images he captured. He took instruction from a noted local photographer, Que Chin, and as his skills improved, his natural eye produced some remarkable photographs. Encouraged by friends in the Evergreen Camera Club and family, he joined the Seattle Photographic Society and began to enter contests. Between 1945 and 1950, Sam submitted prints that were accepted in at least nineteen exhibitions from Seattle to New York, Chicago, Memphis, Baltimore, and Pasadena, among other places.

His two most successful efforts were placement of three prints in the 18th Annual New York International Exhibition of Photography, and in April 1948, he received an award for the print he called *Destitute* in the Seattle

International Exhibition of Photography. The evocative black-and-white portrait of a shabbily dressed older man sagging against a wall was cited as "outstanding" by judges for the exhibition and selected for the permanent collection at the Seattle Art Museum. The image brought national recognition to Sam when it was selected for the *1949 Annual* of the Photographic Society of America as one of fifty photos by talented amateur photographers. In 1951, the society honored Sam with an Award of Merit and designated him a "one star exhibitor" for placing forty acceptances of nine different prints in recognized exhibitions.[34] (See figure 4.)

David Hasson recalls Sam's love for the camera and his talent for creative photography: "He was a very artistic man. He was an artist and he was always curious about art. Basically, photography was that form, . . . and he did some very, very beautiful work. He also had an engineer's mind. He had his own studio where he did all his portrait work and did all of his processing. Many of the professional photographers in Seattle were friends of his and he studied with them."[35]

As an avid outdoorsman as well as amateur photographer, during the spring and summer Sam enjoyed salmon fishing in Puget Sound and swimming in Lake Washington—an easy step out the front door from his Mercer Island house. Apparently, Sam didn't mind the chilly water—his friend Rosie Israel wrote from Los Angeles, asking, "Do you still swim in your icy cold lake?"[36] In the late 1940s, as Sam began to spend more time in eastern Washington, he took up a new outdoor sport, hunting. For a Jew, this was something unusual. Most authorities on Jewish law say that hunting animals for sport is not permissible. Naturally, Sam had his own "philosophy" of hunting. As Robert Hasson put

Above: Sam's award-winning portrait, *Destitute*, 1948.
Below: Sam's Award of Merit, 1951, for placement of 9 different prints in 40 photographic exhibitions.

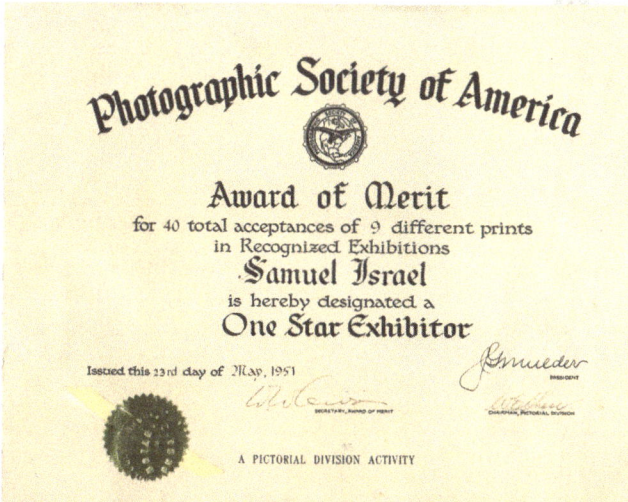

Robert Hasson in his Boy Scout uniform at Sam's place on Mercer Island, c. 1943. Sam was very proud of his nephew, and Robert later credited Sam's enthusiasm for the Scouts to Robert's participation.

it, "He made his own rules." Sam later explained his ideas to a newspaper reporter, who summarized Sam's views for readers: "A strong advocate of Judaism, Israel tries to apply the teachings of the Torah to his own hunting practices, he said. He acknowledged that the Torah forbids sport hunting and only allows a designated person, the 'shochet,' to supervise the slaughtering of animals. The rules are designed to prevent animals from suffering needlessly. While he doesn't follow the precise law, he does try to keep his prey from suffering, he said."[37]

One story recalled by Robert Hasson shows another facet of Sam's hunting philosophy. He says,

They had an advertisement that you could go and shoot elk and deer on this ranch. They're raised, actually bred for that purpose. So, people go along in a Jeep and shoot anything that comes in sight. So, he went there. He saw that they weren't hunting, they were killing. There was no hunting involved. There was this huge expanse of land and deer running around in it, people going around shooting deer. He didn't partake of any of it. He said, "I couldn't do that. I want to go hunting, I don't want to have a sitting duck."[38]

Sam took his nephew Robert Hasson (then a teenager) on one trip, hunting deer on his Soap Lake farm, and other times joined friends on a variety of hunting excursions, including horse-packing trips into the high mountains in search of deer, elk, sheep, and other big game. In 1955 and 1956, Sam devoted so much time to hunting expeditions in Canada and Alaska that he had nephew Robert, who was at the time an elementary school teacher, stay most of the school year at the Mercer Island house.

REAL ESTATE GROWTH AND GROWING PAINS

Through the 1950s, Sam's property holdings continued to grow, though not as fast as in the previous decade. Between December 1950 and January

1951, Sam purchased nine parcels of land totaling approximately 240 acres around Menzel Lake near Granite Falls in Snohomish County. "Sam bought Menzel Lake, so he could go fishing," says Eddie Hasson. "I went there as a teenager, but it wasn't a lot of fun." It was fun for Sam, though. Besides fishing, he had a cabin to stay in during the summers, a canoe for getting around on the water, and Grace. Mrs. Grace McWhirter became Sam's secretary around 1950, answering phones, filing documents, and typing memos. She worked for him for more than a decade (at least to 1961), until she died around 1963. She became a trusted friend, and the two lived together off

Through the 1950s, Sam's property holdings continued to grow, though not as fast as in the previous decade.

and on for many years—a business arrangement, not an intimate relationship. Robert Hasson believes that Grace prolonged Sam's life. "She helped him through his trials and tribulations," Robert affirms, "and did his secretarial work, and cooked for him, and took care of him when he was sick."[39]

In the 1950s, Sam's real estate brought some unexpected financial hassles. One headache was delivered by the City of Seattle in the summer of 1950. Sam and Samis Land Company became embroiled in a legal dispute with the city as one in a series of city property condemnations associated with the construction of the Alaskan Way Viaduct. The Paramount Building at First Avenue and Battery Street stood above the planned Battery Street tunnel, and the city condemned the structure, ordering the owners to move it. The city sought a writ of assistance ordering the King County Sheriff's Office to move ("readjust") the property to an adjoining lot to make way for the construction of the Alaskan Way Viaduct. Samis Land Company, along with its co-owner, Western Life Insurance Company, were awarded $58,857 by a jury in the King County Superior Court as compensation to move the building. After Sam studied the situation with his attorney Joe Diamond (who later became wealthy as "the king of self-serve parking lots in Seattle"), he refused.[40]

Sam fired off a letter to the King County Department of Public Works protesting the court's allotment to move the building as "insufficient." The amount, Sam declared, had been determined on the basis of testimony by "irresponsible professional witnesses" engaged by the City of Seattle. Sam offered the city's experts an opportunity to perform the work for the price they quoted, but they declined. Sam stated that other contractors he had asked to review the site reported that the relocation work could not be done for the amount set by the court. Accordingly, co-owners Samis Land Company and Western Life Insurance Company elected to keep the judgment and notified the city it could cut off a corner of the building to allow the viaduct to pass by without damaging the structure. They offered to give the money to the city if it would move the building.[41]

The judge in the case, Judge Henry Agnew, commented, "It appeared two of the City's witnesses had their fingers crossed when they testified before the condemnation jury that they could move the building for $48,000." Judge Agnew concluded, "The judgment for the value of the building [$58,857] should be substituted and the City then proceed to tear it down, since that would be less costly than moving it." The litigation continued into 1951. In their next court appearance, Samis's attorney, Joe Diamond, argued that the property was valued at $140,000. The city finally offered $110,000 and the sale closed. Further investigation by city officials determined that razing the building would be too expensive, far more than the property was worth. In 1954, the city sold the building to the Catholic Archdiocese of Seattle, which turned it into the Catholic Seamen's Club.[42]

Another headache arrived in the form of the Internal Revenue Service, which audited Sam's income tax returns in 1954 and 1958. Robert Hasson says, "I remember he was so upset he was swearing at the accountant. He said, 'It's all the accountant's fault. I didn't know he did this. I'm going to get sued. I don't want to go to jail!'" As a result of this and other unhappy experiences with the IRS, Sam increasingly became averse to paying taxes. David Hasson recalls, "He had a philosophy that he wasn't going to sell anything, because there was no real reason to sell it. But from time to time, people would come to him and would want to purchase something, and he would say that, 'Yes, I will sell, but I would only do it with an exchange.'" In other words, Sam would defer capital gains tax and related federal income tax liability on the property by means known as a 1031 exchange, a reference to IRS Code Section 1031.[43]

EYES EAST TO SOAP LAKE

Sam Israel's life shifted in major ways in the 1950s. His parents were gone. Julia Hanan had married in 1948. His favorite niece, Sarah, had married

David Alhadeff in 1947, and afterward, he saw relatively little of her as she focused on her own family life. Other nieces and nephews were getting married, and while Uncle Sam was on good terms with his relatives, he remained a lone bachelor among families. In the small Sephardic neighborhood of Seattle, Sam came to be increasingly socially isolated. His financial success allowed him to think more widely about his life. Sam gave up on the prospect of finding a wife and began to look eastward toward Soap Lake, the family's traditional vacation place.

Sam with the original Mariuch, c. 1945.

Sam first bought property in Grant County in early 1946, a few months before the incorporation of Samis Land Company. On April 9, 1946, he signed a contract to buy five lots totaling 251 acres on the southwest corner of Soap Lake from the Northern Pacific Railway for $20,000. The land overlooked the town and became the heart of "Sam's farm." Other purchases in Soap Lake soon followed. Between September 1947 (four months after his mother died) and September 1954, Sam bought eight waterfront lots and other land in Soap Lake. In 1955, he purchased the Bell property adjoining his farm, and in March 1956 added the Zimmer property.[44]

In early 1952, happy to share his place with new neighbors, Sam offered the City of Soap Lake use of his lakeshore land for the Grand Coulee Cavalcade, a nighttime event in Soap Lake during the Columbia Basin Water Festival over Memorial Day weekend. The city agreed, and Sam hired a bulldozer to level the area. An article in the May 12 issue of the *Wenatchee World* featured a photograph of Sam with his faithful German shepherd, Mariuch, with the caption "CAVALCADE SITE SHAPED—Owner Sam Israel, Seattle realtor, surveys the work done on his lakeshore land to prepare it for the production of the Grand Coulee Cavalcade, starlight pageant at Soap Lake May 27–June 1, during the Columbia Basin Water Festival. Stage area has been bulldozed level. Seating will be on hillside to right."[45]

With so many trips to Soap Lake, Sam realized that he needed a place to live in the area. In 1948, he bought the Bontius Building, a two-story structure constructed in 1940 by I. C. Bontius that had a drugstore on the ground level and two apartments upstairs (it later became the Del-Red Tavern).

Eddie Hasson recalls, "One apartment was for my mother and one was for him. We would stay every summer for about seven, eight years in a row."[46]

Toward the end of the 1950s, Sam was ready to move. The time had come to open a new chapter in his life. His vision was clear. He would have

> *Sam gave up on the prospect of finding a wife and began to look eastward toward Soap Lake, the family's traditional vacation place.*

new friends and new properties. His brothers and sister and their families would come to visit. And he wanted his place there to be more than a hobby farm. He wanted a genuine, working ranch with cattle, horses, and even a lop-eared donkey. And dogs. Mariuch the Pooch would have many friends.

Sam kept a journal to track his activities and improvements at the farm between 1957 and 1961. The log (which reveals Sam's poor spelling, among other things) begins, "Dec 21, 57. Arived Soap Lake/Left Jan 27." The details document the immense amount of work he undertook to establish the farm and create a working cattle ranch. He visited for a week or two at a time, and between trips he needed good farm help. Finding dependable men proved elusive. The next entry was pithy and portentous: "DEC 23, 57. JAMES . . . PUT IN JAIL FOR STEALING GAS MOTOR, BARB WIRE, HE IS NO GOOD, JUMPET WIRES OF TRUCK USED IT WIHTOUT CONSENT, USE 230 GAL GAS. 20 DAYS SENTENCE." One hopeful worker after the next was dismissed, for all sorts of reasons: "smokes continuously, did not show any enthusiasm"; "N G" (no good); "no one at farm, no work was done for 10 days." Another man took $220 "for doing nothing"; another "did no work at all, refused to feed cattle, no water on cattle & horses"; and another "left hay on field, left 9 calves to be born, 2 died, very dirty, will not take orders, . . . maybe worked 4 hours a day . . . NO GOOD"; "fired 2 days later

> 1960 91
>
> JUNE   OMAC HATCHER & SON TEL 23
>   MR BERT WASSEL,
>   JOHN LONGBOTTOM OKANOGAN
>
> JULY 5   FIRED ▬▬▬▬▬ HE WAS
>   AS BAD AS THE REST, FAMILY
>   WORST   LEFT FOR VACATION
>   REFUSE TO WORK, PROHIBIT
>   ME FROM GIVEN ORDERS
>   TO PERKINS
>   READS BOOK DURING WORKING
>   HOURS   BROK EVERY PECCE
>   OF AQUIPMENT
>   NO GOOD
>   I WILL NOT OLOW FAMILY
>   ON THE FARM ANY MOR
>   SO HALP ME GOD

Page from Sam's cattle ranching ledger.

for not changing sprinkler"; "quit, no notice"; and so on (spelling, capitalization, and punctuation are the author's for clarity).[47]

The need to find dependable farm labor would plague Sam for years. But he was undaunted. His life felt exhilarating and challenging. Though now in his sixties, he possessed the energy, drive, and money to shape the sagebrush-covered property into his own unique farm.

In July 1960, Sam arrived at the farm to discover his caretaker had taken "vacation." The cattle were unwatered and unfed, and two calves had died. That was the final straw; it was time to relocate. He closed the Mercer Island house, called a moving company, and by the end of the year, was living at his Soap Lake farm.

Figure 3

Properties Acquired by Sam Israel, 1941–1960

NAME	DATE PURCHASED	PAID
Hamilton Building	10/24/1941	$5,500
Army Building*	4/1/1942	$15,950
Hartford Building**	8/23/1943	$39,500
Hardman Building	1/1/1944	$50,000
Drexel Hotel**	7/13/1944	$35,000
Yesler Building**	7/9/1945	$22,500
US Rubber Building**	12/14/1945	$82,500
Schwabacher Building**	1/2/1946	$32,500
Scientific Building**	1/3/1946	$35,000
Telephone Building*	7/1/1946	$40,000
Holyoke Building*	7/1/1946	$40,000
Beacon Hill property	9/12/1946	unknown
Webster-Brinkley Plant	1/13/1947	$250,000
Washington Shoe Building**	6/20/1947	$127,500
Frame Factory Building	8/1/1949	$45,165
Menzel Lakes properties	1950–1951	$13,750

NAME	DATE PURCHASED	PAID
Seventh and Seneca Parking	1954	$1,500
Packard Building	12/28/1956	$85,000
Florence Theatre/Building**	9/24/1958	$6,500
Collins Building**	9/24/1958	$129,250
Northern Hotel (Terry Denny)**	6/13/1960	$55,000
Total		$1,112,115

TOTAL: 21 properties
*Seattle historic landmark
**Pioneer Square Preservation District

Figure 4

Sam Israel Photography

EXHIBITION	DATE	NOTE
Northwest Photographic Salon; Western Washington Fair, Puyallup, Washington	September 1945	*Destitute*, honorable mention
Northwest Photographic Salon; Western Washington Fair, Puyallup, Washington	September 1947	Print accepted
Muncie Camera Club, Annual International Salon, Muncie, Indiana	1947	Print accepted
8th Vancouver International Salon of Photography	November 1947	Print accepted
Victoria International Salon of Photography	1947	Print accepted
Seattle Photographic Society, Seattle International Exhibition of Photography, Seattle, Washington	April 1948	*Destitute* selected for the permanent collection at the Seattle Art Museum
Northwest Photographic Salon; Western Washington Fair, Puyallup, Washington	September 1948	*Doldrums*, honorable mention
San Francisco International Exhibition of Photography, San Francisco, California	1949	Print accepted
International Salon of Photography Camera Club, Port Colborne, Ontario	April 1950	Print accepted
13th National Memphis Salon of Photography, Memphis, Tennessee	July 1950	Print accepted

EXHIBITION	DATE	NOTE
Photographic Society of America Annual Exhibition, Baltimore Museum of Art, Baltimore, Maryland	October 1950	Print accepted
2nd International Asheville Photographic Society Exhibition, Asheville, North Carolina	1950	Print accepted
Chicago International Exhibition of Photography, Chicago, Illinois	1950	Print accepted
Western Canada International Salon, Winnipeg, Canada	1951	4 prints accepted
Rochester International Exhibition of Photography, Rochester, New York	No Date	Print accepted: *Destitute*
Lewis County Camera Club Exhibit	No Date	Print accepted
Evergreen Camera Club of Seattle, Washington	No Date	Print accepted
Foothill Camera Club, Pasadena, California	No Date	Print accepted
18th Annual New York International Exhibition of Photography	No Date	Prints accepted: *Western, Trawler's Nest, White Russian*

CHAPTER 4
Refuge and Returning, 1960–1973

Opposite: Sam stands in front of a wall at the new campus of the Hebrew University in Jerusalem, October 1973. Behind him are the names of Founders who contributed funds for construction of the campus.

Casa mia, nido mio.
(My home, my nest.)

GROWING THE FARM

Soap Lake lies nestled into the Channeled Scablands of the Lower Grand Coulee on the east side of the Cascade Range near the geographic center of Washington State. The lake covers some two square miles and, for centuries, has been a gathering place for those seeking relief from illness and injury in the medicinal healing waters. Before white settlement, local Native American tribes called the place Smokiam, meaning "healing waters," and brought people and animals there for extended stays.

Soap Lake is one of only eleven meromictic lakes in the US; that is, its two layers are distinct and have not mixed in thousands of years. The top layer of water measures up to eighty-one feet at the deepest point and is heavy with some twenty-three minerals, giving the water a slick or "soapy" feel and producing a foam that gathers along the shore. Below is a thick mud layer, rich in stronger minerals with concentrations of microscopic life-forms. This mineral-rich water and mud have attracted health seekers from around the world.

The town of Soap Lake, located on the southern shore of the lake, was incorporated in 1919. By then, it had become a thriving spa and resort community with four hotels and a couple dozen rooming houses, as well as small businesses that catered to visitors. The population grew slowly, and when Sam Israel was planning to make his move, the little town boasted a population of about 1,600, plus as many tourists staying at sanitariums and recuperating in bathhouses.

After Sam's many trips to Soap Lake over three decades, the area felt like a return home, to a place filled with pleasant memories of his mother and family, and with a geography and climate that reminded him of Rhodes. The climate is desertlike, marked by warm summers with temperatures averaging in the nineties and chilly winters with frequent subfreezing temperatures and several inches of snow. Annual rainfall is typically less than nine inches; on average, there are 320 sunny days per year. Basalt cliffs rise on the east side of the lake, and on the west side gently sloping, sandy, brown hills are covered with bunchgrass and random clusters of drab green sagebrush.

Sam acquired waterfront lots on the slope west and north of the City of Soap Lake, where he enjoyed a serene view of the blue lake and the little town. In many respects, his farm represented a kind of refuge, a place of new horizons and new faces, where Sam could leave behind the disappointments that had left him a bachelor in the family-centric Sephardic community of Seattle. With more land here, he could expand well beyond the first attempt at farming he had made on Mercer Island.

Gradually, Sam made improvements to the property, working to bring his vision into reality. Ground was cleared of brush and rocks, Sam often driving the Caterpillar across the land himself. He moved dirt and rocks to create a pond near his bunkhouse. He hired truck drivers, carpenters, and crane operators and had a well dug and a pump installed. Ditches were dug to channel irrigation water. Contractors built fences, corrals, several garages, and outbuildings. Sam purchased cattle, a few horses, and a donkey and planted alfalfa to feed the animals and an apple orchard. He bought grain and other feed for the cattle and horses, and there were the typical, frequent veterinarian bills. Several hundred acres were leased to neighbors, who planted wheat and other dryland crops.

Sam lived in a small, one-room wood house—more of a bunkhouse or cabin, roughly seven feet wide by nine feet long—that was sparsely furnished, containing only the bare necessities of life. It was, says Eddie Hasson, "modest, to put it mildly."[1]

At the far end, there was a small bed with slats and a twin mattress. The tops of two plain wood dressers served as counters. Next to the bunkhouse stood the pump house, which had a cement floor, a shower, a washing machine, a toilet, and a tiny kitchen with a stove and refrigerator, plus a plain table with a couple of chairs. During the warmer months, Sam slept outside on a cot. Nearby were refrigerators—not plugged in and not cold—that he used for storage, including food for his small group of rescue dogs. The pack of strays, usually numbering a half dozen and all affectionately named Mariuch—individually and collectively—were a happy if noisy group of mixed breeds, mostly German shepherds. "He lived that way," recalls Eddie Hasson, "for at least 25 years."[2]

Above: Sam feeding the "Mariuch." Below: The two-bedroom house built by Sam for Bona and Albert, c. 1970.

Around 1970, Sam had a house built for Bona and Albert and their family. It had a kitchen with cabinets, a brown vinyl-covered couch, a Formica-top table and a couple of chairs, and (later) a Sony television. There were two bedrooms and a tiled bathroom. Sam had built the house for Bona's family, and he refused to move into it when they were not at the farm. Bona lost patience with him. "My mother was just anguished," says Eddie Hasson. "She screamed at him, 'You can't do this! You have to live there! You have to move in!'" Reluctantly, after several years, Sam agreed and finally moved into the house. Sam had his bedroom, and when Bona and her family visited, they had the other bedroom.[3]

Sam brought a couple of vehicles from Mercer Island and locally purchased several more. Soon, the property was home to a small and odd fleet. In 1958, the inventory included the early 1940s red-colored White truck (it had been used to haul tons of rubber heels to recycling in 1943 and for a long time had been parked in front of the house at 1805 Spruce Street); a 1941 Dodge panel wagon (a WWII-era army surplus ambulance that Sam had converted into a hunting vehicle; he later returned it to the house on Mercer Island); a 1947 Willys Jeep (still at the farm today); a 1950 International half-ton pickup; a 1951 Frazer; a 1953 Willys pickup; a 1955 International truck; a 1957 Volkswagen "Bug" sedan;

and a 1957 Volkswagen truck. Later, Sam added other vehicles to his motley fleet, including a 1951 Pontiac, a powder-blue 1960 Pontiac, a passenger bus, and several motorcycles and Vespas. In addition, there were tractors, bulldozers, road graders, a dozen or more three-wheeled mail trucks, and a host of farming equipment. Sam filled four to five acres with an astonishing variety of equipment and construction materials, including concrete conduits of various diameters ranging from two to eight feet, as well as bricks, wire, telephone insulators, and odd pieces of metal.

As years passed, vehicles, equipment, and materials fell into disuse, and the farm grounds became "littered with useless items," in Eddie Hasson's words, many of them from government surplus sales. Sam's friend and real estate agent Jack Patrick recalls this story: "He mentioned to me one time that, 'You know, I don't know what's wrong with me, but the only thing I enjoy is accumulating things,' and that's what he enjoyed. If he had bought a camera, he'd have 30 or 40 of 'em, and he just loved to accumulate things.... He was always interested in everything."[4]

As a fifteen-year-old, Dana Behar occasionally visited Sam, usually with a cousin or a couple of high school friends. Sam, he said, "had a natural sense for bargains, which was how he bought his real estate. If it was cheap enough, he would buy it whether he needed it or not." One day Dana quizzed Sam about the accumulation of useless things on the farm: "I said, 'What do you have all this stuff for?' He said, 'Well, if you need it, it's there.' I said, 'When are you ever going to use it?' He said, 'Oh, I'll get to it next time around.' He would always say that, 'Next time around.' I said, 'Why did you buy it?' He said, 'Well, I went to the county auction, and it was 5 cents on the dollar.'"[5]

The activities at Sam's farm demanded enormous amounts of time and energy. Sam finished many projects while abandoning many others at one stage or another. He built a greenhouse around a fig tree that he brought back from a trip to Rhodes in 1973, but the building never got a roof, and after a couple of years the tree died. He had a manufactured home intended for use as a guesthouse brought to the property but never got around to connecting the utilities, and it fell into disrepair. The "dream house" of his imagination had a courtyard with a fountain at the center, but he stopped at the foundation. His efforts to construct housing left several block foundations and a "cluster of ramshackle cabins," in the words of one journalist.[6]

Sam's enthusiasm for new projects remained high, while the drive to complete lower priority ones faded as months and sometimes years passed. His nephews agree that Sam had a lot of ideas but had trouble completing things. Among the unrealized projects was Sam's Acropolis. He planned to build a partial replica of the Rhodes Acropolis, a picturesque ruin that stands on a cliff above the village of Lindos and dates to the Hellenistic era when the Greeks built a temple to Athena in the sixth century BCE. Built on a prominent hillside, Sam's Acropolis would be seen from the other side of the lake. There would be three Doric columns, and perhaps it would remind people of the ruins in Rhodes or Greece. "He had this place picked out, and he had the cement blocks put in," says Victor Hasson, "but he never finished the Acropolis."[7]

Sam's nephew David Hasson thought Sam's habit of not completing things was his biggest weakness as a businessman. "There was so much going on in his head that he just would go from situation to situation and was never able to really sit down and plan and do a complete project from beginning to end," declares David. "Things would go a certain amount completed, and he would lose interest and go on to something else. He was a man of ideas, and on all topics. It wasn't just real estate; he just was a man who was constantly thinking."[8]

Finally, good farm help appeared when Sam met Duane Scheib (1927–2014). A local man who had grown up on a farm, Scheib had served in the US Air Force during World War II, operating heavy equipment for four years. Following the war, Scheib worked various jobs in construction and heavy equipment prior to joining the Washington State Department of Highways, where he retired thirty years later as supervisor of state highways for Ferry County. Then he started Scheib's Equipment Sales in Soap Lake and spent another twenty-five years doing the work he loved most, buying and selling big equipment. At some point during his time with Ferry County, when Scheib was about thirty-five years old in the early 1960s, he went to work for Sam, and their relationship continued after Scheib opened his own business in Soap Lake. He spent twelve years with Sam, typically seven days and up to thirty-five hours or more a week, to supplement his highway department salary. Scheib brought his knowledge of heavy equipment, plus the skills of an experienced ranch hand who knew how to care for livestock. Over the years with Sam, Scheib ran machinery from Sam's collection—backhoes, Caterpillar D9 bulldozers, tractors, and other equipment—to dig ditches, level ground, plant trees, and do a host of other chores. Scheib helped break (or, to use today's terminology, "gentle") horses, feed cattle, assist calving, build Sam's swimming pond, move rocks, and build roads. Scheib later fondly recalled his experiences with Sam: "This is just a fun place. He loved it here. He hired and fired 35 men the first five years I worked for him. He wanted it done his way and that's it. If they didn't do it, up the road they'd go."[9]

The two men became good friends and sometimes went on hunting trips together. Sam paid Scheib for his week's work every Sunday night without fail and usually gave him a gallon of ice cream to take home to his daughters. "He was very kind that way," recalls Scheib. Sam gave him a bonus at Christmastime, or a gift, such as a hunting rifle. Only once did Sam miss the Sunday night payment. Scheib recalls, "One time he was so sick down in Soap Lake Hospital that he couldn't pay me that night, and he felt sorry for months and months after that, apologizing. I said, 'Sam, that's okay.' He paid me that money. As sick as he was, within a day or two he paid me anyhow. He apologized, but he paid me every week except for that one time. I said, 'It's okay, Sam.'"[10]

SAMIS HEREFORD RANCH

The story of the rise and demise of Samis Hereford Ranch is both fascinating and sad. It began in the spring of 1958, when Sam launched plans to develop one of the finest cattle herds in Grant County. On April 12, 1958, he traveled to an auction in Fall City, Washington, where he purchased registered Hereford cattle for breeding stock from the W. E. Boeing estate, including twelve steers and heifers, four calves, and one bull. The next day, Sam drove to Chehalis and added another four head of registered Herefords. The core of his new enterprise arrived at his Soap Lake farm three weeks later on May 7 and 8. In November 1959, he added sixty calves to the herd. By November 1961, the Samis Hereford Ranch counted more than one hundred head, including sixteen bulls and three milk cows.[11]

The effort lasted less than a decade. Eddie Hasson explains:

He wanted to go to Israel and he just couldn't. He told me that he decided to sell the farm—I'm sure this is how he said it—when a calf was stillborn. The calf died in the cow's womb because, he says, "I did not have the strength or wherewithal to pull the calf. The legs

---

Samis Ranch buys registered Herefords

In an effort to give Grant County one of the finest Hereford herds in the county, Samuel Israel of the Samis Ranch of Soap Lake recently purchased some breeder stock on the coast. The cattle will be moved to the Samis Ranch within the next month and visitors will be welcomed as soon as the Herefords are settled in their new home.

On April 12, Mr. Israel purchased 17 head of registered Hereford cattle from the W. E. Boeing Estate farm at Falls City, Wash. These cattle combine the Royal English Champion bloodlines through Free Town Contrite, and the best bull from the Patterson Land Co. dispersion sale of 1950, Samis Ranch also has the Wyoming Domino Heir W 134th bloodlines.

On April 13, Mr. Israel purchased four head of registered cattle from West Cascade Hereford Breeders association at Chehalis. These are Wyoming Hereford Ranch bloodlines through WHR Proud Mixer, and Court Lionheart, NHR Pueblos Domino, and Golden Nugget.

The Samis Ranch is located just west of Soap Lake.

were out. I didn't know how to do it." He called the veterinarian, but he came too late. He says, "That's when I knew that you can't have a farm unless you're able to do that." So, he decided to sell all the cattle.[12]

In late 1966, Sam came up with an idea that he hoped would save the herd—donate them to the State of Israel. He began by exploring the possibility of giving his prize bulls to Israel with the Israeli consulate in Seattle, who hopefully would take up the matter with the Ministry of Agriculture. Months passed with no answers. A year later, despite an Ephrata veterinarian's glowing report on the value and quality of Hereford cattle for crossbreeding with dairy cows, and the benefits Israel could reap, the effort fell through. Sam had no recourse but to let go of his herd.[13]

In December 1967, Sam summoned his nephews Robert and Irving to the farm. They put together the extensive registrations for the Herefords. A colorful flyer announced the "Samis Hereford Ranch Herd Dispersal Sale" to take place on December 16. The auction of 250 head of Sam's registered Hereford cattle was held at the Central Washington Livestock Market in Quincy. The sale of premium registered stock included 20 three-year-old bulls and 40 two-year-old bulls. Sam hoped to reap a substantial profit, but it wasn't to be. He had waited too long—the registered stock documentation had become obsolete.

Robert Hasson recalls, "Sam didn't like to neuter any of them. He's like, 'I can't cut their balls off.' So, what happened was the herd's value went down to no more than just regular cows. When it got to the point where it was useless to keep them, he auctioned them off." Most of the cattle sold only for the price of meat, because the buyers beforehand had colluded to pay only $600 a head. The big sale netted a meager $29,564—about half of the herd's value. A half dozen head were unsold, and Sam kept them at the farm. On the drive back home from the auction, a disappointed Sam said to Robert and Irving, "Well, there goes another million

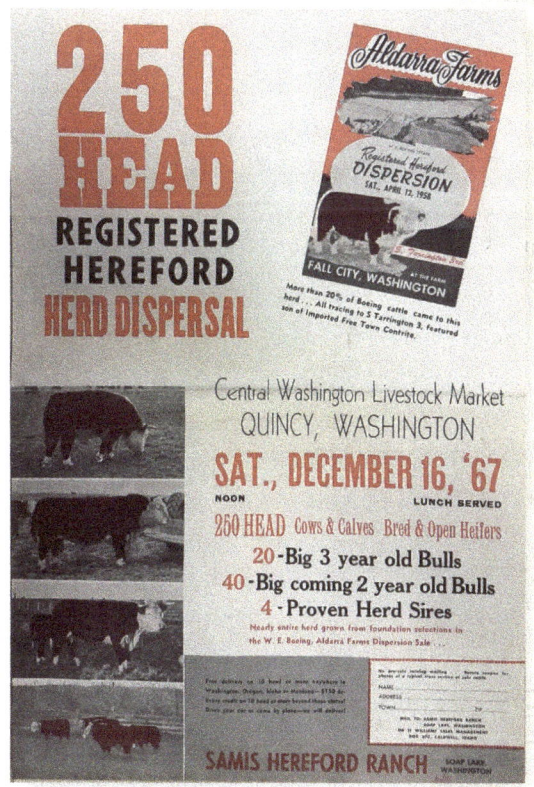

Poster for the herd dispersal sale, December 1967.

At the herd dispersal sale, December 1967.

dollars." Several years later, as Sam reflected on the failed enterprise, he observed, "It's been no fun. It's been the most expensive thing I've ever run into, expensive luxury." He declared it an utter "disaster." It marked the end of Sam's nine-year venture into the world of registered cattle breeding.[14]

The two dozen horses and several donkeys that Sam gradually gathered on the farm met a different fate. He told the story during a court trial in 1980:

> *They were going to the auction. And then there were three men bidding. There was a lot of horses being sold. They take the horses like they do cows. They don't ride them or anything, just bring them in three, four at a time; three or four bidders in there. One man bought all of mine. My horses are not broken. They're just wild horses. And the ones that were broken are too old, that I used to ride myself. But the*

> *rest of it, they're good horses, you know, not just wild horses, but they haven't been ridden. I asked him, "What are you going to do with them?" They take them to Snohomish, and they butcher them. . . . They freeze the meat. They take it some place in Canada; from there they fly direct to France. I said, "That's against my religion, that we cannot butcher. I cannot let anybody eat anything that we're not eating ourselves. Killing horses for food, cats, dogs, that's prohibited in Torah."*[15]

The horses and donkeys returned to Sam's farm. They grew old, and many died; the rest remained until after his death in 1994.

"ONE-SHOT SAM," TROPHIES, AND PUPPIES

Sam's love of hunting and photography continued to find ready outlets after the move to Soap Lake. He took dozens of photographs and video footage of farm life—the dogs, the cattle, the horses, the donkey, and many of the improvement projects, as well as the family and friends who visited. He also began planning special trips to hunt big game in Canada, Alaska, Wyoming, and the mountains of northeast Washington. Family and friends had come to know him as "One-Shot Sam." The nickname referred not to his excellent marksmanship but to his unique style of hunting—his philosophy of hunting. When the game was in his sights, he would take only one shot, and if the animal was looking at him, he would not shoot; if he missed, he would say, "God does not want me to shoot this animal."[16]

Sam's hunting expedition in October 1961 to the Northwest Territories in Canada brought both success and notoriety. On October 16, Sam bagged a world-record bison (wood buffalo). He was thrilled and planned to enter the trophy in *The Guinness Book of World Records*. He had the head stuffed by a professional taxidermist and posed for a photograph, his face beaming with pride. Unfortunately, the proud moment did not last. After the taxidermy, the head shrunk and was a quarter-inch short of the record. The

Sam hunting, September 1962.

Above: Sam hunting in British Columbia, 1960. Inset: Sam with his near-world's record bison, 1962.

story, featured in a Seattle newspaper, carried the header, "The Shattered Dream of a Mighty Hunter."[17]

Sam's love for dogs was well known to his family and Grant County locals. He always had a pack of dogs at the farm, and neighbors with an unwanted pup would take it to Sam's place, knowing he would take care of it. Eddie Hasson recalls the time when one of his rescues had five puppies and Sam put an ad in the newspaper: "Free puppies at Samis Ranch." Nobody showed up. "Then," Eddie recalls, "he decided to put another ad in, and it said: 'Calamari puppies for sale at the Samis Ranch.'" The clever use of *calamari*, "squid" in Greek, was all it took. "People wanted to go out there and find out what was a Calamari puppy," says Eddie. "They'd come out there and the kids picked up the puppies, and they fell in love with the puppies. Sure enough, the puppies all sold."[18]

FARM AND FAMILY

Many of Sam's family members, friends, and a few persistent journalists made the trek to his farm from Seattle in the 1970s and 1980s. Regardless of the visitor, Sam greeted them in his usual attire—baggy khaki pants, a casual shirt (blue chambray or plaid flannel), shoes with no socks, and a soft old hat. He and his barking pack of rescue dogs would meet the visitor at the gate, which was adorned with several No Trespassing and Positively No Smoking signs. And Sam was usually packing a loaded shotgun.

Sam happily took photos of his visitors, family especially, of course. There are snapshots of them with Sam's "props"—posing in front of an old wagon or riding on the tractor or the Jeep. Sam liked to be in the photos with family members too. He sometimes wore a red fez that Victor had brought him from Israel in 1972, and sometimes he sported a Panama-style fedora. Judging by the numerous photos of Sam in the fez, he clearly enjoyed wearing it, perhaps recalling his boyhood in Rhodes when he, his father,

Aerial view of the farm, c. 1985.

and Morris wore similar headgear for special occasions and a 1911 studio photograph.

Most of those who traveled to Sam's farm were relatives. Sam's brothers John, Nissim, and Morris came occasionally. His older brothers David and Jack never made the trip. On March 22, 1962, Jack Israel died at age seventy of a heart attack. In Sam's later years (his sixties, seventies, and eighties), after the move to Soap Lake, the brothers' relationships gradually evolved. The contentiousness and often harsh tenor of earlier times slowly became mellower, more congenial. Eddie Hasson describes Sam as more courteous, friendly, and affectionate with his brothers. "They would usually sit down and just have free-ranging conversations about the old days and politics," Eddie says, "and, of course, Sam was always right. You never argued with him." Eddie recalls one particular conversation between Sam and Morris: "Sam was sure he was born in 1899. Uncle Morris, who was kind of a meek man, says, 'Sam, I have the book that has the dates of birth for us.' They would put the date of birth in the book that they would go to a synagogue with, a treasured Jewish book. He said, 'I was born May 10, 1900.' Sam said, 'No, you're not. You can't be. I was born in 1899.' Uncle Morris would say, 'Okay, Sam,' and they'd go to the next topic. He knew he wasn't going to win."[19]

Sam stands at the gas pump on his farm, c. 1972.

Dana Behar got similar treatment. "He didn't have conversations," says Dana. "He would pontificate." You were required not only to listen but also to look at Sam as he talked. Dana replicates Sam's high-pitched voice and accent, recalling, "Sam would say, 'You look me in the eye when I'm talking to you, see. You got to look at me in the eye.' He would go on forever, and if you broke the stare, he would get furious, and you had to continue to look at him until he was done with the story."[20]

Sam especially enjoyed visits with his sister Bona; her husband, Albert Hasson; and their children and grandchildren—Robert and Louise Hasson and their children (Sara and Adam); Eddie and Marguerite Hasson and their children (Albie, Joey, and Randy); David and Michele Hasson and daughters (Tama, Bonnie, and Shannon); and Victor Hasson and Marilyn. Eddie and his family made the trip at least once a year. Eddie, a CPA with his own

Top: Last gathering of the siblings at Sam's. Left to right: Sam Israel, Morris Israel, Bona Israel (seated), Albert Hasson, Nissim Israel, John Israel, summer 1977. Middle: Sam and a favorite camera, 1984. Bottom: Eddie Hasson family at Sam's farm. Marguerite, Eddie, Albie; above: Randy and Joey, 1983.

Left: Marilyn Hasson, 1963. Above: Mike and Daisy Israel, c. 1985. Below: Sam and Sarah Azose, great-niece, 1988.

accounting firm, came more often after 1968, when he became Uncle Sam's bookkeeper. Sam's relatives knew him as well as anyone at the time. The visits were memorable for each of them.

Sam's nephew Robert remembers numerous trips to the farm. "He would call me all the time," Robert says. "'Robert, come over, I'm sick. Robert, come over, I need some help.' So, I would go over and spend a couple days. I'd bring over some goodies that my mother made, his sister—*biscochos de huevo*, crackers, cookies. He would do that with other relatives too."[21]

Robert, Sara, and Adam Hasson, August 1977.

Adam Hasson recalls, "Sam loved to make us look out across the lake, and he would say, 'Now *this* is God's country!'" Dana Behar visited during one high school spring break, about a week before Passover. Robert and Bona were there at the time, and Sam was excited to have family around. Dana, who found his great-uncle "such an unusual character," recalls, "He loved the holiday, and he loved to hear Robert sing, so Sam said, 'We're going to do Passover right now.'" Dana objected: "But, Passover is not for a week." Sam insisted, "We're going to do it right now." So, they celebrated Passover Seder a week before Passover.[22]

The memories of Bona and Albert's sons offer a series of windows into Sam and his world in the later decades of his life.

David Hasson recalls:

> *I always brought my kids with me because that kind of softened everything with him, and he loved kids. . . . He wanted us to visit him all the time under his conditions, and so he was very, very generous. He was generous with my children. When they graduated out of high school, he sent them to Israel. He always photographed them every time they came over. We have amazing pictures of the kids that he had taken, and always dressed up in cowboy outfits and with horses and stuff.*[23]

Victor Hasson recalls:

> *If there was ever true love between brother and sister, it was Sam and my mother. She would always be in contact*

with him. Every Pesach, every holiday, my mother would send baked goods to Soap Lake by Greyhound. My mother used to make borekas de spinaka, she used to make travados and mustachudos, and all these old things that Sam loved. Of course, he would complain about it because he was always trying to watch his weight.

Before I would leave the ranch on my visit, he would make sure I had enough oil and gas. It was always a ceremonial good-bye. "Look at your car. Going to make sure that you have gas. And when you get home, you call me."[24]

Opposite, top: David Hasson family visiting Sam. David, his daughters Bonnie and Tama, Michele's daughter Shannon, and Michele, 1983. Opposite, bottom: David Hasson, Bona, Bonnie, Michele, Tama, c. 1984.

Eddie Hasson recalls:

He would be just so excited when we showed up because he was so lonely. When we'd go there, the kids would go crazy because they wanted to go out and play. "No, no!" Sam would say, "You sit here, and I'll tell you about this." He dominated the conversation. He could care less what anybody else had to say.

He used to have a wall that had the photos, and also a little shelf, and he had his Sabbath candles. He would light the candles every Friday night, and he had some Hebrew this and Hebrew that. It was like a little bit of a memorial wall, family wall, at the farm.[25]

Robert Hasson recalls:

I admired him. I enjoyed his company. I even enjoyed listening to him talk as he went on, and on, and on, and on. He was deadly honest. He was helpful to people that he liked, and he was generous to the Scouts, and he was a generous man in many ways.

You don't cross him. I crossed him once. Once, and it had to do with him boasting about how he helped the

Sam with Eddie Hasson's family; Albie, Joey, Marguerite, Sam, and Randy, c. 1984.

family, how he made them all what they were. I was thinking at that time about my father. My father was an underachiever. He was really a smart guy and here he was stuck being a grocer. So, I said, "Uncle, what would happen if you left your hands off of your family, let them go naturally the way they were going to go, without you butting in?" He said, "There's the door." He kicked me out. Then he called me the next day. He says, "Come over," and he apologized, but you don't cross him.[26]

Robert's wife, Louise, found Sam unforgettable. She was, to use Robert's words, "adversarial with him." Louise was forthright and strong with Sam. "He didn't like that," said Robert. Sam would say to her, "You're persistent, aren't you?" and she would reply, "Yes, I'm persistent."[27]

Louise felt moved to put her experience with Sam into a poem, "Meeting Uncle Sam," which she later included in a volume of published poetry.

> There was no pleasing him
> without being servile. Women
> in their place was his realm.
> So he playfully teased,
> "Are you having a good time?"
> Knowing full well his macho retreat
> was not welcomed. As you cooked he
> acted surprised, referring to you
> as a "mishkia", the obedient
> woman who serves.
>
> It was a "men only" space.
> A paper plate on the counter garnished
> with a scattering of arsenic
> to control flies, red sand on wimpy white.
> The kitchen otherwise reasonably clean,
> but not scrubbed. Old shirts and hats
> on a hook, dishes from everywhere
> in the cabinet, muddy shoes loosely
> assembled in the entry.
>
> He was lonely and talked into forever,
> his blue eyes twinkling with mischief.

> You should never disagree.
> That was not allowed. He was the master,
> the Uncle, the millionaire recluse,
> hungry for life, yet retreating from it,
> cunning, an artist with the camera,
> a hunter, and skilled raconteur.
> Someone to be worshipped
> from afar but never challenged.[28]

One occasional visitor was Rabbi William Greenberg, who served as leader for Congregation Ezra Bessaroth from 1962 until he retired in 1990. Rabbi Greenberg made an annual circuit through eastern Washington, Oregon, and Idaho, to certify Ore-Ida brand potatoes as "OU," Orthodox Union, that is, kosher. Rabbi Greenberg always made a point of stopping to spend a couple of hours with Sam. Later, Sam selected the rabbi to sit on the Samis Foundation's original Board of Trustees.

Visitors looking for a donation or government bureaucrats intent on imposing some regulation received a gruff dismissal. Sam, says Dana Behar, "had kind of a strong libertarian streak; he hated anyone who was trying to interfere with how he was living or trying to get money from him." When Dana spent a few days with Sam during spring or summer breaks, he would hear Sam's long, complaining tales of the latest incidents. Dana recalls:

> *The stories were all about the injustices he suffered from fat county tax assessors or whatever. He would say, "That fat bastard came by, and he told me that I can't do that on my land, and I told him get the hell off my property, see, then I got my shotgun and put a couple shells in it, and I shot in the air, and I said, now you get the hell out of here, see."*
>
> *Sam was disgusted with hypocrisy, or luxury, or excess. A solicitor looking for a donation found trouble. Sam would say, "And he came by, and he drove a Cadillac, and he said he needed money. I said, 'What the hell, you're driving a Cadillac, see. Look what I drive—I got a Willys Jeep!'"*[29]

TO ISRAEL AND RHODES, AND BACK

For years, Sam dreamed of going to Israel. Advertisements in eastern Washington newspapers by El Al Israel Airlines served as a frequent reminder, keeping the idea alive. The hardest part was getting the time away from all of his obligations at the farm.

In the summer of 1972, he resurrected the idea of shipping what remained of his prized herd of Hereford cattle to Israel. This would give him a way to connect with the Jewish homeland and do a good deed at the same time. He contacted the Hebrew University of Jerusalem in June, offering to donate nine registered Hereford cows and their calves to the School of Agriculture. On September 20, a long letter arrived in Sam's mailbox from Yair Mundlak, dean of the Levi Eshkol School of Agriculture at the university. Mundlak praised Sam for his generosity but in the end politely declined the offer.[30]

A year later, Sam decided the time had come. He purchased round-trip airfare and made arrangements with Bona and Albert to take over duties at the farm. The itinerary began with a flight from Spokane to New York, then to Israel, returning via Athens, Greece, with a short side trip to Rhodes, then Athens to New York, and finally to Spokane. He would leave for his three-week adventure on October 11, 1973, and the plane would land in Tel Aviv the following day. However, the Arab–Israeli War, known to Israelis as the Yom Kippur War, erupted on October 6, delaying his trip. It ended on October 25, and Sam left five days later.[31]

At the beginning of November, Sam boarded a plane in New York, the first El Al Israel Airlines flight to Israel after the war. He arrived in Tel Aviv and was met by his nephew Victor Hasson, who had graduated from the University of Washington School of Dentistry (DDS degree) in 1973 and moved to Tel Aviv soon afterward. Victor vividly recalls Sam's visit. Before leaving Soap Lake, Sam had called and asked Victor to find him a cabin. "He doesn't want to go to the Hilton; he doesn't want to go to any of these big hotels; he was a simple man," says Victor. He found a hotel that had small cabins and made arrangements. "It was the first time that I saw Sam really happy," Victor recalls. After a few days, Sam bused to Jerusalem. Here, he chose a room at a luxury hotel, the King David, which was nearly empty and offered a substantially discounted rate. As the only tourist, he had free range, wandering into the kitchen and getting to know the cook. Soon, he was making his own breakfast.[32]

Sam, ever the avid photographer, took hundreds of photos, mostly color slides. The images include Victor; Morris's son Robert; Morris's granddaughter Gayle, who at the time was living in a kibbutz outside Jerusalem; and many nearby tourist destinations. One day, Sam boarded a bus and made a memorable trip south to Masada. He was one of the first tourists after the Yom Kippur War to walk among the ruins of the cliff-top fortress.

Sam atop a wall overlooking the Old City of Jerusalem, built during the 16th century by the Ottomans, October 1973.

He looked over the Dead Sea and recalled how Jews rebelling against the Roman Empire held out for months, until a Roman offensive in the spring of 73 CE ended with the suicide of more than nine hundred rebels.

Equally memorable was Sam's visit to Rhodes. He found the city and skyline little changed since his departure. Mandraki Harbor was larger, but the horizon was still marked by one- and two-story houses of mud and concrete and waving green fronds of date palms. He walked the same hills, narrow cobblestone streets, and ancient ruins that he had walked as a teenager. The great castle and massive walls built by the Knights of the St. John Hospitallers still enclosed *la Juderia*. He strolled past small shops and the fountain where he had collected water in a bucket as a boy. Many buildings looked exactly the same, and he found numerous houses where the old family names were carved in stone above the door. He took photos of the Acropolis at Lindos, several medieval walls and buildings, the Kahal Shalom Synagogue, and Mandraki Harbor, as well as the house he had known as a child.

It must have been a strange experience; so much looked the same after five decades, yet so much had changed, particularly after Greece took

La Juderia, from Sam's visit to Rhodes, October 1973.

possession of the island in 1947. At his family home, now inhabited by a "nice Greek family," to use Sam's words, he had hoped to buy his father's old cigarette maker, but it had been sold. Sam took photos of local children, but none were relatives since any family left on Rhodes had been murdered by the Nazis in 1944. Many houses remained empty; others stood in ruins. They, as well as five synagogues and numerous landmarks, had been destroyed by bombs during World War II, including most of the Alliance school that Sam had attended as a teenager. In *la Juderia*, streets trod by Sephardim for centuries had their Ladino names changed to Italian names in 1938, then changed again to Greek names after World War II. Sam strolled along *la Calle Ancha*, but that, too, had been altered, becoming Piazza Principe Umberto di Savoia under the Italians, then Pindarou under the Greeks.[33]

The exhilaration Sam felt during the trip to Israel only grew after his return to Soap Lake in late November. "He had a very deep love for Israel in his heart," affirms Rita Israel Calderon. He came back energized and determined to make a difference in people's lives, especially in the lives of Jews and Israelis. It was, as Eddie Hasson says, "the highlight of his life." Sam had always done *mitzvot*, but after his trip to Israel and Rhodes, his charitable works became more elaborate, more numerous and frequent, and more generous; it is likely that that journey can be credited with inspiring the creation of the Samis Foundation six years later.[34]

Eddie Hasson says Sam couldn't stop raving about how wonderful the country was and saying, "We have to do things to help them." Sam assembled a slideshow and began going to grade schools, high schools, church groups, and civic organizations in Grant County to talk about Israel. "He called it 'on the circuit promoting Israel,'" recalls Eddie. "He would start the slideshow with a tape recorder and play his favorite song that began, 'When Israel went out of Egypt'—it's in Hebrew and my brother Robert sings it—and he ended the show with the sunset over Mandraki Harbor in Rhodes." In November 1974, Sam spoke at the Holy Trinity Lutheran Church during Fellowship Hour at the invitation of the pastor. He was invited to give speeches in the late 1970s and early 1980s at Soap Lake High School on Judaism and the Middle East, the history of Judaism, the sources of religion, and "what happened during the Second World War to the Jewish people." Students and teachers alike appreciated Sam's talks. One teacher wrote to Sam, "Many commented that they thought that you had been very effective, a significant person in the fate of Soap Lake, and certainly a person to remember."[35]

Sam also enthusiastically promoted Israeli wine. He bought Carmel brand by the case and arranged for one of his brothers or nephews to bring it from Seattle. "Whoever came to the farm," says Eddie Hasson, "he'd always give them a lecture about Israel, and he'd give them a case of Carmel." Sam's promotion of all things Jewish got a boost from the 1973 book by Simon Wiesenthal, *Sails of Hope: The Secret Mission of Christopher Columbus*. Most of the book discusses the history, persecution, and fate of Jews in Spain, but the part that sparked Sam's imagination was Wiesenthal's presentation of years of research that offered convincing evidence that not only was Columbus Jewish but his voyage to the New World in 1492 was in reality an effort to find a safe, new homeland for Jews who had been expelled from Spain.[36]

Sam gradually acquired a small collection of books, many in Hebrew—gifts from rabbis, although he couldn't read Hebrew, only Ladino and English. Mostly, Sam read magazines—*National Geographic* (he had hundreds), as well as several hunting and photography magazines. Wiesenthal's book was another story. Sam gave copies to the libraries in Soap Lake and Ephrata and handed them out to friends and even some Christian church groups that he let meet in his buildings. He gave Eddie Hasson a box of the books, telling him, "Make sure you distribute these books. This is important for everybody to know." Eddie sent copies to the Seattle Hebrew Academy, friends, neighbors, and his brothers David and Robert.[37]

Sam's affection for Israel also led him to make substantial donations to Jewish organizations in the US and Israel. Just before his trip in 1973, Sam endowed the Samuel Israel Scholarship at the Hebrew University of Jerusalem, and the same year he gave $20,000 to the United Jewish Appeal in New York, half of which was earmarked for the Emergency Fund. In 1974, he contributed the same amount and in the two following years made donations of $10,000. Later, in 1986 and 1987 (and perhaps other years), Sam donated modest sums to the Jewish Television Institute and became a charter member.

In his mid-seventies, Sam remained vital and robust. He continued to battle officious bureaucrats who he believed were infringing on his rights. Still, Sam's energies were gradually waning. His age and health were an issue as he faced the challenges of managing real estate both west and east of the Cascades, as well as several major legal hassles that hit him in the 1970s and 1980s.

CHAPTER 5

Real Estate, Mitzvot, and Triumph, 1974–1989

Opposite: Last gathering of Sam with siblings and their spouses. Seated: Juliette Israel, Gentil Israel, Violet Israel, Bona Hasson; Standing: John Israel, Morris Israel, Sam Israel, Nissim Israel, Albert Hasson, summer 1977.

Quien muncho se aboca, el culo se le vee.
(He who bows down too low exposes his ass.)

SAM'S HEALTH

While Sam carried much of his youthful exuberance into his sixties and seventies, he was forced to transition from athletic hiker to walker, an unpleasant change for a man who had prided himself on improving his physique and maintaining fit condition through his fifties. He remained active on the farm, but his capacity for exertion decreased each decade, and although he had given up whiskey and smoking, he steadily gained weight. This deeply troubled him. He kept a bathroom scale in the kitchen and watched the numbers climb, marking his weight in writing on the wall or a calendar, punctuating each rise with dramatic exclamations, such as "Oh my God, I'm too fat!" and *"Stupido!"* and "No More!"

In late 1977, Sam's oldest brother David Israel died at age eighty-seven. Like the rest of the family, David suffered for years from diabetes, and in his last year he had a leg amputated. Four months after David's death, in March 1978, Sam's younger brother Nissim died. Then, at the end of the year, Bona's husband, Albert, died. "The passing of my father devastated

Victor Hasson visiting the farm, April 1981.

him," recalls Victor Hasson. "My father was almost like a brother to him." Victor recalls the days that followed:

After we buried him, Sam wanted me to come to the farm. I get there, and he's crying. The first thing he wanted me to do was to light a candle and say kaddish. I was still religious, and you don't say kaddish without a minyan. I said, "Uncle, we don't have a minyan." He says, "You're going to say kaddish. On." Of course, my mom was devastated. He would call my mom and try to calm her down. Every time after that, I would come, we would light a candle and say kaddish. It didn't matter what time of the year it was, that's what we had to do.[1]

SAM'S VISION: LAYING THE FOUNDATION FOR THE FOUNDATION

Fully aware of his own diabetes, weight, and other health issues, and the fact that his mother, sister, and brothers all had diabetes, Sam, as never before, began to consider his mortality and his legacy. He was single, with no children to inherit his estate. In 1976, more than a year before David's death, Sam began to write and rewrite versions of his will and to sketch out ideas for a foundation that would carry on the management of his properties. Initially, Sam envisioned "a foundation for the benefit of beneficiaries in the State of Israel," including Hebrew University. He planned to leave some cash to family members, and to assign the bulk of his estate to benefit institutions in Israel. The first attorney that Sam employed, a Seattle lawyer who was "not Jewish," advised Sam that his plan was impossible under US tax regulations. Sam fired him, because the man "lacked enthusiasm or understanding necessary to accomplish the goal."[2]

The second attorney reached the same conclusion as the first one. Being Jewish did not spare him a summary firing. A third lawyer told Sam he needed some non-Jews on the board, because he couldn't have a foundation with religious limits. Sam fired him too.[3]

An early, undated draft on Sam's Soap Lake letterhead stationery offers a more developed description of his vision for the foundation. His document, titled "Rough Draft, Distribution of Funds to Charities," lists eight areas for funding:

1. Hebrew schools in Seattle
2. A Jewish cemetery "for the entire community"
3. "Any Jews that wish to return to the Promised Land"
4. Orphans, widows, and poor people
5. Scholarships for outstanding students to attend any university in Israel
6. Archaeological work and museums in Israel
7. Protection of wildlife in Israel and maintenance of wildlife parks
8. Victims of emergencies or catastrophes anywhere in the world[4]

Sam wanted to write the foundation document himself, but the attorneys refused to cooperate. Eddie recalls, "Sam was very, very frustrated because nobody would get it right. Of course, we talked about it, and that's when I suggested Irwin Treiger. I said, 'He's a nice Jewish boy and he would know what you want.'" Eddie and Irwin (1934–2013) had been friends since college, when they both attended the University of Washington, where Treiger had graduated from law school in 1955. On one of Sam's visits to Seattle, Eddie introduced him to Treiger, who was practicing law at the prestigious firm of Bogle & Gates.

Treiger was a highly regarded tax attorney with a national reputation for his expertise in trusts, estates, and foundations. He was known for his sharp wit and an exceptional ability to listen to his clients and find solutions for their legal needs. His notable legal and civic career spanned more than five decades, with leadership in many organizations in the Jewish community and the wider Seattle community, including roles as president of the Jewish Federation of Greater Seattle and president of the Seattle Foundation among others.

The two men "hit it off very, very well," in Eddie's words. From the start, Treiger knew the key to working for Sam. "I didn't try to tell him what to do," he said. Treiger prepared the paperwork to Sam's satisfaction, and the organizing documents for the nonprofit Samis Foundation were filed with the Office of the Secretary of State in Olympia on December 19, 1979. From then on, Treiger was Sam's primary attorney. The two worked well together, and for Treiger it was a memorable relationship. Years later, he recalled his time with Sam: "I would never say he was jovial in any of my experiences with him, but he wasn't cold either. I mean, he talked, he liked to talk, and he talked a lot, and he was very outgoing in that sense.... He was an unpredictable guy in many, many ways. He did some things that absolutely shocked me at times.... I admired him for what he had done during his lifetime.... I really enjoyed working with him. But, you know, he had his rough spots, no question about that."[5]

Sam's plan was to transfer one property to the foundation after the first year and to see how it worked. "He was very cautious," says Eddie Hasson, "and wanted to make sure everything was running smooth." Eddie's trip to Sam's farm in May 1981 began the process of foundation funding. The two sat down, and Eddie showed Sam the rental income total for the foundation's first property. Sam decided where he wanted the money to go, Eddie wrote the checks, and Sam signed them. The next year, Sam transferred a second property to the foundation, and the process repeated until the foundation held four income-producing properties. The Samis Foundation still held only four properties at the time of Sam's death in 1994, but the process for the fledgling operation had proven sound, and Sam was pleased.[6]

Sam receiving award from the Caroline Kline Galland Home, clipping from *Grant County Journal*, June 5, 1972. Left to right: Sam Tarshis, Sam Israel, Hank Wolf.

PHILANTHROPY: DOING *MITZVOT*, SAM STYLE

Sam Israel had been doing charitable deeds and making donations to organizations since at least the 1930s. In the Seattle area, Sam was a long-time and devoted supporter of many Jewish and secular causes. He contributed to the Red Cross, the Community Chest, and Congregation Ezra Bessaroth. He made notable donations to the Jewish Federation of Greater Seattle, the Seattle Hebrew Academy, the Caroline Kline Galland Home, and various Israeli charities.[7] Although most of Sam's donations went to Jewish organizations, he continued to support other causes. Among them (perhaps not surprising, considering Sam's love for mountain hikes) was the 1975 American expedition to climb K2, the second-highest mountain in the world, led by Jim Whittaker, the first American to reach the summit of Mount Everest (in 1963), for which he gained immediate and lasting fame in the US.[8]

In November 1984, Sam paid off the mortgage debt of the Seattle Hebrew Academy (SHA). Sam had always supported local Jewish causes, but it was a family connection to SHA that proved a boon for the school. Eddie Hasson says, "I think that what got him started specifically with the Seattle Hebrew Academy and the idea of a Jewish education was when my children went to the Academy." On one of Eddie's trips to Sam's farm, he told his uncle that the school was deep in a mortgage they couldn't pay off, about $78,000.[9]

One day, SHA president Barry Ernstoff received a phone call from Sam, who asked if he knew the balance due on the school's loan. Ernstoff recalls their conversation:

> *I told him that I knew the balance more or less, and Sam proceeded to give the exact number of the balance owing on the loan, including both dollars and cents. He then told me that he had sent a check in that exact amount to the bank to pay off the loan. And at the end of our conversation, he asked me to assure him that we would never mortgage the school building again. I told him that for so long as I was president of the Academy or active on the Board, I would not allow the building to be mortgaged again and thanked him for his generosity.*[10]

On behalf of the academy, a board member wrote a glowing letter of thanks to Sam. "I was moved to tears by your kindness, generosity, and by the truly outstanding thoughts expressed in the letter you sent, that was read by your dear nephew, Eddie Hasson," he declared, noting that there were "few people in this community who have the heart that you do."[11]

Daisy Israel adds an important detail that reflects a hallmark of Sam's philanthropy: "I do remember a conversation around the table where the school gave Sam the naming rights to the school, the Seattle Hebrew Academy. And I thought, 'Isn't that great. It'll be called the Isaac and Sarah Israel School, like the Benaroya Hall and Stroum Jewish Community Center. Everything has a name. And the school will be named for our grandparents. And Uncle Sam said, 'No. You don't give to be honored.' He says, 'You give quietly.' And that was his code."[12]

At the same time, Sam was very particular about where his money went. It was another aspect of his "my way or the highway" attitude, to use Eddie Hasson's words. Three examples illustrate how this played out.

Sam disliked being solicited, even by organizations to which he'd previously donated. Josh Gortler, who served as executive director of Kline Galland Home for several decades, once traveled to Sam's farm to ask for a donation. To Gortler's surprise, he was met at the gate by Sam himself, wielding a gun and surrounded by his pack of barking dogs. Gortler drove off and did not look back. The unpleasant exchange did not affect Sam's donations to the home, and in later years, Gortler earned widespread respect (and an honorary doctoral degree from Yeshiva University) for his local and national leadership in care for the elderly.

Sam wanted to be in complete control of where his money went. Once, a carpenter did some work for Sam but declined payment because of Sam's stature in the community and reputation as a generous man. Sam insisted and paid anyway. The carpenter decided to donate his proceeds to a conservative synagogue in Seattle, thinking this would please Sam. It didn't. When Sam heard of the donation, he was furious that "his" money was being given to a conservative synagogue.[13]

Though he did not give in order to receive recognition, Sam believed that, on occasion, his generosity made him exempt from certain rules or social mores. An incident that earned Sam no small amount of buzz in the Seattle Jewish community occurred one Shabbat in 1981 when he visited Sephardic Adventure Camp (SAC), an annual summer camp first organized by Rabbi Solomon Maimon of Sephardic Bikur Holim (SBH) in the mid-1950s. (Since the 1980s, SAC has been run jointly by SBH and Congregation Ezra Bessaroth.) Earlier that summer, Eugene Normand, a PhD in nuclear engineering who worked at Puget Sound Power and Light and who also was head of SBH's Youth Committee, as well as the husband of Rabbi Maimon's niece, Esther, was helping organize the adventure camp at Sun Lakes-Dry Falls State Park. Normand had read about Sam Israel in recent *Seattle Times* articles and had the idea of inviting Sam to visit the camp, since the park was near Sam's home, some seventeen miles north of Soap Lake, near Coulee City. Normand wrote to Sam but never heard back from him. Normand later recalled, "I thought that was the end of the story. I was wrong." He recounts the awkward events that unfolded:

> *It seems that Mr. Israel received the letter, knew where the SBH camp was going to be held, and decided that it would be a nice gesture on his part to pay the camp a visit. He would*

be able to bring his slide projector and show the campers his slide show about Israel.... The day that he decided to visit our camp at Sun Lakes was Saturday, Shabbat. To observant Jews, there are lots of restrictions on what activities can and cannot be performed on Shabbat.

Thus, when Mr. Israel showed up with his slide projector, I knew right away that was going to be a problem. However, the bigger problem was that the outer entrance to the camp had been locked, and so it was very difficult for an outside person to gain entrance to the camp. This was probably done

> Sam paid off the mortgage debt of the Seattle Hebrew Academy. Sam had always supported local Jewish causes, but it was a family connection to SHA that proved a boon for the school.

because it was Shabbat, the day of rest, and no visitors were expected on this day.... I can't recall if he told me how he had gotten in, but I do know that it took him a very long time, probably an hour or more, to reach someone who would let him in....

So, there he was, storming in, holding some of his slide projector material, and very upset because it had taken him so long to be able to get through to our campsite.... I remember that I spent something like 20–30 minutes talking to him, trying to calm him down, but it wasn't easy. Part of his dress was a .45-caliber pistol which he had in a holster. For sure, you don't see those on Shabbat, and you don't see those on people you meet during everyday affairs, but we know that Sam was very different in how he conducted himself....

> *I had a difficult time trying to nap that Shabbat afternoon, the job of trying to calm down Sam Israel had gotten me worked up and exhausted.*[14]

Sam, frustrated and angry, left, vowing he would never give money to the camp. And he kept his vow. However, since his passing, the Samis Foundation has supported the camp with grants every year.

> *In 1981, Sam, at age eighty-two, was the largest single landowner in Seattle. One newspaper went so far as to tag him "Tops in State Property Holdings."*

THE CARETAKER: PHILOSOPHY AND PRACTICE OF REAL ESTATE

At the root of Sam's accumulation of property lay a keen awareness of the complex amalgam of personal, family, and Jewish history. For him, collecting properties was a means of gaining security, a way to feel he would not become a man like his father, who saw his savings in Italian lire evaporated by inflation, or like fellow Jews who had been persecuted for centuries. He explained to one reporter: "It's the nature of the Hebrew, being persecuted for centuries, never being able to be a citizen. . . . Jews couldn't buy land for many years. We were pretty safe in Turkey, we could own land, but by nature Jews protect themselves. It was a curse of God, that they should be strangers in every land but the promised land. . . . It's by nature that you seek protection. All foreigners are the same way. . . . They don't believe the government owes them anything. They need wealth."[15]

In 1981, Sam, at age eighty-two, was the largest single landowner in Seattle. One newspaper went so far as to tag him "Tops in State Property Holdings." His properties, an eclectic assortment of buildings, parking lots, vacant land, timberland, and lakefront lots, were spread out from King and

Snohomish Counties in western Washington to Grant and Douglas Counties in eastern Washington. (See figure 5.) David Hasson explains part of the reason for the widely dispersed holdings: "There'd be a building downtown that he would want, and the estate included 40 acres of someplace in the Olympic Peninsula, a piece of property on Vashon Island, someplace way up north by Marysville. He basically, probably sight-unseen, bought those parcels with the building and these things kind of accumulated."[16]

As Sam Israel's stable of properties grew, journalists occasionally sought him out to ask why he had acquired so much real estate. Sam told one writer he was holding the properties "in trust for the poor." Similarly, James Horrigan, a vice president at Coldwell Banker who assisted Sam for years after his longtime friend Henry Broderick sold to Coldwell Banker, told a reporter that "Israel frequently mentions that the Bible instructs him to keep his property. He says God put it in his trust to benefit the poor, and that's what he intends to do with it. I'm positive he means it." Sam explained to the journalist, "I came up from the ranks. I don't need luxuries. I am a simple man."[17]

Sam revealed a second facet of his philosophy, also based in his Jewish faith, in another interview. "Never count your blessings," he said. And high on the list of Sam's blessings were his properties. Sam always paid as little as possible for a building or lot. James Horrigan explained to a reporter, "Low down payment was the key. The total price was less important, particularly if it was a corner property, or it fit with his strategy of land assemblage. He was shrewd and had a lot of vision. He bought in Skid Road when you couldn't give it away. He knew it would be valuable one day." Some people have asserted that Sam was so averse to owing money on a mortgage that he typically bought a property outright; however, that is not the case. His financial ledgers and income tax files reflect money owed on many properties that he had acquired on contract. Paul Fetterman, who at one time served as Sam's attorney, told the press, "Israel would buy many properties on contract; he would make a small down payment, and as soon as he had money for another down payment, he would buy more property."[18]

To another reporter, Sam summarized his philosophy and formula for success in real estate: "Pay cash if possible, write checks only for large purchases, never use credit cards, and never, never pay more for something than it's worth." Of course, there were other basics, like saving money and living frugally. In Sam's case, by the time he was in his seventies and eighties, he was living on little more than $300 to $400 a month. He received a salary from the Samis Land Company, as well as a Social Security check monthly, and saved most of it.[19]

When asked by journalists about his "worth," Sam refused to answer. It didn't matter anyway, he said, though "the IRS and my accountants probably wouldn't agree." His brother John had told a reporter that Sam was "a multi-multi-millionaire." Sam scoffed at the idea. "My brother talks too much," he said. "My properties are low-class properties."[20]

Washington Shoe Building, built 1890.

After Sam moved to the farm, he managed his properties in Seattle by phone and mail, and with the help of his brother John. Sam kept files on each of his Seattle buildings, so he had ready access to the purchase price and down payment terms, names of tenants, rents due, and so on. In Seattle, John used Sam's old office in the Washington Shoe Building at 406 Occidental Avenue South and was Sam's "eyes and ears," in Eddie Hasson's words. John worked for Sam for most of his career, beginning with his start in the shoe repair business, then at Wingfoot Shoe Repair until Sam gave the shop to John in 1954. Six years later, the shop's building was condemned, Wingfoot ended its four-decade life, and John, known as Uncle Johnny to his nieces and nephews, went to work for Sam as properties manager in Seattle until about 1980. As usual, Sam maintained control of everything. Eddie Hasson describes the brothers' business relationship:

> *Uncle Johnny worked for him for 50 years, pretty much his career was working for Sam. . . . Johnny did all the leasing, but Sam would always set the rents. And if Johnny said, "Well, you can't afford that. How about we can do this." No such thing. Sam set the rent, this is it. There was no negotiation.*
>
> *Sam was so controlling, and if there was a property that Sam wanted a tenant to look at, he'd tell him, "Now, John, you take them to the property, show them the property. Don't answer any questions. Don't say nothing. Just show them the property. This is it." And John would say, "Okay, okay."*[21]

At times, the expression of John's and Sam's distinctly different personalities created tension in the relationship. In contrast to Sam's business-focused energy and savvy, John's style was more relaxed and family-centered. Marilyn Hasson Henry recalls, "Uncle Johnny had other qualities that perhaps Sam did not value." John, she notes, was "the most loving and devoted husband and father. Because of his relaxed style of work, Uncle Johnny was often home tinkering and kibitzing with the family. . . . Uncle Johnny's contribution to the family was that of love, compassion, and quiet devotion." Adam Hasson remembers John in a similar light. "Uncle Johnny had a very playful sense of humor and loved to tease," he recalls. "His wife, Auntie Julie, would sometimes pinch him in response to all his ribbing and call him a 'pinchon.' The word 'pinchon' in Ladino means troublemaker, and I always thought there was a connection between that and the pinches!"[22]

When John got too old to manage the properties, Sam called on Eddie's brother David. David, who then was a practicing architect in Seattle, provided another level of property management that John could not. Eddie Hasson recalls that Sam phoned David in the middle of the night, saying, "I need someone to look at these buildings and tell me what needs to be done. What I need to do is basically maintain them so that the next generation comes together, that they can go ahead and see what they can do with it, or if we get someone who wants to do some work, develop it, we can do that." Sam kept rents very low, and fixing things like a broken toilet were the tenant's responsibility. Eddie Hasson says, "Sam's not going to fix it. You don't like it? Move out." If there was a roof issue or a structural issue, David would hire a contractor for the repair work.[23]

As Sam aged, so did his properties. Over the years, most of his buildings were rented out and occupied, mainly on the ground level, and Sam tended to do minimum improvements. Typically, he kept rents below average for the Central Business District and Pioneer Square in downtown Seattle, so tenants were less likely to complain. At the time that David Hasson became property manager for his uncle, Sam was in his late seventies, and many years had passed since he had been close to the Seattle real estate scene. Most of his limited knowledge came from television news broadcasts. "He really felt that he was too old to make a difference," says David Hasson.[24]

Sam had little confidence in others but trusted nephews David and Eddie Hasson. Every so often, a realtor or developer would approach Sam with a proposition to buy one of his properties or get a long-term lease. Real estate agents who telephoned Sam with an unsolicited proposal received a gruff rebuke, earning him a reputation as cantankerous and difficult to deal with. In 1980, Sam described at length his style of dealing with outsiders—that is, nonfamily members—who sought him out. The least welcome group were "promoters" and agents seeking a real estate listing:

> *They call me. "Can I come over and see the—"*
> *[Sam] "What is it you want?"*
> *"I want to talk to you about that property."*
> *[Sam] "It's not for sale. It's not. I don't want you to come."*
> *That's my answer time and time again.*
>
> *I have to see who he is and why. No broker's going to come over and ask me question. I'm just talking about promoters or anybody else that comes over and wants a listing and talk about it. I don't talk to them unless I know who it is.*
>
> *In other words, I won't turn my back on any development that the city has to be taking care of. But I'm not going to bother with any broker or promoters of any kind. I have to know who it is. I was told he was the president of the bank, or vice-president, and he came over to my place himself. And he come in with the manager of Sears and Roebuck Company. He became a real estate man. And I chase him out, that's it.*
>
> *When I found out he's fishing around or something of the kind, I said, "Nothing doing. It's not for sale." And that stops them all. That's it.*
>
> *Sometimes when somebody wants a piece of property, that there is possibility that they could make a deal, and then I generally ask the question: "Do you have an opinion what the property's worth?" When they come over with a rotten proposition, then that's it. That's the end of it. . . .*
>
> *If a man ever offers me an offer, he cannot come back with an offer. He is out of the picture. No one can bargain with me. . . . When I put up a price, that's it. No discussion. No negotiation. A year from now I might change my mind higher or lower. But if somebody made an offer, he can't come back two weeks later and boost up the price.*
>
> *Anybody that comes over—only the ones that I think that he will be entitled to buy the property.*[25]

Not surprisingly, very few people got past Sam's farm's big front gate festooned with No Trespassing signs. Once, around 1976, two women from Mercer Island, one a broker and the other a prospective buyer, arrived unannounced. Sam and his dogs met them at the gate. "I cut them pretty short, in five minutes, that's it," Sam recalled. Aside from his basic mistrust of promoters and developers, Sam preferred to live alone and to be left alone, "like the Turks would call it, solitude. I want to be with the dogs, and cats, and birds, and cows, and horses. I want to be alone, except for family when they come over; they're welcome to come at any time," he emphasized.[26]

He did try a couple of times to make the deal, "but he got burned," says David. "As brilliant as he was, he was isolated, and he didn't really get the whole picture on some of the things that were happening. So, his philosophy was, 'I am not going to do any development, I'm just going to let it sit there for the next generation.'"[27]

For obvious reasons, most property developers considered Sam an "obstacle to progress." City bureaucrats, whom he considered "always wrong," were often on the receiving end of brusque, critical letters and angry phone calls from Sam. One recipient of a phone call from Sam remarked, "You really had to hold the phone 12 to 18 inches away from your ear. He would bellow." Some in Seattle, notably historic preservationists after the 1970s, when federal, state, and local preservation regulations were enacted, grudgingly called Sam an "accidental preservationist," acknowledging that ultimately he had played a positive role in saving many of the city's turn-of-the-century brick landmarks.[28]

At the same time, Sam had many supporters outside the Jewish community who recognized his contributions to the city. In April 1982, George E. Benson, a member of the Seattle City Council, invited Sam to attend inaugural ceremonies on May 29, 1982, for the Waterfront Streetcar. "You, more than anyone in the city, as part of the Local Improvement District, are responsible for the Waterfront Streetcar," Benson wrote.[29]

One of the few properties Sam sold was the Union Trust Building in Pioneer Square at 119 South Main Street. Shortly after an earthquake on April 13, 1949, rattled the Puget Sound area, an architect phoned Sam to report that the building had been seriously damaged. One story, according to Eddie Hasson, is that the architect convinced Sam to sell the building by exaggerating the damage and repairs that would be needed. Sam agreed to sell the building to developer Ralph Anderson. The new owner renovated the building and raised rents, which substantially increased the property's value. In 1968, the Foster/White Gallery opened next door, paving the way for Pioneer Square to become a vibrant arts district in the decade that followed. Although Sam had no interest in remodeling buildings, according to David Hasson, Sam later felt he had made a mistake. His goal was to preserve the buildings—keep the roof fixed and rent the street-level storefronts. "A lot of the buildings, if he had not owned them, would be parking lots," says Eddie Hasson. "But he kept the buildings going by just getting the rents from the storefronts."[30]

In the 1980s, Sam's "caretaker" management of his properties clearly helped not only low-income residents who rented rooms but also other members of the community. In Pioneer Square, Sam master-leased the upper floors of some buildings, and those tenants divided up the spaces and leased mainly to artists, helping nurture the Seattle art scene for over two decades (until gentrification and city housing regulations ended the unofficial live-work spaces).

In 1983, Greg Kucera was an ambitious young man who wanted to open his own art gallery. He looked at various locations and determined that he wanted to be near Pioneer Square. "There was this particularly challenging block on Second Avenue," recalls Kucera, "and Sam held the lease to the Corona Building, the Hartford Building, the building across the street, and the Butler Garage Building. It seemed like all roads pointed to Sam Israel." He decided on a space in the Corona Hotel building at 608 Second Street, where he hoped to get a "very affordable" lease of $350 a month for 1,800 square feet. He vividly recalls how Sam became his first landlord:

Above: Corona Hotel, built 1903. Below: Hartford Building, built 1929.

At the time I was opening, it was end of the recession in Seattle and the rest of the country, the beginning of the "Reaganomics" era. It turned out to be fortuitous for me to open at that moment. I had no business experience prior to that in owning a gallery though I had worked at Diane Gilson's gallery for the prior few years. Based on my financials, I was not what you would think of as a guaranteed reliable tenant. But, I really wanted the space even though the area was almost *completely derelict, partially because Sam owned and controlled it and wouldn't redevelop it. There was a liquor store on the corner; next door to my space was a club space called the Gorilla Room, which was a notorious punk rock place. Across the street was the 611 Bar, a really low-class gay bar; drunken people, drag queens getting in fights out front on the sidewalk; drug peddling; obviously a lot of sketchy stuff going on, a "den of iniquity" there. It was a funny time to open there, but Sam insisted that I speak to him by telephone, even though David Hasson, his nephew, was the leasing agent. So, I got on the phone with Sam and described my little business plan and my first time owning a business. He was surprisingly lenient with me. He said, "All I care about is you pay your rent on time." I said I would do that. He leased me the space for $350 a month. It was perfectly clear from the get-go that Samis Land Company was not going to put one dollar into that space, it was all going to be me paying for the remodel. It was a terrifying prospect, really, but the space was so cheap it was worth doing it that way.*[31]

Kucera remodeled the space through the summer and opened the Greg Kucera Gallery on October 3, 1983. Creating an attractive and viable business took no small effort. The space was "completely wrecked," he says, "filthy inside" from being vacant for decades. With the help of several friends, Kucera put in drywall over the old plaster and made various other improvements. He would work with the crew all day, then go to dinner, and then return to do some of the tasks that could be done by one person, like patching all the holes in the ceiling with chicken wire and plaster. When he started moving some old shelving in the back, he discovered a $5 bill taped to the underside of one of the shelves. "It was from about 1928," Kucera notes with pride. "It was the first dollar I ever made owning my own business, and I have it in my office today. I took that as a good omen that the space was going to work out for me."

Good omen or not, Kucera faced a rough start. The winter of 1983–1984 proved extremely cold, and Kucera had no money to put in any kind of heat. "I was freezing to death in there," he recalls. Word reached Sam, probably from David Hasson, and soon Sam had a heater installed above the front door at his expense. "It was the only time he was overtly generous with me, but it helped a lot," Kucera notes. The gallery slowly prospered and grew. A few years later, Kucera added another 1,500 square feet and then, with his

Galland Building, built 1906.

partner, Larry Yocom, opened Gallery Frames in a small space also near Second Avenue and James Street.

It was not only Greg Kucera who benefitted from Sam's real estate philosophy and practice but also artists, other galleries, and the community of Pioneer Square as a whole. "It can't be overestimated how important Sam was to the artistic community here," emphasizes Kucera. He continues:

> *There were a number of artists who were his tenants over the years, well-known Seattle artists, and there were quite a few galleries who leased his spaces over the years, for example,*

Lynn McAllister, Cliff Michel, Linda Cannon, and others.... You could open a business for very little money at that time, partially because Sam wasn't interested in developing his spaces, but he didn't mind if somebody else fixed them up, and that made it possible to open a business on a very modest budget. For art galleries that's a very important thing. Galleries tend to proliferate where there is very cheap rent but, because of the nature of their business, they raise the tenor, the quality, of the neighborhood.[32]

The story of the Galland Building is another graphic example of Sam's philosophy at work. Located at the corner of Second Avenue and Seneca Street in the Central Business District, the six-story masonry building was built in 1906 and, for most of its life, housed a department store. After more than sixty years, the Galland was aging, empty, and valued at $250,000 when Sam acquired it in 1969 in exchange for the Telephone Building, which had been condemned by the City of Seattle. Sam thought the appraised value was too low and convinced the city to raise its valuation to $300,000. When the exchange was completed, Sam donated the extra $50,000 to the Kline Galland Home. In May 1972, the Kline Galland Home honored Sam with a special plaque, saluting him for "his business acumen and financial expertise in the recent sale of its property resulting in increased annual income to better serve its residents and enabling it to be acclaimed as the outstanding home for the aged in the State of Washington."[33]

As years passed, the Galland Building followed the pattern typical for many of Sam's properties: the ground floor was rented to several specialty retail stores, and the upper levels were used for warehouse space or left empty. In 1986, that changed.

In 1985, one block up the hill at 1201 Third Avenue, Washington Mutual Bank had engaged Wright Runstad & Company to develop a fifty-five-story skyscraper. But the Galland Building (then called the Galland & Seneca Building) posed a problem for Wright Runstad. Victor Alhadeff, a longtime associate of Sam's and now a Samis Foundation trustee, describes the events that unfolded next:

The developer reached out to Sam and explained that they were going to build this beautiful new high-rise, and the tenants needed to know they would have an unobstructed view, so he wanted to buy the Galland & Seneca property to protect the view for his tenants. Sam said, "No, not for sale." That was the end of the conversation.

The guy called back and said, "Mr. Israel, you don't understand, we're building this building and the whole value of it is this beautiful view; and it's not about price, I'll pay you whatever you want."

Sam said, "It's not for sale."

The guy said, "But, you don't understand, we're building this big building, and the tenants have to have an unobstructed view."

Sam said, "Your problem, not mine." So, finally, Sam did say, "It's not for sale, but I'll rent it to you."

The guy said, "I need to have a protected view for the life of the leases, 25 years." Sam said, "Fine, I'll lease it to you for 25 years, but, I want the lease to be on one page." It was a fixed dollar amount that escalated every year for 25 years. He said, "One page—the rest of all of that stuff is to your benefit, not mine, and I don't understand it. Here's the rent, you stop paying, I get the building back. It's simple. One page."

So, in comes the agreement, a standard 50-page lease. Sam doesn't open the envelope, he just returns it unopened with a little hand written note: "I said one page." They finally did get it to one page, and that lease did happen.[34]

Construction on the building, initially known as the Washington Mutual Tower and now as 1201 Third Avenue, began in 1986 and was completed in 1988. Today, the Galland & Seneca property is ground-leased by the Samis Foundation and is the site of the 2+U complex, completed in 2020 by Skanska USA. Two connected office towers—the Qualtrics Tower that rises thirty-eight stories and a second tower of eighteen stories—offer sweeping views over downtown and Puget Sound. The building complex, which includes an "urban village" with working areas and free rehearsal spaces for arts and cultural programs, stands adjacent to the Seattle Art Museum and Benaroya Hall and is a beautiful addition to the Seattle skyline. As a ground lease, the property will generate steady and growing income for the Samis Foundation, all because of Sam's simple business model: "I'm not going to sell, but I will lease."

Victor Alhadeff praises Sam's farsightedness. "Sam knew that Washington Mutual had to maintain that building because they wouldn't want the neighborhood going downhill," he notes. "This is a story of how tough Sam was—'your problem, not mine.'" The philosophy of not selling was firm, but there was a reasonableness in Sam. He found a different way of solving the developer's problem, but on his terms, and forcing the deal to be simplistic. "He didn't like legal documents," says Alhadeff. "He liked simple, easy to read, easy to understand documents, almost like handshake deals." It was a beautiful example, says Alhadeff, of how Sam's philosophy of real estate continues to affect so many lives. He smiles. "It was brilliant simplicity."[35]

> *As a man whose word could be trusted, Sam expected the same integrity from friends and others with whom he did business.*

THE DICK TALL AFFAIR

As a man whose word could be trusted, Sam expected the same integrity from friends and others with whom he did business. In 1979, Sam handwrote an agreement with Richard "Dick" Tall on a sheet of lined tablet paper for a property exchange, fully expecting the transaction to flow smoothly. It did not.

Three years earlier, in 1976, Sam received a phone call from Dick Tall. Sam knew Dick's brother, Leonard Tall (1924–1998), founder of Tall's Camera Supply and CX Corporation, who for many years had rented space from Sam in the Galland Building and whom Sam highly respected. Dick Tall introduced himself as Leonard's brother and said he wanted to come visit Sam and talk about his twenty-acre lot on the south end of Mercer Island. The parcel was zoned for residential housing, and Tall wanted to develop it. But the conversation ended quickly, Sam later recalled. "We didn't discuss nothing. It's not for sale. I'm not interested and that's it, finished." Sometime later, Tall called again, saying he wanted to come over to Soap Lake and talk to Sam again about the property. Sam described the events that followed when the case came to trial in 1980:

> *He was friendly, very smooth-talking, very friendly, very nice. All right. We start discussing. He tells me he wants to go into developing, okay, to buy the property. I said, "I am not interested in selling the property." That's all. I didn't want to put any price on or nothing on it. . . .*
>
> *He was getting pushy, pushy. And every time I said, "No, no, no." And then, "What the hell are they selling the lots for?" And he gave me idea. . . . I was curious to know what's happening up there. I'm getting old and that property does not produce any income. It's a dead property. And I'm trying to make a foundation.*[36]

Tall cited a general figure for the property's value and promised to send Sam a listing book for properties in the area, which he did after some months. Even after Tall's second visit in 1977, Sam told him, "Not for sale. Not interested. I don't want to bother with it." Another year passed. After Tall's third visit to the farm, Sam finally agreed to sell the parcel to Tall for $1 million, but only as an exchange. Sam would direct Tall to purchase certain properties in Seattle, and when the total value reached $1 million, they would exchange properties in accordance with IRS Code Section 1031, which prescribed the rules for a tax-deferred property exchange. The term on the agreement was one year.

Despite the fact that Sam had written the contract himself and no attorney had reviewed the agreement, things started off well. Tall acquired the Butler Block, then the Broderick Building. As the one-year time limit approached, Sam picked out the Forest Hotel and a three-lot parcel identified as the Stetson-Ross Plant. At that point, Tall ran out of money and, more importantly, realized that the properties he had acquired for Sam were worth substantially more than the lot on Mercer Island. Tall informed Sam that he could not complete the final purchase and declared bankruptcy.

The two men then became adversaries in court. The trial of Samis Land Company, represented by Irwin Treiger and two other attorneys from Bogle & Gates, versus Dick Tall's business, Columbia Pacific Industries, took more than a year. Court proceedings lasted a week, and in February 1980, Sam appeared in Superior Court at the Grant County courthouse to testify. After the customary oath was administered, Sam took another oath, this one in Hebrew. Tall's attorney, Henry M. Aronson, asked Sam to translate. Sam obliged but put Aronson in his place:

> SAM: *That oath is for Hebrews only, but I will spell it out. If you want to know what it is, you may find out when you go to Seattle—if you don't understand it—and they will tell you what it is. But, I will spell it out.* Barhuh bahuh dayan aemet. . . . *You may find it out. It is very simple to find out. I'm sorry you don't understand it.*
>
> ARONSON: *Could I ask you to briefly explain it for us?*
>
> SAM: *I would rather not to. It's a Hebrew prayer; sacred to me, very sacred. It means to me a prayer, full submission to the will of God. I will interpret it to Mohammed religion, but I will not translate it in the Hebrew meaning. We have same meaning with the Arab's Mohammed.*

Eddie Hasson recalls, "Sam was a riot, but he was a very sympathetic witness on his own behalf." At the conclusion of the proceedings, the judge ruled in favor of Sam and ordered Tall and Columbia Pacific Industries to deliver "specific performance" in accordance with the terms of the contract. In the end, the litigation brought Sam (Samis Land Company) ownership of the Broderick Building, the Stetson-Ross Plant, the Butler Block, and the Forest Hotel. After the trial was over, Eddie Hasson, Irwin Treiger, and the other attorneys representing Sam went to Treiger's office. They popped the cork on a bottle of champagne, but Sam refused to join in. "No, I won't drink champagne," he said. "This is a sad day because two Jews had an argument and it was in the newspapers. It's very, very bad for the Jewish community. It's a victory but it's not a celebration."[37]

For Dick Tall, the end of the story was more tragic. He was bankrupt and a broken man. A few years after the trial ended, on December 6, 1985, Dick Tall died at the age of forty-five.

Broderick Building, built 1923.

Gatewood Hotel, built 1898.

THE GATEWOOD HOTEL AFFAIR

When it came to his properties and the opinions of local bureaucrats, Sam Israel was not one to bow down. He readily tackled city hall, state and federal agencies, or anyone he felt was treating him unfairly or trying to take advantage of him. Sam's disinterest in selling or improving his aging buildings increasingly made him a target of both developers and advocates for historic restoration or civic improvement. It was only a matter of time until the conflicting notions about Sam's properties in Seattle spilled over into the press and the courtroom. Among the most prominent incidents were those involving the Gatewood Hotel, which occurred in late 1984 as the Dick Tall trial slowly moved to conclusion. "Sam cared about the homeless," states Eddie Hasson. "He cared for the common man. That's the story of the Gatewood."[38]

One confrontation with the City of Seattle ended well for Sam. The city in the 1950s had passed an ordinance to tax areaways beneath the streets and sidewalks in front of property owners' buildings. In the 1970s and early 1980s, they reimposed the fees. Virtually all of the affected property owners coughed up the money. Not Sam Israel. He filed suit, claiming it was unconstitutional for the city to charge property owners for use of their own property. In 1987 and again in 1988, after the city appealed, the court ruled that the city's assessment of $39,000 on fourteen of Sam's buildings was, indeed, unconstitutional. Sam's attorney, Ralph Brindley, told reporters, "Everyone else had knuckled under. Sam doesn't back off from anything." (Today, the fees are considered reasonable, with different rates for occupied and unoccupied buildings.)[39]

Sam regularly appeared in the newspapers of his adopted hometown in Grant County, but he tended to avoid Seattle journalists. When his property holdings and associated litigation did attract the interest of reporters, Sam kept his comments relatively short and pithy. A colorful exception was an interview in July 1981 with *Seattle Times* reporter Carey Quan Gelernter. Her articles featured accompanying photographs of Sam that included an unflattering shot of him wearing an untucked flannel shirt and a soft hat, howling with his dogs.[40]

One writer, Candace Dempsey, proved both amiable and adept at portraying Sam and his world, in the process winning Sam's invitation to return and capturing aspects of Sam's life seldom of interest to journalists. After giving Dempsey his requisite long lectures about Jewish history, Sam told her, The Torah says you never deliberately hurt anyone. But if someone hurts you, you can take an eye for an eye." When Dempsey asked, "Do you ever feel like building something to leave behind you?" Sam's answer was thoughtful and revealing, as Dempsey reported: "'What do you want me to build?' he wonders, chuckling and slapping himself on the knee. 'I'm too old . . . all my girlfriends have been six feet under for twenty years. I get up every morning and say, 'Thank God, I made it through another night.' He says he isn't lonely up on that hill, but adds he regrets never marrying. 'I ask the girls and they say no. I ask again and they say no. So, I don't ask anymore. I wasn't good enough, just a shoemaker.'"[41]

Sam had purchased the Gatewood Hotel at 101–111 Pine Street (First Avenue and Pine Street) on October 30, 1975, for $200,000. The building, a four-story brick structure, had ninety-six single rooms for rent on the upper three floors and a tavern, furniture store, and gift shop on the ground floor.

The housing crisis downtown made the Gatewood one of the few inexpensive sources of shelter for homeless and poor citizens. In 1984, the tenants were the low-income and destitute who could find no other place to stay, including "retired loggers, retired mill and railroad workers, people that lost a limb, people on a pension," says Eddie Hasson. The rooms, which were rented for $4 a night, were also typically occupied by transients and families with little or no income. Eddie continues: "They had a little room and they would go to the coffee shops, they'd go here and there. That was the homeless. But it was then that these buildings started to get rehabbed. There's no room for the homeless in a rehab. They want people that are going to pay $500 a month not $50 a month. You could just see how it was affecting the homeless. They were being squeezed out of their housing and they're out on the street."[42]

Sam had never seen the Gatewood Hotel building, and in fact believed he had purchased a normal hotel with customers and maid service. He raised the rent and leased the Gatewood to Ray Armistead, who managed the property. But in 1984, Armistead had trouble meeting lease payments and started evicting tenants. The evictions brought a suit by the City of Seattle and a whirlwind of media attention. Newspapers, especially the *Seattle Times*, published articles condemning "absentee landlords" and implicating Sam Israel. The turn of events was a shock to Sam.[43]

Sam had never accepted a request to be interviewed for television. The Gatewood events changed that.

KING-TV, owned by KING Broadcasting Company in Seattle, was one of a handful of stations in the country that gave their journalists freedom to develop in-depth stories, and a one-hour documentary on housing issues, *Shelter from the Storm*, became a project for one of the station's brightest young reporters, thirty-year-old Jack Hamann, in late 1986. In the mid-1980s, housing in the Belltown neighborhood had become a growing concern after the city began moving to develop the area where many single-room-occupancy (SRO) hotels were located, including the Gatewood Hotel. The worst SROs were "eyesores," and low-income residents lived in filthy conditions with poor lighting, peeling paint, broken plumbing, and other clear signs that the building owners had no regard for the health and safety of renters.

As Hamann interviewed residents and searched out owners, he discovered that many of the buildings in the worst condition belonged to Sam Israel. Hamann heard stories about Sam that painted him as a heartless, uncaring slumlord. "I became determined to reach Sam," recalls Hamann. The effort took several weeks. Finally, in late fall, after an exchange of letters, Sam agreed to an interview. Hamann and photographer Diana Wilmar drove to Soap Lake and took hotel rooms for the night. The next morning, they telephoned Sam, and he arranged to meet them at the gate to his property.[44]

"I was not prepared at all for what we found; it was jaw-dropping," Hamann says. Sam, as usual, was dressed in his casual farm clothes, driving the beat-up old pickup he often took to town, accompanied by the Mariuch. Hamann recalls, "It was a mess of a ranch, with abandoned trucks, rusted vehicles, tractor parts, two donkeys, and barking dogs." Other absentee owners Hamann had met or heard about were living in comfort, enjoying the wealth they made off cheap rents and minimal investment in their properties. "Clearly, Sam was not living high on the hog," Hamann says.

Also, to Hamann's surprise, Sam was friendly and accommodating. Hamann, in his trademark low-key, personally engaging style, strolled around the property and toured the bunkhouse with Sam, asking questions while the camera rolled. KING-TV broadcast the interview on December 30, 1984. The news anchor opened the story with the question, "Saint or Slumlord?" and described Sam Israel as "a very elusive and controversial man." The Hamann interview, which was incorporated into the one-hour documentary, is remarkable for two reasons: it is the only television interview of Sam, and the footage offers fascinating glimpses into Sam's personal life, faith, and philosophy. A few selected scenes are notable:

> *HAMANN: To begin to understand Sam Israel, you must first know that he is a deeply religious man. He says he accumulates so much property because he needs protection, protection from the persecution that has plagued Jews since the time of Moses.*
>
> *SAM: This thing has happened for two thousand years, it was the curse of Moses, the gift to the Jews, the going away from the Promised Land. They will be spread out across the face of the Earth. And they will be persecuted by all the nations of the world. That is the curse. . . .*
>
> *HAMANN: Samis is also the name of his charitable foundation. When he dies, all his money will go to the foundation, to be managed by ten prominent Seattle businessmen.*
>
> *SAM: They will make the decisions on what to do. And my instruction not to sell unless they have to, try to lease as much as humanly possible, and to have income for the foundation that it may run for 50 or 100 years; to help the poor, the sick, any disaster, any place in the world, of any religion, of any people, they don't have to be Jews. . . .*
>
> *HAMANN: I guess the question I have for you, are you happy? You have all of the property and you've had a long life, but are you happy?*

SAM: I come from the ranks. Money has never support me, and I have never had any use for it. And was I still a cobbler, it would have been exactly the same. I try to do the best I can to protect the interest of my properties, the interest of the peoples, the district, and the City of Seattle. And I'm not out to benefit myself few dollars at the expense of the neighbors and the property owners in the vicinity, in the City of Seattle. I don't need the money.

HAMANN: Sam Israel believes he has been wrongly portrayed as some kind of villain. He says he cares very much about Seattle's future, and he spends a lot of time these days thinking about his own future.

SAM: I'm 87 years old, next month I'll be 88 years old. When I get up in the morning, I feel it's a gift of God, that I'm living that day, and I'm not out to make money, or to hurt anybody. Now, what's gonna happen to me now? Some of these mornings I may not wake up. Every morning I thank God for it, it's a gift from God. One morning you'll read, and I'm not going to wake up. If they catch me in the morning, early in the morning, that I'm dead, before sunset, I'll be six feet underground. They'll take my body and they'll wash it with soap and water, and they will wrap my body with a piece of white cloth. That is a bed sheet, we call it "mortaja" [shroud] in Spanish. With the white sheet, the richest of the rich and the poorest of the poor, white sheet. We come naked and we go naked, that's the book, that's the way we live. Money don't mean nothing, can't take it with us, we believe in our books and we practice. . . .

HAMANN: Sam Israel has a vision for downtown Seattle. He wants it to be a gleaming center of commerce, a vibrant, commercial magnet for world trade. So, he keeps many of his buildings deserted, he says, while he makes plans for those buildings to someday be torn down and replaced with skyscrapers. There are many however, who believe his vision is actually destroying key parts of the city. . . .

When he bought the Gatewood Hotel several years ago, Israel thought it was a real hotel with maid service and daily customers. He had no idea it served as permanent housing for low-income people. He admits he hasn't been to Seattle in ten years. . . .

What do you say to the people in Seattle who would say that you take care or care more about your dogs than you do about the people who are on the streets of Seattle who would like to live in your buildings?

SAM: *They live in the buildings and they are destroying the property, deteriorating it, that would cause more damages to the neighborhood, to the business people that are*

"When I get up in the morning, I feel it's a gift of God, that I'm living that day, and I'm not out to make money, or to hurt anybody."

there, and to the City of Seattle. Those people, unfortunately, I feel sorry for them, they drifted away from society, from life, whether by alcohol, dopes, whatever. It is up to the government, to the city, to go ahead and try to restore them, to bring them in, to do something about it. If we don't, we are gonna having trouble. . . .

HAMANN: *Israel hopes that someday the Gatewood and other old hotels will be torn down and replaced with gleaming office complexes. And all the low-income seniors who will no longer have a place to live, where should they move? But out in the country is where they should come?*

SAM: *That's right. Enjoy the, what is the beauty of the country, the splendor, of the beauty. And look it here, how peaceful it is, how nice it is. And then when they retire, like this one here, put the horse in the pasture. Now, I'm in a pasture, I belong here, I don't want to go anyplace else.*

It didn't take Sam long to have second thoughts about the interview. One week later, he phoned Hamann. "You can't use anything I told you," he commanded. Hamann politely replied that the story about him and about the Gatewood would run. Sam persisted. "I just don't want to do it." Hamann, unruffled, replied that the story would air, people would get to hear Sam's side of the story, and it was important. Sam's response came angry, fast, and hard: "Then, I put a curse on you, I put a curse on your children and all who follow you!" The reporter later recalled, "I was more amused than threatened. He sounded like my Hungarian grandmother. I told him, wait until the story is aired, then see what you think and get back to me. I guess he was OK with it—I never heard from him." After the broadcast, however, Hamann did receive a cordial and complimentary note from the Samis Foundation (probably written by Eddie Hasson) thanking him for the accurate portrayal of Sam, a rarity at the time for Sam Israel. Years later, as Hamann recalled the interview and his visit to the farm, he noted, "Sam is on my list as one of the most interesting people I've ever met."[45]

The Gatewood Hotel affair gradually came to an amicable resolution. According to Eddie Hasson, Sam telephoned him and said, "Can you get the Pike Place Market Association or anybody to rent the buildings? I'll give them a good deal. I'm looking for a tenant. I'm in trouble." Eddie reached out to Ernie Sherman, owner of Pacific Plumbing Supply Company and chair of the Property Management Committee of the Pike Place Market Association. Sherman connected Sam with Plymouth Congregational Church, which was assisting the city in solving problems with low-income housing. Sam sold Plymouth the building for $1 and agreed to give them a long lease on the land. Sherman recalls how the events developed:

> *The Gatewood was located on First Avenue across from the Market and was an eyesore inside and out, so the Pike Place Market Association thought. I agreed to try to lease the Gatewood for the Association. Through Morrie Piha and Eddie Hasson, it was arranged that I could go to Soap Lake and meet with Sam and attempt to make a deal. I flew to Moses Lake, and then drove to Ephrata, where I met Sam for the first time. He showed me all the properties he owned in the area, and then we went to his ranch. We talked for a long time about any and everything. He was an amazing guy, and I think he liked me—I know I liked him. We agreed on the terms of a long lease that we both signed, and I caught a night flight back to Seattle.*[46]

By September 1985, city officials and interest groups, the Plymouth Congregational Church, and the US Department of Housing and Urban Development reached an agreement that would provide federal rent subsidies and a path to renovation of the hotel three years later. Although Sam continued to receive bad press over the matter, Michael Carroll, head of the Seattle Preservation and Development Authority, praised Sam for being "most cooperative in working out details of the plans for the renovation of the building and the lease." Carroll acknowledged Sam as an important member of the Gatewood Hotel Project Team and noted, "We discovered that once Mr. Israel makes a verbal commitment, there is not fear there will be any subsequent changes that vary in any way from his word."[47]

In March 1989, Sam, who a month before had suffered a stroke, agreed on a twenty-five-year lease to the Pike Place Market Preservation and Development Authority. The Seattle press termed the agreement "historic," considering Sam's long-standing reluctance to involve himself in low-income housing projects and his belief that his properties in downtown were too valuable to be used as housing. In 1991, Eddie Hasson, who had been appointed Sam's guardian following the stroke, and his brother David Hasson approved redevelopment for the Gatewood. By the time Sam passed in 1994, the Gatewood was "a bright and successful low-income building operated by the Plymouth Housing Group."[48]

REAL ESTATE EAST AND INVESTING IN THE FUTURE

From the 1950s through the 1980s, Sam had invested in his new home territory. The variety of acquisitions was amazing—buildings and vacant lots in downtown Soap Lake and Ephrata, waterfront lots, potato farms, wheat farms, and miscellaneous pieces of sagebrush-covered land. Sam was known for standing on the courthouse steps when the county assessor auctioned properties that had gone into foreclosure for failure to pay taxes. On one occasion, Sam (using Samis Land Company) purchased the Wylie Chrysler dealership building in Ephrata at public auction for $150,000. On another, he bought waterfront property in Moses Lake, sight unseen, only to find out later that although the lot was more than 165 feet deep, the lakeside measured only 8 feet wide. He also purchased property in the small, unincorporated town of Beverly, which lies on the west bank of the Columbia River just south of the Vantage Bridge. Jack Patrick was the real estate agent who worked on many of Sam's purchases. "Sam, was not the easiest one to deal with in the world," says Jack, "but he was very straightforward, and you knew where he stood on anything."[49]

Over the course of three decades, Sam's holdings in eastern Washington became substantial. In Ephrata, he owned nineteen properties totaling 25 acres. In Moses Lake, he acquired three properties totaling 9 acres, including waterfront lots. In Soap Lake and the immediate vicinity, Sam bought thirty-five pieces of property that totaled 2,524 acres. Elsewhere in Grant County, he acquired thirty properties amounting to 13,028 acres. In all, Sam's eastern Washington holdings counted eighty-seven properties totaling 15,586 acres, valued in 1995 at more than $4 million.[50]

Inevitably, Sam's property interests and willingness to tackle intrusive government agencies head-on brought conflicts and lawsuits. Among the most publicized were Sam's disputes with the Grant County Irrigation District Commission and the Quincy-Columbia Basin Irrigation Project.

The completion of Grand Coulee Dam in 1942 had far-reaching effects for both hydroelectric power and agriculture. Congress authorized the Columbia Basin Project in 1943, and after World War II, construction began on a network of irrigation systems that spread across central Washington. Under the authority of the US Bureau of Reclamation, canals, reservoirs, and large concrete siphons were constructed to carry the water that would irrigate hundreds of thousands of acres. In the vicinity of Soap Lake, Sam's farm and other surrounding properties began receiving water from the Quincy-Columbia Basin Irrigation Project in January 1956.

The Bureau of Reclamation's regulations allowed irrigation water for only 160 acres per farm unit. Property over that amount was considered "excess land" and not entitled to irrigation water from the project. In addition, the bureau's excess land policy required landowners to sell all but 160 acres at a dryland price set by the bureau within ten years after water from the Second Bacon Siphon and Tunnel reached the area.

Sam owned two tracts totaling seven hundred acres, one acquired in 1946 and another in 1961. On one parcel Sam's tenants farmed dryland winter wheat with good returns of forty to fifty bushels an acre, so he saw no need to sell the land deemed excess. In 1963, he brought his objections to the Irrigation District Commission, but they refused his request to withdraw property from the excess designation. Sam filed suit, which eventually landed the case in the US District Court and the US Court of Appeals, Ninth District. Ten years later, in 1973, the court sided with the irrigation district and the federal government.[51]

Three years later, in August 1976, Sam became the photographer for the Second Bacon Siphon and Tunnel (which ran from Bacon Coulee to Soap

Lake from Dry Falls) and worked on contract for the San Francisco–based project builder, Guy F. Atkinson Construction. Though Sam had lost the suit, he continued fighting the irrigation district and Bureau of Reclamation into 1977. Since he and other farmers had planted dryland winter wheat on some seven hundred acres, there was no need to be part of the district at all, nor to sell his land. "It's against human rights," he told the court. The bureau's land policy, he emphatically insisted, was unconstitutional because it deprived him of the right to sell his land at a fair market price. He spent thousands of dollars on legal fees, all to no avail. Ultimately, after court cases and a number of district commission hearings, the government prevailed; the district denied Sam's request to withdraw his land, and the matter ended.[52]

THE FIGHT FOR CLEAN AIR

It wasn't just disagreements about water and excess land that got Sam in trouble. In the spring of 1971, Sam's environmental concerns placed him at odds with the Grant County commissioners and the Purdy Company, a recycling business that had earned a reputation for polluting the air. The company, founded in 1950, operated more than fifty recycling facilities in the Midwest and the West, including one near Chehalis, Washington. Purdy had purchased twenty-two acres of land a couple of miles northeast of Ephrata near the Municipal Airport and on March 11, 1971, announced plans to open a railroad car recycling and metal salvage yard, which they anticipated would employ forty or more people and recycle three thousand railroad cars a year. Purdy's practices included dismantling railroad cars, selling the metal, then burning the remaining parts, which threw enormous black clouds into the air. The prospect alarmed many local citizens, including Sam.

Purdy applied to the Grant County Planning Commission for a certificate of occupancy and a building permit. The commissioners hoped to avoid the issue, saying they had no authority to deny the Purdy application. Immediately, Sam placed an ad in the next *Grant County Journal*: "My only request is that the Commissioners VOTE ON THIS ISSUE to see whether they want the Purdy Company in Ephrata or not. They cannot convince me they do not have the authority any more than Pontius Pilate did not have the authority to stop the crucifixion of Christ, a crime I'm still paying for."[53]

Sam's vocal opposition inspired local high school students to protest, and his ad ignited a furor. On the evening of March 24, two dozen shouting

WHY POLLUTION?

Who am I fighting?

... Not the Purdy Company but the Grant County Commissioners. For more than a week now and at their meeting last Monday their answer has been the same. They say they have no authority to stop the Purdy Company from coming here. At the meeting Monday I was trying to prove they do have that authority. My only request is that the Commissioners VOTE ON THIS ISSUE to see whether they want the Purdy Company in Ephrata or not. They cannot convince me they do not have the authority anymore than Pontius Pilate did not have the authority to stop the crucifixion of Christ, a crime I'm still paying for. The next Commissioners Meeting pertaining to pollution is April 5. All interested please attend.

Samuel Israel

Sam's ad placed in the *Grant County Journal* during the fight against Purdy Company, March 25, 1971.

students stormed the residence of Mayor Harry Drittenbas, demanding a hearing and a permit to hold a protest march in downtown Ephrata. The mayor agreed, and on the following day, a public city council meeting was held. Sam and many others spoke to the issue of the protest march, as well as the prospect of Purdy's operation seriously polluting the air around Ephrata and Soap Lake. After lengthy discussion, the council agreed that the group could "parade, as long as they parade in an orderly fashion as any other group is allowed to do." The following day, the students and others—carrying signs paid for by Sam—held an Ecology Parade through downtown Ephrata on Basin Street.

Two weeks later, on April 12, the Grant County Planning Commission met in a packed-room public session. Sam spoke before the commission, claiming that burning railroad cars would result in major air pollution in the area. Nonetheless, the Planning Commission recommended approval of Purdy's application for a certificate of occupancy and building permit on their site. Three days later, in response to Sam's request for another public meeting, the Board of County Commissioners took up the matter. Sam, now recognized as "the leading opponent" of Purdy's operation, appeared at the hearing, where for two hours he and others urged the county commissioners to reject Purdy's application. The effort failed. The commissioners declared that Purdy was "within its rights" to operate the recycling facility and on April 13 issued the certificate and permit to Purdy.

The company lost no time. The same day, a handful of blowtorch-wielding workers began cutting metal from the first ten boxcars, and late that evening—in the middle of the night—set fire to the remnants. Sam and the other Purdy opponents were out of options. Gradually, Sam turned his attention to other matters. The Purdy scrapyard operated from 1971 to the late 1970s, when stricter state and federal air pollution regulations sharply reduced operating profits and the facility finally closed.

PRESERVATIONIST FOR WETLANDS

A few years later, in the 1980s, the conservation group Ducks Unlimited, a nonprofit dedicated to the preservation of wetlands, honored Sam for his "appreciation and enhancement of wildlife in the region." In 1982, Sam made a deal with the State Department of Fish and Game that

Eddie Hasson in Jeep at site Sam donated to the Washington State Department of Game, 1982.

allowed the department to manage his property at Lake Lenore. The department would "improve and protect the land," as well as construct an access road and manage hunting and fishing. The state erected a large sign, and Sam was especially proud of their efforts. "Why should I deprive people of hunting?" Sam told the reporter covering the story. "My land has always been open to hunters. Only now the Game Department can do a better job of protecting it. Land really belongs to no one. It's just for us to use." A similar arrangement followed in 1984, after Sam acquired another parcel in the area, giving him ownership of most of the land between Soap Lake and Lake Lenore. This time, the arrangement with the Game Department for public access and hunting on his property included Little Soap Lake, and Sam told a reporter he wanted people to "use the lake and appreciate God's creation. . . . All I ask is for the public to keep the lake clean and obey Game Department rules." Sam also let a local motorcycle club ride on his property, requiring only that they sign an agreement stating that Sam was not responsible in the event of an injury.[54]

GOOD NEIGHBOR SAM

Sam with his International pickup, visiting in Ephrata, c. 1987.

Sam had positive regard for his Grant County neighbors, and for the most part they felt the same about him. He praised them to one reporter as "hard-working, God-fearing people." While some held a negative view of Sam, including one who thought Sam wanted to take over the county and make it "his own little kingdom," most of the townsfolk in Soap Lake and Ephrata thought Sam was "nice." In his later years, Sam became something of a legend, a recluse mostly seen by locals driving around Soap Lake and Ephrata in his war-surplus Jeep or well-worn International pickup. Some simply didn't know him and didn't know what to think. Tracy Warner, a writer for the *Wenatchee World*, said, "To most people, Sam is that rich guy up on the hill. He's got vacant lots all over town, and some people say they're eyesores. They say, 'Here's this millionaire and he lives in a dump, dresses like a bum and drives around in an old Jeep half the time.' They can't figure him out."[55]

Sam took photographs of Grant County's varied scenery, courthouse personnel, and wildlife. In 1981, his photos of local landscapes were displayed at the Moses Lake branch of Seattle First National Bank. The reporter for the *Columbia Basin Herald* who covered the story, Nancy Wolf, asked eighty-two-year-old Sam what kept him going with the desire to record history. She got a clear answer: "His love for his fellow man," she wrote, "the deeply ingrained belief that all are equal, and perhaps most of all, that he is 'his brother's keeper.'"[56]

There were many who appreciated him, like those associated with the Scouts and Christian women's groups whom Sam let use his buildings for meetings. He also earned the affection of many Christians with a surprising and generous gesture in September 1983. Sam had learned that the United Methodist Church in Ephrata was looking for a bell to place in its newly completed church bell tower. So Sam set to work locating a bell. He purchased a three-hundred-pound bell and donated it to the church as a "token of good will between Jews and Christians."[57]

Longtime residents of Soap Lake Bonnie Holt Morehouse and her husband, Keith Morehouse, relate a story about Sam from the 1970s. As a teenager, Keith worked at a RadioShack in Ephrata and recalls that Sam would come into the store every month to get a free battery. On one visit, Sam wanted to buy an expensive antenna for his television. "Keith advised him that he didn't need that expensive antenna because his property was right by the new reflectors built up at the farm," says Bonnie. Sam bought the cheaper one and was pleased. Bonnie says, "He later told Keith that he got great reception and was appreciative of Keith's honesty."[58]

Marina Romary, Soap Lake mayor from 1981 to 1986, was another local who liked and appreciated Sam. Born in 1938 in Soap Lake, Romary was the daughter of Greek immigrants. She had known Sam as a youth and recalled, "He liked to come around and talk with the Greeks and my dad and John Pappas, and he was just part of the community." Jack Patrick, owner of Jack Patrick Real Estate and Sam's broker as well as friend for many years, tells a similar story: "He would drive into Ephrata almost daily, stop at one end to visit a friend, drive across town to visit another friend, and then get back to the farm at 3 p.m. to watch wrestling on TV." Eddie Hasson saw no indications of anti-Semitism among Sam's Soap Lake and Ephrata neighbors: "Everybody knew he was Jewish in Soap Lake," Eddie says. "He carried it on his arm."[59]

In 1980, one local resident of Soap Lake, Kathy Nopson, was moved to write a letter of support and consolation to Sam. "I was not living in this city during the time that you suffered deceit and malignment by some of the people," Nopson wrote, referring to Sam's fight against the Purdy Company. "You are a deeply religious man who has been brought up on wisdom, forbearance and humility." Nopson acknowledged "the validity and extent of your misgivings about this city and its people," but urged him to reconsider recent events, which she explained as the behavior of "delayed people," and to "forgive the misdeeds of the past."[60]

At the same time, Sam was deeply afraid of being burglarized. Sam had also encountered ill-tempered bikers and others, as well as thieves who stole sand, gravel, and other small objects from his property. He lived alone, and in his later years, as his health declined, he grew more and more concerned (perhaps to the point of paranoia, suggests Eddie Hasson). He certainly had valid reasons. For one thing, he kept a stash of money handy but hidden. He lived on a small portion of the monthly stipend from Samis Land Company and Social Security checks. He saved a small amount for regular expenses in a bank checking account, a large sum in savings, and cash in a hidden box. After his death, Eddie Hasson found that box, which contained $100,000. In addition, Sam had many cameras and guns around the farm—the kind of easy-to-sell or pawn items that would attract a thief. As a hunter and gun collector, Sam felt comfortable keeping a pistol, rifle, or shotgun handy. "I would never go to his farm after 10:00 at night," says Eddie. "Never. If I did, I would yell, 'Uncle, it's Eddie!'"[61]

Robert Hasson offers another perspective. Sam's fight against the Purdy Company created "a lot of enemies," says Robert, "because there were many people who worked there who were afraid of losing their jobs. Sam always carried a weapon with him, and he was always afraid of being kidnapped. He lived in fear because he knew he had a lot of enemies." Duane Scheib, Sam's longtime friend and ranch hand, offers a similar picture of Sam's concern for his own safety: "With all the money he had, he was really afraid somebody was gonna come and kill him. He slept in this little shack over here. He had six-shooters under his pillow. He had 30.06s [rifles] sitting there loaded." In 1982, Sam told a journalist who had noticed a pistol strapped to Sam's waist, "A lot of damn fools think I have money buried on my property. That's nonsense."[62]

Sam certainly had neighbors who plainly did not like him, for one reason or another. But Sam had a larger goal in mind. He once remarked, "They have called me names and they have cursed me. But they did not know then they were very fortunate that I controlled the lake." He opposed private property developments that would restrict public access. "The lake has to be developed for resorts only, with people coming from all over the United States instead of going to Europe," he said.[63]

Saturday Bazar; Eddie Hasson, Bona, Marguerite, Joey, 1984.

Among the pieces of real estate that Sam acquired was an empty lot in Ephrata at 1100 Basin Street. In May 1984, he decided to put the property to work for the community. He had a sign made proclaiming "Bazar," and invited farmers, merchants, and craftspeople to set up a tent, table, or booth on Saturdays to sell their wares. Poles were planted to raise the Turkish flag and the US flag. Townsfolk loved it, and so did Sam. He wanted it to be successful, and every Saturday he would set it up, usually sitting with a tape deck playing Greek music that carried over the small crowd. He delighted in giving dollars to kids—and $20 each to Eddie and Marguerite's children—urging them, "You've got to spend it," to help support the vendors. "He was always there, and he encouraged people to spend money," recalls Eddie. When Sam's sister, Bona, was there, says Eddie, "he would make her raise the flag so that he could photograph her raising the flag."[64]

142 REAL ESTATE, MITZVOT, AND TRIUMPH

The "Blue and White Building" in Ephrata, c. 1986.

Press coverage in the *Columbia Basin Herald* and the *Wenatchee World* helped promote the idea, affirming Sam's intention "to recreate the excitement and atmosphere of the bazaar in downtown Ephrata," which would be "good for the community." Anyone was free to peddle their wares, from garage sale items to a car or a horse. "Even pigs, if they are little and cute," Sam joked. For him, the project felt like a meaningful way to contribute to the community. He told the *Herald* reporter, "In my religion, there's no smoking or drinking or chasing girls allowed. The only enjoyments in life are eating and helping people out." The *Wenatchee World* noted, "Turkish bazaars hold fond memories for Israel. The Turks were very honorable and wouldn't steal, he said."[65]

THE BLUE AND WHITE BUILDING

While Sam's efforts to be a good neighbor in Grant County earned him the goodwill of many members of the community, that road was not always smooth, especially when property was involved. In late 1985, a tussle arose over what Sam would come to call the Blue and White Building. Sam bought the Homestead Building in Ephrata, a one-story structure with a basement that he rented to Homestead Electric, a shop called the Fragrant Way, and an office suite. On Sunday afternoon, December 1, the Homestead Building caught fire. The fire department arrived and found the door locked, but rather than break it down, they went to Sam's farm to get his permission, as the building blazed. By the time the firefighters returned, the building was gutted; only one door and two walls remained. The city declared the building a public nuisance and in March 1986 sued Sam to have it removed. Sam countersued, charging that the city and the fire department were negligent in fighting the fire.[66]

Sam was irate. He hired a consulting engineering firm that reported the walls were structurally sound. Rather than demolish the walls, Sam had them painted bright blue and white, the colors of the Israeli flag. Eddie Hasson says, "Sam made a big statement. It was known as the Blue and White Building for ten years. He wouldn't touch that building, he would not fix it up." The case in the Grant County Superior Court dragged on through 1987 and was finally settled in February 1988. Sam agreed to add additional bracing to the walls, which satisfied the Ephrata city engineer, and the suit was dropped. Eventually, the building's remains were demolished, and the Rotary Club paid for paving so the lot could be used for community parking.[67]

ARCHAEOLOGY AND WILDLIFE PHILANTHROPY

While some private property owners shun archaeological investigations, Sam welcomed them. In August 1958, an archaeology team from Washington State University had spent a couple of weeks on Sam's property on the southwest corner of Soap Lake, excavating three native pit houses estimated to be three hundred to six hundred years old. A local newspaper account had included a photo of the team and a folksy note: "Shortly after this picture was taken, Samuel Israel, owner of the property on which excavating is being done, arrived with an ice-cold watermelon for the crew." In the summer of 1976, Northwest Archaeological Associates, a consulting firm based in Seattle, was conducting exploratory excavations at several sites in the Lower Grand Coulee area, including one on land owned by Sam. The archaeologists unearthed a campsite and house pit from the late prehistoric/pre-European period that yielded thousands of artifacts. The findings were impressive and delighted Sam, though they did not appear in published form until 1997, three years after his death. Still, his contribution is firmly recorded for posterity.[68]

In the late 1980s, Sam learned of excavations in Israel at Jericho and Herodium, conducted by Ehud Netzer, archaeologist, architect, and professor at the Institute of Archaeology at the Hebrew University of Jerusalem. Netzer had begun his work in 1972, and fifteen years later it was producing notable results that occasionally caught the attention of journalists and others outside the academic world. Sam decided to support Netzer, and in June 1987, via the Samis Foundation, donated $15,000 to the project. Netzer invited Sam to visit Herodium with him on his next trip to Israel, but Sam's health was declining, and he never made the journey.[69]

Dr. Yossi Leshem, then a young zoology professor who was studying bird migration, had orchestrated Sam's connection with Netzer. In 1983, Dr. Leshem, a self-described "keen birder" who had combined his activities in bird conservation and education with an academic career, was a PhD student at Tel Aviv University (he later joined the faculty). Since 1971, he had been associated with the Society for the Protection of Nature in Israel (SPNI), an organization established in 1953 that focused its efforts on conservation of Hula Lake in northern Israel, a unique habitat "of an exceptional biological diversity" and a wintering spot for hundreds of millions of birds on one of the world's largest migration routes between Europe, Asia, and Africa. In 1979, Dr. Leshem established the Israel Raptor Information Center, which later became the Israel Ornithological Center, a part of the SPNI, and he was founder and director of the International Center for the Study of Bird Migration in Latrun, Israel.

Dr. Leshem contacted Sam after hearing of him through an acquaintance in Tel Aviv who knew Sam's nephew Victor Hasson, who mentioned that Sam not only was a man with "many assets" but also was "very keen on nature and wildlife." Dr. Leshem reached out, mailing Sam booklets, videos, and other information on bird migration and SPNI activities, describing SPNI's conservation work on behalf of animals mentioned in the Bible that were becoming extinct in Israel, and the group's efforts to educate the public, especially young people. "We soon found that Samuel Israel was that rare combination of a warm human being," Dr. Leshem later noted, "with a soft spot in his heart both for Israel and for wildlife and its protection."[70]

Sam's first donations in 1983 were used to promote and support a research project headed by Dr. Leshem on bird migration, jointly sponsored by SPNI, Tel Aviv University, and the Israeli Air Force. The IAF had suffered eleven combat airplane crashes from collisions with migrating birds, which had cost the lives of three pilots and more than $200 million. As a

Sam with Scouts, 1986.

result of the project, the collision rate dropped by 76 percent, saving uncounted lives and an estimated $1.5 billion.

After that project's success, Sam made regular donations to Dr. Leshem's work and SPNI. "In a short time, we became the grateful recipients of the first of a series of yearly generous contributions from Samuel Israel," Dr. Leshem proudly says.[71]

SCOUTS AND HONORS

In the 1980s, Sam also made many efforts to support local Boy Scouts. He had been enamored of the Scouts since his nephew Robert Hasson had been involved in the youth group. Robert recalls, "He didn't have children, and those were kind of his children. He liked to have them around at apple time,

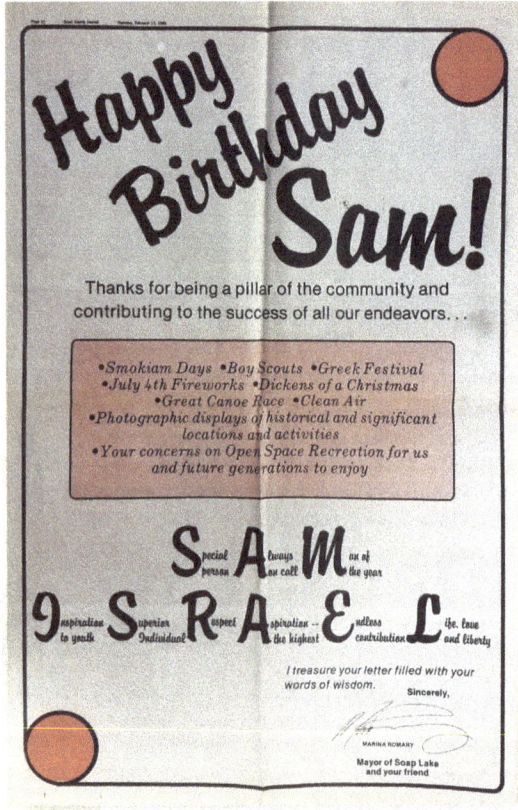

Above: Boy Scouts patch, "Camp Israel, 1989." Below: "Happy Birthday" poster, 1987.

when they would come and pick apples. He'd give them punch and snacks, and they still do that."[72]

In May 1987, Sam surprised the local Scouts with a huge gift. He designated his property on the west side of Soap Lake for Scout use, and in Sam's honor, the area is named Camp Israel. Tim McNamara, troop leader of Ephrata–Soap Lake Troop 44, presented a plaque to Sam designating him "Honorary Chief Scoutmaster." The following year, the Scouts gathered at a huge camporee at Camp Israel. Later, Sam also recognized the Girl Scouts too, offering to pay for the uniform and dues of any girl who wished to join the Columbia Basin Girl Scouts.[73]

David Hasson recalls Sam's dedication and generosity to the Boy Scouts: "Sam was very much part of the Boy Scouts, and he set up a program that any person who wanted to become a Boy Scout and could not afford a uniform, he would buy their uniform. He also told them that it's important that you save for college, that education was the most important thing. So, every time a person would join the Boy Scouts, he would set up a bank account for them with $50."[74]

Sam's many contributions to the community over the years earned the warm regard of Soap Lake mayor Marina Romary. On Sam's birthday in February 1986, Romary placed a full-page ad in the *Grant County Journal*, proclaiming, "Happy Birthday, Sam." The ad read, "Thanks for being a pillar of the community and contributing to the success of all our endeavors: Smokiam Days, Boy Scouts, Greek Festival, July 4th Fireworks, Dickens of a Christmas, Great Canoe Race, Clean Air, Photographic displays of historical and significant locations and activities. Your concerns on Open Space Recreation for us and future generations to enjoy."[75]

Grand Marshal at the Greek Festival parade in Soap Lake, May 1987.

Romary later recalled Sam's reaction: "I had taken up that ad in the *Grant County Journal*. Well, he was tickled with that and he appreciated that. And what was in the ad told him how we felt about him. Because I don't think Sam knew that people did feel that way about him. That he was a pillar of the community and that we loved him for it."[76]

Sam's generosity and high profile made him a popular selection as grand marshal for the Greek Festival in Soap Lake, held on Memorial Day weekend (May 23–25) in 1987. Romary recalls the story:

One year I asked him to be grand marshal at the Greek Festival Parade. And I'd asked him before, this time he said yes. And so, we were doing belly dancing in the street after the parade. We had a bunch of girls in costume, and Sam came to me in the office. He says, "Marina, I forgot my money. I don't have any money. Can you loan me some money in ones, one-dollar bills?" So, I get 40 dollars out, 40 dollars in ones, and gave it to him. He went out exactly out front of the office where they were doing the dancing and spent all that money of course with the Greek belly dancers as they're dancing around.

And the next day on the stage, Sam called me up to the stage, and he said, "Marina, you loaned me some money yesterday, and I want to pay you back." And so, he handed me an envelope, and there was $1,000 in it. And he said, "And that's for a donation to the Greek Festival so they'll have more."[77]

Above: Greek dancing at Soap Lake Greek Festival, Soap Lake, May 1992. Below: Sam and the Boy Scouts, Sam's 90th birthday celebration, February 12, 1989. Caleb McNamara (boy standing on left) with his father and scoutmaster, Tim McNamara.

SAM'S NINETIETH BIRTHDAY

At age ninety, Sam Israel reached the peak of his popularity in his adopted town. On Sunday, February 12, 1989, a grand celebration was organized to honor Sam's ninetieth birthday. Sam invited Boy and Girl Scouts and the general public from the Columbia Basin to celebrate his birthday at the Grant County Public Utility District auditorium in Ephrata. Sam announced his plans to talk to the young people about their responsibility to take over the leadership of the country as they grew older. Dressed in a casual shirt and pants, Sam donned a red fez and took the stage to speak to the audience of some 350. He told stories of his youth and gave the youngsters his best words of wisdom. He told them that he still had the first $10 he deposited in a bank when he moved to the US from Rhodes in 1919. Sam's recipe that helped make him a millionaire, he said, was captured in a Turkish saying: *Buzuluram buzulman*, meaning, "I will break myself before I break you." In other words, add dollars to your savings accounts and have the same attitude, not to break those dollars. "It worked for me and I think it can work for you," he told them.[78]

Good for his word, Sam set up savings accounts for any Boy or Girl Scout who attended the birthday gathering. One member of the audience asked Sam if he planned to develop his property, echoing an old rumor that had circulated for decades. Sam's answer probably surprised the man: "The people of Soap Lake don't realize how lucky they are that I control about three-fourths of that lake that I don't sell. . . . The time for it is getting right. Unfortunately, old age has sneaked up on me. I'll have to get somebody else that has the ability, that has the capital." After the crowd sang "Happy Birthday" to Sam and he blew out the candles on his cake, one member of the audience asked if he had a birthday wish. "Yes," he said with a smile, "to be with you into the next century."[79]

Another special tribute to Sam arrived in his mail on March 2, 1989. The Soap Lake High School's Board of Directors planned to award Sam the degree of "Honorary Graduate" at the June 1, 1989, graduation ceremony. The award declared, "In recognition of your contributions to the welfare of the youth of the Soap Lake region and recognizing your public counsel to the young people regarding the high importance they must give to their own education, and further recognizing your many contributions to groups of young people and to needy young individuals." The students wanted to include a picture of Sam in their yearbook with an inscription. The district superintendent James Marta praised Sam "for the many good things you have done for our area, including community contributions, scouting, wildlife support, and just for being the model citizen you have demonstrated yourself to be."[80]

Fate intervened before Sam could attend the ceremony. The years of adventures, fights with bureaucrats, hunting, fishing, photography, travel, feeding the dogs, and farm projects were over. Sam's life and livelihood—his vast collection of properties—were in the hands of three of his Hasson nephews and the fledgling Samis Foundation. The sands in Sam's hourglass moved into the final years. He would not be with the Scouts into the next century.

Figure 5

Seattle Properties Acquired by Sam Israel, 1961–1994

NAME	DATE PURCHASED	PAID
Seneca Building	1961 and 1966	$69,000
Fifth and Yesler Lots	9/14/1962	$23,500
Liberty Parking Lots	5/18/1966	$393,750
Mottman Building**	3/7/1967	$54,000
Atlantic Street Lot	2/1/1968	$16,500
Galland Building (Galland & Seneca Building)	1969	Property exchange for Telephone Building; $250,000 appraisal
Rainier Beach Property	10/13/1970	$850
Corona Hotel**	10/19/1970	$95,000
Army Parking Lot	9/1/1975	$83,700
Gatewood Hotel*	10/30/1975	$220,000
Broderick Building	12/12/1980	$356,000 property exchange

NAME	DATE PURCHASED	PAID
Stetson-Ross Plant (3 lots)	12/12/1980	$144,000 property exchange
Forest Hotel	12/12/1980	Property exchange
Butler Block (Butler Garage)**	12/17/1980	$500,000 property exchange
Second and Bell Building	2/28/1985	$225,000
Total		$1,181,300

TOTAL: 15 properties
***Seattle historic landmark**
****Pioneer Square Historic District**

CHAPTER 6
The Epic Season, 1990–1994

Opposite: Sam with Marguerite Hasson and Bona, c. 1984.

Buen corason haze buen caracter.
(A good heart makes for good character.)

IN THE HANDS OF GOD

On February 5, 1985, John Israel died of a heart attack at age seventy-four. John, like the rest of the Israel family, suffered from diabetes and heart trouble and had been in and out of hospitals for five years. Sam lost a brother for the fifth time, but this brother was ten years younger than Sam. Of Sam's generation, only he and Bona remained. The experience must have been startling and sobering.

Two years later, an appointment with a Moses Lake doctor, E. Michael Graham, revealed serious issues with Sam's heart due to diabetes. Afterward, in a letter to the physician, Sam wrote at length of his concerns. "By nature, I am a person that worries a lot," he stated. "Ever since you examined me, I spend half the nights awake with nightmares." Graham had told Sam he could have a stroke at any time or even drop dead, and Sam pointedly told him, "THAT IS IN THE HANDS OF GOD, especially when a man is 88 years old."[1]

Health concerns plagued Sam into the next year. He had trouble sleeping and often felt ill, so he began to see a doctor in Ephrata. Bona told Sam,

"You need to see a specialist," and he agreed. She arranged for him to see family member and cardiologist Dr. Alex Sytman at Providence Hospital in Seattle. Eddie Hasson picked up his uncle at the farm and brought him to the city. As they neared Providence, Sam suddenly told Eddie, "Turn here, then turn left there." After few more turns, they stopped in front of the old family house on Spruce Street. "I was surprised," Eddie recalls. "We looked at the house, and the owner, a Mrs. Jones, was outside changing light bulbs. Sam hailed her, 'Hello, Mrs. Jones,' and she saw it was Sam and invited us to come in." When the two entered the house, says Eddie, "I was astonished. Everything was exactly like it had been when I was six years old, and we moved from there. Even the coat tree still stood in the entry. The house seemed huge when I was six, but now it looked so small, it was such a surprise." After a short visit, they bid Mrs. Jones goodbye and drove to the appointment. Sam stayed for five days of testing at Providence, but Dr. Sytman concluded there was little that could be done to improve Sam's declining health.[2]

In late February 1989, just days after the celebrations of Sam's ninetieth birthday, he began feeling seriously ill.

By the summer of 1988, Sam's health was having a serious impact on his business. In April, Irwin Treiger, representing Sam and Samis Land Company, filed suit against Seattle Metro (Municipality of Metropolitan Seattle), challenging the city's local improvement district assessment to finance a bus tunnel in downtown. Four months later, in August, when Treiger checked in with Sam about moving forward with the suit, Sam's reply was terse and uncharacteristic: "I have been very sick lately," he wrote. "I have more than enough to handle just taking care of myself and my business. I am no longer interested in trying to fight the evils of this world. JUST FORGET IT."[3]

Six months later, in late February 1989, just days after the celebrations of Sam's ninetieth birthday, he began feeling seriously ill. He telephoned

Eddie Hasson and sister Bona, who traveled to Soap Lake to care for his animals. Sam's friend Jack Patrick took him to Columbia Basin Hospital in Ephrata, where he was diagnosed with pneumonia. From there, Sam was taken to Central Washington Hospital in Wenatchee, and on February 26, he suffered a stroke. On March 14, he was discharged and transported by ambulance to Providence Hospital in Seattle. Robert Hasson drove to Soap Lake to take care of the farm, while Eddie drove his mother back to Seattle.[4]

At Providence Hospital, Sam was met again by Dr. Alex Sytman. With a diagnosis of multiple issues including stroke, diabetes, and coronary and cerebral artery disease among other things, surgery was not a viable option, especially given Sam's age. There was little that Dr. Sytman could do. Sam stayed at Providence for three weeks. Sytman and the family had hoped to transfer him to the Kline Galland Home, but no rooms were available. In early April 1989, Sam was moved to the Keiro Nursing Home, where he waited for space to open at the Kline Galland Home. After two months, a room became available, and Sam was transferred in early June. He would live his final five years there.[5]

SAM'S CEMETERY

For many years, Sam had contemplated what would happen upon his death. One of his earliest and deepest desires, inspired by his love for the Jewish people as a whole and the maxim "kol Yisrael arevim zeh ba-zeh," that all Jews are responsible for one another, was to create one cemetery for all Jews in Seattle. Eddie Hasson says, "I think it was on his mind in the thirties." According to Victor Hasson, Sam had plans for the cemetery long before writing his will. Sam's first drafts of the plan for the Samis Foundation's distribution of funds listed the project as the number two priority, after education in Jewish schools in Seattle. His intent was clear: "At the present time I'm trying to acquire land to establish a Jewish cemetery for the entire community. If I accomplish this before my death, support the cemetery, whatever the needs may be."[6]

Sam talked to his family and friends often and at length about the Jewish cemetery. Eddie Hasson tells the story: "He hears about the politics of this cemetery versus that cemetery. He thinks that that's terrible. There's too much politics. He wanted to have one cemetery for everybody, and they'd all be buried right next to each other. There's no reserving, there's no nothing. He said, 'And then the rabbis will have their own section and we'll line them up. Every time one dies, they'll be right next. Line them up just like that."[7]

Victor Hasson recalls one of many conversations with his uncle about the cemetery: "I looked up at him and he started to smile, and he says, 'Para los muertos y Satan.' So, it's for the dead people and Satan. Then he started all over again, writing another will, and another will, and another will." Several times Sam attempted to buy forty-acre parcels of timberland in the Issaquah area from the Washington State Department of Natural Resources, hoping to exchange them for some of his properties in eastern Washington of equal value. Sam even floated his cemetery plan with different rabbis. But the grand idea never worked.[8]

THE FARM IN TRANSITION

Once Sam was moved into assisted living, his nephews faced the major task of dealing with the vast collection of things he had gathered over the years. Many were in the Seattle warehouse: cameras, lights, and other photography equipment, all professional-grade and very expensive. More challenging was Sam's collection of stuffed game trophies that he had amassed over the years, including deer, moose, elk, and bison, among many others. Several dozen of the trophy heads, all with serious infestations of maggots and other issues, were taken to a taxidermist and cleaned, then passed on to different taverns that were tenants of Samis buildings (including the one on the ground floor of the Gatewood Hotel), which were happy to display them. The near-record bison went to Jonas Brothers Taxidermy. When the bill for cleaning and restoration came back at $4,000, they offered not to charge for the work if they could keep the trophy; Eddie agreed.[9]

Sam's Mercer Island place posed a major challenge in its own right. The property had become heavily overgrown; simply getting to the house was difficult. Blackberries and brush covered the grounds, virtually cloaking several dilapidated cars and a motor home. The prospect of removing those alone was daunting. Then there was Sam's once prized brick house, which burglars and vandals had ransacked several times, and teenagers had repeatedly used for partying. Rodents had set up colonies, and the old furniture was rotting. The roof had leaked, adding mold and mildew to the cleaning headaches.[10]

These problems paled next to the challenges in eastern Washington. While Eddie remained in Seattle, Robert took the lead in Soap Lake. Eddie phoned Robert, saying, "Sam's not coming back to Soap Lake. I want you to

Eddie Hasson at Sam's farm, c. 1990.

hire a mover and move everything that's movable at the farm to the warehouse." Robert was stunned but got the job done. It took the better part of a week. Sam's farm had become, in Eddie Hasson's words, "a graveyard of old autos and equipment." Outbuildings and warehouses were filled with farm equipment and various kinds of supplies. Few of the vehicles had titles, which added to the workload. Eddie and Robert tried to find buyers and managed to locate a few. They donated the steam shovel to the Grant County Historical Museum. In the house were file cabinets with Sam's business records.[11]

Eleven dogs roamed the farm; a nearby family (Del and Sheryl Parrot) took them in. A bull and a donkey were parceled out to other neighbors. Eight horses stayed on, the last one finally passing in 2010.

Robert devoted many hours to dealing with Sam's guns. "There were guns all over the place, and they were loaded," says Eddie. "There was about 100 guns in one state of repair or another, and pistols." Robert recalls, "He had guns all over the house. He had guns under the pillow and everywhere."

Robert called the Grant County sheriff, who came out and unloaded the weapons. A day later, Robert called the sheriff again. "I found more guns," he said. The sheriff came out again. Eddie finishes the story: "There was one place on the farm that was like a greenhouse. In the middle of the greenhouse was Sam's fig tree that he got from the Isle of Rhodes. But, there Robert saw some boards, and he pulled the boards up, and there was a whole pit full of guns. So, he had to call the sheriff out a third time to unload the guns that were in this pit that was next to the fig tree."[12]

Finally, Robert rented a big truck, loaded it, and brought everything to store in a warehouse in Seattle.

LIFE AT THE KLINE GALLAND HOME AND BEYOND

The Kline Galland Home was not to Sam's liking, perhaps in part because he had to wait for a room to open. He told Dana Behar, "They make it like a luxury hotel. One person to a room. They should put bunk beds in there and stack them ten high; put mattresses in the hallway and put them all in there." But at least there Sam had the company of relatives who came to see him regularly. Bona was devoted to her brother, visiting him daily for five years. Her daughter Marilyn recalls, "I accompanied her on many Sundays. Occasionally she could not face a visit so she would ask me to go instead. Although I said 'yes,' in the end, she and I would go together." Eddie and David Hasson took turns visiting Sam on alternating days, each spending an hour or more with him three to four days a week, and other family members visited on weekends. They did their best to explain to Sam what was going on during his periods of alertness. In a limited way he did understand, at least enough to know that he needed to allow Eddie to run the business and David to manage the properties. He often asked about "going home," apparently meaning to the old family home on Spruce Street, or perhaps his Mercer Island house. Sam's body and mind were gradually, steadily deteriorating, and his need for round-the-clock care made such a notion impossible.[13]

Another physician, Dr. Scott Pollock, diagnosed a number of physical issues and noted that the stroke had left Sam with impaired speech, limited use of his left arm, and a significant degree of left-side body weakness. He received physical therapy daily, but improvements were minimal. His brain had been seriously damaged, and accordingly his memory and judgment were impaired as well. Sam exhibited mild, intermittent dementia, and though he showed alertness occasionally, he was often incoherent, unable to focus, and unaware of what was going on around him.[14]

A young man named Michael Toobert began working with Sam as his massage therapist, then became Sam's companion and primary caregiver, working five days a week from 2:00 p.m. until 10:00 p.m. Eddie Hasson describes Toobert as "a character." Toobert shirked the Kline Galland Home's rules by bringing his dog, who became the pet of all the tenants. One of Toobert's efforts to help Sam adds a bittersweet story to Sam's sunset years at the home. Eddie Hasson recalls the events:

> *Michael was the one that found Sam's old girlfriend in San Francisco.*
>
> *He'd had a stroke, he wasn't himself—he wanted to marry that woman because he never had a chance to marry her. Sam told Michael her name, Julia Hanan, and she lives in California. He started searching and searching. He learned that she was living in a nursing home in San Francisco and her husband had passed away. So, Michael got hold of her and said, "I have an old friend that wants to talk to you." So, Sam talked to her and said, "You come to Seattle. I want to marry you."*
>
> *So, Michael said, she said, "Oh, thank you, Sam, thank you very, very much. I loved you, too. You were a wonderful man, but I can't marry you. I'm just too old and I just can't do it, but I'll always think of you." She tried to make him feel good. That was the last contact with her.*[15]

THE LECLEZIO AFFAIR

Sam had been at the Kline Galland Home for only a short time when a strange man began dropping in to see him. For a while, few were aware of him, and everyone, including his nurses and Michael Toobert, seemed to think that he and Sam were old friends. That turned out to be a convenient misconception fostered by the visitor. "We kept wondering who he was and why he was showing up," says Eddie Hasson. A few weeks later, they found out.[16]

The man was Louis Leclezio, a real estate developer who wanted to purchase Sam's Mercer Island property. In March 1990, Leclezio began meeting regularly with Sam, and one day he showed up with some papers for Sam to sign.

Sam signed an earnest money agreement on June 1, 1990. In exchange for Sam selling the Mercer Island home and two acres at Faben Point to him for $3 million, Leclezio promised Sam that he would bring him to the house, where he could stay as long as he was alive. Leclezio apparently thought he had made a good deal for himself, especially since the price offered for the property was below its actual fair market value. "It was a deal," emphasizes Eddie Hasson, "that Sam in the old days—in his right mind—would never have signed." There could be no stronger proof that Sam was mentally incompetent.[17]

Michael Toobert saw that Sam was unhappy, and as soon as he learned what had happened, he telephoned Eddie Hasson. Eddie and David Hasson moved to take legal action to protect Sam and his holdings, and to make certain no one could ever again take advantage of him. In June 1990, Eddie, via Sam's attorney Irwin Treiger, hired a neuropsychological consultant, Wendy B. Marlowe, PhD, ABPP, to evaluate Sam. Marlowe met three times with Sam between June 18 and July 2 at the Kline Galland Home and presented her evaluation report to Irwin Treiger in early July. A week later, Treiger submitted a petition for guardianship to the King County Superior Court. On July 27, King County Superior Court commissioner J. M. Muckleston appointed an independent social psychologist, Gail H. Banks, as guardian ad litem for Sam.[18]

For the next two weeks, Banks conducted a thorough review, including a series of interviews with Sam, his caregivers at the Kline Galland Home, his physician, his attorney, and several family members. On August 15, Banks submitted the "Report of Guardian Ad Litem" (which included Marlowe's evaluation report) to the King County Superior Court. Banks found Sam minimally responsive and unable to understand his rights or to answer simple questions. He showed confusion, easily lost focus, and had a "lack of ability to understand me or what we were discussing." Banks reported that Sam's physical and mental capacity were substantially limited and that he was incapable of managing his personal or business affairs. "Mr. Israel requires protection and assistance in areas of mental and physical care and treatment," Banks concluded. "His degree of incompetence requires the appointment of a general guardian of his person and estate." Eddie Hasson was "the appropriate person" to be Sam's guardian, declared Banks, and she recommended Eddie's appointment for "an indefinite period of time."[19]

During the court hearing in late August, attended by Eddie and David Hasson, the reports on Sam's condition were reviewed, and Eddie testified that Sam "really was unable to sign leases and carry on the burdens of owning all these buildings. So, he agreed to it." On August 31, King County Superior Court commissioner Maurice Epstein signed documents declaring Sam Israel incompetent and appointing Eddie Hasson as Sam's legal guardian.[20]

Louis Leclezio filed suit against Eddie Hasson a year later in July 1991, claiming that Sam had been competent at the time he had signed the agreement. Lengthy negotiations on terms of a closing agreement between the two sides brought few results. The litigation dragged on for three years and ended up costing hundreds of thousands of dollars in legal fees. Eddie Hasson recalls, "After many months of hassle and many appraisals, we settled on $3.6 million. Leclezio still kept up with delays. The final document was for $3.6 million plus interest from the previous closing, which he didn't meet, to the new final closing date of January 20, 1994. He also didn't keep that one. That was the end of it." The property remained with the Samis Foundation.[21]

THE SEFER TORAH AND OTHER FINAL TRIUMPHS

> *Therefore, write down this poem and teach it to the people of Israel; put it in their mouths, in order that this poem may be my witness against the people of Israel.*
> —Deuteronomy 31:19

According to Jewish tradition, the words from Deuteronomy 31:19 present the *mitzvah*, or commandment, that every Jew write a Torah scroll, an obligation that can be fulfilled minimally by purchasing one letter via a scribe writing the Torah scroll.

Sam's family, as a loving gesture that showed their gratitude for his decades of caretaking, facilitated the creation of a beautiful Sefer Torah that today resides at Congregation Ezra Bessaroth. This was a highlight in Sam's journey of returning during his final years.[22]

In early 1991, Sam and his family were considering Sam's forthcoming ninety-second birthday. Victor Hasson, who at the time was visiting from Israel, suggested a Sefer Torah to be donated to Ezra Bessaroth. Sam liked the idea and commissioned Victor to have the Sefer Torah prepared when he flew back to Israel. Victor found the *sofer* (scribe) to make the Sefer Torah, which was to be done in strict accordance with tradition and in honor of the

Page from Sam's Sefer Torah.

memory of Sam's parents; coincidentally, the *sofer* had the same last name as Sam's mother's family, Biton.

Sam's Sefer Torah bears a unique feature that signifies the time in which it was written, during the dark days of the first Persian Gulf War. While Rabbi Biton was at work in early 1991, Iraqi Scud missiles were striking Tel Aviv. To mark the event, Rabbi Biton stretched the parchment, on the column of script on which he was working—the section of the Torah dealing with the Israelites crossing the Red Sea, the *shira*. Victor returned to Seattle with the new Sefer Torah in early August.[23]

> *Sam's family, as a loving gesture that showed their gratitude for his decades of caretaking, facilitated the creation of a beautiful Sefer Torah that today resides at Congregation Ezra Bessaroth.*

On August 18, 1991, the morning dawned clear. It would be splendid weather for a special day—the official dedication and presentation of a new Sefer Torah donated by Sam Israel to Congregation Ezra Bessaroth. Ceremonies began at 10:00 a.m. at the Kline Galland Home, where Rabbi Yamin Levy spoke to the assembled group, describing the procedure that would ensue, as the new Torah was carried from the Kline Galland Home to the synagogue's sanctuary. First, the *hechal hakodesh* (Holy Ark) was opened and the new Sefer Torah handed to Sam. Two of the home's Torahs were also taken out to accompany the new Torah to the sidewalk, one carried by the rabbi of Bikur Cholim-Machzikay Hadath and the other carried by Rabbi Solomon Maimon, rabbi emeritus for Sephardic Bikur Holim.

Then, a colorful and lively procession walked the two miles north from the Kline Galland Home to Congregation Ezra Bessaroth. Michael Toobert pushed Sam in his wheelchair, and Sam's family (the Israels and the Hassons), plus various other members of the congregation, took turns carrying the Sefer Torah under a *chuppah* (marriage canopy) along the

Above: Sefer Torah parade, from Kline Galland Home to Congregation Ezra Bessaroth, August 18, 1991. Left to right: Isaac (Ike) Azose, Michael Toobert pushing Sam in wheelchair, unknown, Robert Hasson. Below: Sefer Torah parade, from Kline Galland Home to Congregation Ezra Bessaroth, August 18, 1991. Left to right: Eddie Hasson, Randy Hasson, Michael Toobert pushing Sam in wheelchair, Bona Hasson, Morrie Capeluto, Jewel Capeluto, Norman Behar, Jerry Cohen.

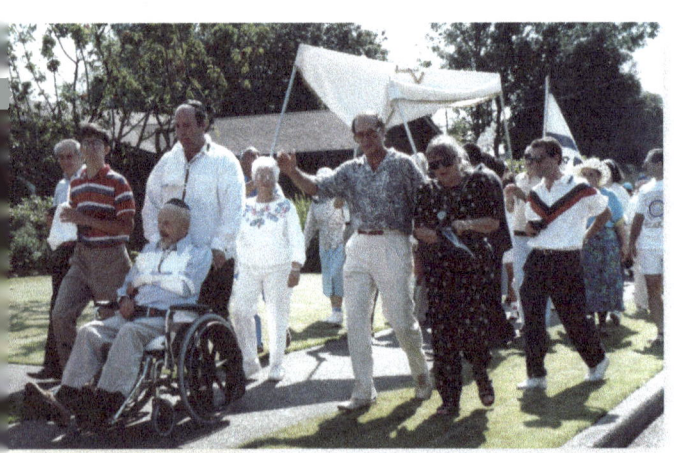

sidewalk. The group of some three hundred marchers stretched for blocks, with a Seattle Police Department motorcycle escort blocking traffic at intersections for everyone's safety. The enthusiastic celebrants, representing all three Orthodox synagogues in the Seward Park area, joyously sang and danced along the route.

At Ezra Bessaroth, the dedication ceremonies included speeches, songs by the choir, recitation of blessings, and a few remarks from Sam, effectively repeated to the assembled group by Rabbi Levy: "He told us a very touching story that last year, for his 92nd birthday, he was wondering what he should get himself and couldn't think of a thing, until his nephew, Dr. Victor Hasson, suggested a Sefer Torah to be given to the Ezra Bessaroth." Sam was brought in his wheelchair to the *tevah* (reading desk) to recite the blessing before and after the reading of the Torah. The day was later described in Ezra Bessaroth's newsletter, *Clarion*, as "wonderful" and "for many a once-in-a-lifetime event." Equally important, recalls Eddie Hasson, "I think Sam enjoyed the whole affair; he was very happy." Isaac "Ike" Azose, the hazan for the congregation, notes, "We use Sam's Sefer Torah all the time because it is one of those that is not so heavy that it doesn't take a very strong person to be able to lift it prior to reading it on Shabbat or the holidays."[24]

The dedication ceremonies for the Sefer Torah were among a handful of bright moments in Sam's final years. Sam had been chosen as "Honorary Parade Marshal" in the 1990 Memorial Day weekend celebrations in Ephrata. Two years later, there were more tributes. In early May 1992, the Ephrata Babe Ruth League and the Ephrata Lions Club dedicated a new flagpole at center field in Bambino Park to Sam Israel to honor him for "his long-time support for youth activities in the Ephrata-Soap Lake area." Sam had donated the sixty-five-foot pole, which was moved from one of his properties to the park by a combined effort of realtor Jack Patrick, the City of Ephrata, and the Grant County Public Utility District. At the same time, on the west side of the mountains, Sam and his family appeared on a poster for the *Quincentennial Sepharad Exhibit* at the Seattle Center Pavilion, May 21–June 21, 1992, organized to recognize the five hundredth anniversary of the expulsion of Jews from Spain. The poster for the *Scenes of Sephardic Life* exhibit featured the portrait of the Israel family taken in 1915 in Rhodes.[25]

In late May 1992, Sam was proclaimed honorary grand marshal of the Soap Lake community parade and Greek Festival over Memorial Day weekend. Bona, Eddie, Robert, and David had Sam transported by ambulance and arranged for him to spend three days at a local nursing home. In the parade down Main Avenue, Sam rode in a convertible alongside longtime friend and former mayor Marina Romary. The festivities were his final public appearance.[26]

As Sam's physical strength waned and his mental state deteriorated, he had the regular companionship of his sister, nephews, and nieces (besides his nurses and Michael Toobert). Sam's nephew Victor Hasson periodically visited from Israel and recalls Uncle Sam in his last years: "Rhodes was on Sam's mind a lot in his final years. His childhood started to come back to him. He would tell me stories about his childhood, which was strange, because my father would not mention Rhodes." Sam would sometimes have his slides out and constantly rearrange them. "Toward the end," says Victor, "he couldn't tell which were Rhodes and which were Israel." For High Holidays gatherings, they brought Sam to Bona's house. Victor Hasson describes Sam's final Pesach in April 1994:

Above: Scenes of Sephardic Life, poster 1992. Below: Sam riding in car with Marina Romary, May 1992. Sam was "Honorary Grand Marshal" of the Soap Lake community parade and Greek Festival over Memorial Day weekend.

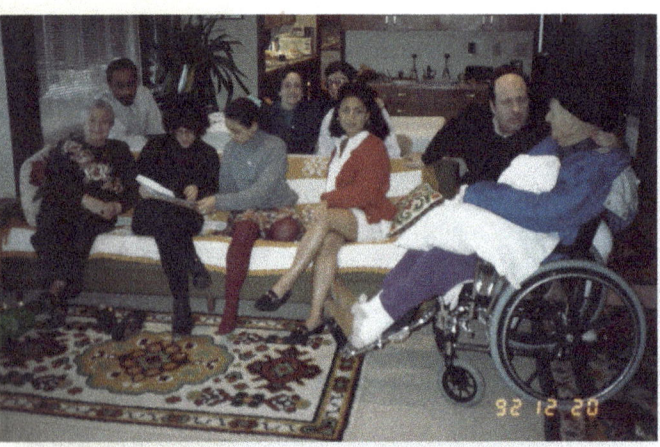

Hanukkah at Bona Hasson's home, December 20, 1992. Left to right: Anna Gold, Bobby Henry, Joanne Lipson, Mira Henry, Marguerite Hasson, Randy Hasson, Risha Henry, Michael Toobert, Sam.

They told me Sam's not going to come. And I said, "What do you mean, he's not going to come? I don't care if you guys have to get a series of ambulances and 25 caregivers, I want to see him at our Seder table." They got the ambulance and caregiver, and they wheeled him in. We would say the Haggadah, and I remember when he got to one part, he put his hand on my hand, basically to stop me. He said, "Esto." And I figured out . . . esto. He wanted me to say it in Ladino.[27]

Robert sang Sam's favorite song from the Haggadah, and Sam's eyes remained closed, as they did the entire evening, recalls Adam Hasson, "but he was listening." It was the last time Sam left the Kline Galland Home.[28]

THE PASSING

Sam faded slowly, as do many elderly stroke victims. In early June 1994, the family could no longer communicate with him, and he was placed on a feeding tube. That lasted a week. On Saturday evening, June 11 (2 Tammuz 5754), Sam passed quietly. Funeral services were held on June 13 at the Seattle Jewish Chapel, and Sam was buried with other members of his family in the Sephardic Brotherhood Cemetery in north Seattle. He was survived by his sister, Bona, and numerous nieces, nephews, and extended family. Daisy Israel offers a touching memory of the funeral:

The day of his funeral, after the funeral, in the caravan we were driving out to the cemetery, and I told Mike [Daisy's husband], I said, "We're not going the right way." We were going up to Capitol Hill. Where they were taking us was past the Seattle Hebrew Academy. All the students were lined up on the sidewalk for blocks with their hand on their chest as we drove by, to honor him. And I thought at that point, here's my Uncle Sam's tribute. . . . I think it needs to be said, because there are stories and there are reputations, but we in the family know that he never did it for honor, he never did it for publicity. He just did it quietly, because for some reason or another, in his mind and in his heart, this is what you do with your wealth. . . . But he never wanted his name in neon lights, and we always knew that.[29]

The larger Seattle community had mixed responses. To his credit, Seattle mayor Norm Rice sent a heartfelt letter to Sam's sister, Bona, extending his and his wife's, Constance's, sympathies, remembering Sam for his "courage to follow his own dreams," and noting that Sam's "good works in the Jewish community and in support of education are well known and will live after him."[30]

Public announcements of Sam's passing followed an interesting if predictable pattern. The major Seattle newspapers focused on Sam as property owner. The *Seattle Times* tagged him "Owner of Many Seattle Buildings." Another writer highlighted the landowner profile with the title "Israel's Empire to Remain Intact." The *Seattle Weekly* took the most negative angle, using the snipe (some would say insulting) line "Low-Rent Sam." The well-regarded journalist Rick Anderson hit the mark, calling Sam "Seattle's Least Understood Landlord." The community newspaper *Jewish Transcript* got closest to the full story, remembering Sam as a "Shrewd Businessman, Community Benefactor," and headlining "Sam Israel's Legacy: The Samis Foundation."[31]

HEADSTONE FOR A SHOEMAKER

Eddie and David Hasson developed the headstone that stands on Sam's plot at the cemetery. They talked with various family members as well as Rabbi Maimon and decided on a simple inscription. The most prominent words, apart from Sam's name, are "A Shoemaker" at the top of the stone and "For We Are Our Brother's Keeper" at the bottom. Also inscribed in Hebrew are the first two verses of Psalm

114, Sam's favorite music from the Pesach Seder: "When Israel went out of Egypt, Jacob's household from a people of alien tongue, Judah became His sanctuary, Israel his dominions." Eddie Hasson explains the background: "Sam's motto was 'We are our brother's keeper.' As a Jew, we're responsible for one another. That's why he was always so upset when a Jew would get into trouble. He thought that was the worst thing. They should be humble and not put their names on buildings or synagogue plaques. He thought all that was terrible. That's the way he felt, and he quoted that so many times."[32]

AN EPIC SEASON

Sam Israel's journey took him from *la Juderia* on the little Island of Rhodes to Seattle, from Seattle to Soap Lake, and finally back to rest in Seattle. For three generations over nine decades, many people in many ways shared large or small parts of that sojourn. Eddie Hasson says of his part, "The journey has been amazing, absolutely."[33]

Other members of Sam's family, as well as associates and close friends, have voiced similar sentiments. Their own personal histories intertwined with Sam's, and the experience was unforgettable, the impact lasting, indelible. Rita Israel Calderon describes Sam as "a man before his time. He was doing the things that made him happy, way before it was the thing to be doing." Irwin Treiger says, "He was a man of all seasons in many respects. I mean, photographer, hunter, this, that, but he really wanted to establish something that would preserve the Jewish religion, . . . and Jewish education was his primary goal." Rabbi Solomon Maimon praises the Samis Foundation as "one of the greatest things to happen to any community of America." Robert Hasson says, "Sam would be very proud; the Foundation is what he would want."[34]

Eddie Hasson reflects on how history might have turned a different direction: "I always think back, if that person that rejected Sam had said, 'Okay, you can marry my daughter,' there wouldn't be a Samis Foundation, because he would be married and have four kids like the rest of us."[35]

David Hasson offers a unique footnote to his recollection of Sam: "He really said that it's up to the next generation to do what he wants to do to complete his legacy. Sam told me that after he died, from time to time, he'd come back and give me further instructions. I have not heard from him recently."[36]

Clockwise from top left: Robert Hasson, 2013; Victor Hasson, 2012; Eddie Hasson, 2012; David Hasson, July 2017.

CHAPTER 7

The Land Abides

Opposite: Shed on Sam's farm, October 2017.

Si Mose morio, adonay quedo.
(Moses may be dead, but God endures.)

THE SEASONS OF SAM'S LIFE

As we look back at the span of years allotted to Sam, the seasons of his life begin to take form. Each was marked by distinct or predominant energies, patterns, coloration, geography, disappointments, triumphs, and transitions. Sam was stamped by his era and his Jewish-Rhodesli culture, and in turn he left his own mark on the times and events in which he moved. The mighty stick of wealth that he possessed, the sharp and dominant mind he wielded, and the robust physique he developed served to enhance his impact on the people and places that came into his orbit.

Sam's childhood and youth, from 1899 to 1919, were the formative period during which his family and life in *la Juderia* of Rhodes provided a nurturing environment for his maturation. As a bright and ambitious nineteen-year-old immigrant in Seattle, Sam established a successful shoe repair business. As he prospered during his twenties, he began to acquire property. He had several reasons, largely associated with a strong motivation for security. He learned that, for the long term, there was more security in owning property than in cash and so began investing profits in real estate. He succeeded beyond his or others' expectations.

In the quarter century between the end of World War I and the end of World War II, Sam led a robust lifestyle, joining YMCA friends on climbs of Mount Rainier and other mountain treks, going to dances in stylish clothing, and pursuing young women in hopes of matrimony. But he failed to marry, a fact that later in life he said was a genuine regret. He had a large extended family, including many nephews and nieces, but no wife or children, or the kind of home and comfort a nuclear family provide. He was a hunter most of his adult life, an activity that combined his love of the outdoors with a collector's—and nervous property owner's—affection for firearms, which also embody the essence of protection and security.

After World War II, windfall profits from contracts with the US Army enabled Sam to acquire a substantial number of properties and spurred him to incorporate Samis Land Company, and he shifted to full-time management of his growing real estate portfolio. At the age of sixty-one, Sam left the small Seattle Sephardic community that had been his home for four decades and moved to Soap Lake. He remained energetic and productive as he matured into his eighties; though he became more reclusive, he maintained close bonds with his extended family.

As Sam matured, his active, healthy lifestyle gradually slowed, and his natural tendency to gain weight began to show. His body transformed from the muscled and slim physique he developed in his twenties and thirties to a stout form verging on pudgy in his sixties. By his seventies and eighties, Sam was clearly overweight, heavyset, and to one observer, "plump." Yet, in his elder years, his battles with government policies, as well as his various public philanthropic activities, drew the attention of journalists, occasionally thrusting him into the public spotlight.

At age ninety, Sam had achieved many of the goals he had set his mind to over the decades. Though he did not seek public praise for his generosity, it came anyway. The proud days of enjoying family gatherings, sipping coffee with a handful of friends, and helping his neighbors in both Seattle and Grant County ended abruptly soon after his ninetieth birthday when he was felled by a stroke. Yet, even in Sam's last years and his physical decline, accolades followed him, bringing a large measure of recognition for his good works.

From his youth, Sam had been a caretaker. He took care of his brothers, educating and financially supporting them in the shoe business and the grocery business. He took care of his parents in their old age, providing for their home with him. He gave generously to his family and to community

Sam's 93rd birthday celebration, at Bona Hasson's home; Robert Hasson, Sam, David Hasson, 1992.

organizations. His 1973 trip to Israel and Rhodes stamped him forever with the desire to help fellow Jews in America and in Israel.

Sam's lifelong commitment to something larger than himself emerges as his greatest legacy. Through the donation of properties to the Samis Foundation, his powerful caretaker energy—his unique, quiet style of being his brother's keeper—lives on.

VISITING RHODES

Among the many visitors to Rhodes in recent years is Sam's nephew Victor Hasson. His experience speaks eloquently to the past and present of the island's Jewish residents. For more than twenty-five years, Victor has returned every year to Rhodes at least once, usually on Yom Kippur.

The flight from Tel Aviv is less than an hour, and package flight and hotel deals are relatively cheap. At first, the island was something of a mystery to Victor. "The first few years," he says, "I would rent a moped and jazz around the island. I didn't know anything about Rhodes, I didn't know all the Jews were in a quarter, I didn't know about the Holocaust. I didn't know about anything." Over time, that changed. For Victor, the trip became a pilgrimage, a way to touch some vestige of the old family homeland. Until the last couple of years, when health issues began to interfere, Victor attended Yom Kippur Holiday services at the Kahal Shalom Synagogue, which he led with his longtime friend Sam Amiel, and the anniversary memorial held annually on July 23 in honor of murdered Jews.[1]

In 2011, Victor asked the Samis Foundation to donate a new set of holiday prayer books produced by Hazan Isaac Azose, president of the Sephardic Traditions Foundation. Azose has served as hazan at Congregation Ezra Bessaroth for more than three decades and specializes in publishing Hebrew and Hebrew–English liturgies in the unique traditions of Rhodes and Turkey.

The Samis Foundation agreed. In November 2011, Samis sent thirty Rosh Hashana Mahzor books and, in September 2014, sent fifty-six Yom Kippur prayer books to the Jewish community of Rhodes for delivery to the Kahal Shalom Synagogue. The books carried a special dedication bookplate: "In loving memory of Sam Israel," followed by the abbreviation z"l for *zikhrono livrakha*, or "may his memory be a blessing." Today, people—mostly second-generation Rhodeslis—travel from many countries for the memorial and stay for several days. It has been gratifying for Victor to help make the contribution. "The eve of Yom Kippur and right after Yom Kippur the synagogue is packed; all 56 books are used," he says proudly.[2]

> *Kahal Shalom Synagogue*
>
> *In Loving Memory of*
> *Samuel Israel z"l*
> *A proud citizen of Rhodes,*
> *supporter of the State of Israel*
> *and founder of*
> *The Samis Foundation*
> *Seattle, Washington*

Bookplate for prayer books prepared by Isaac Azose and donated to Kahal Kadosh Shalom Synagogue by Samis Foundation.

THE LAND ABIDES

In early October 2018, Eddie Hasson and I visited Sam's farm. We had the good fortune of enjoying a fair autumn day, with cloudy skies and

Eddie Hasson at front door of Sam's bunkhouse, October 2018.

cool temperatures. In the three decades since Sam lived here, many things had changed. The maple, poplar, and pine trees planted in the 1950s and 1960s had grown tall, offering cool shade for the summer months. Gone were the acres of aging vehicles and farm equipment. Only a few rusted pieces of machinery lay scattered here and there, and the old red 1941 White truck stood solidly on four flat tires near Sam's bunkhouse. The apple trees that Sam had planted were loaded with bright red fruit, and Eddie picked several bags, as he has every year for decades. The pool lay calm beside the house that Sam had built for Bona and Albert and their children. Beyond the edge of the pool, the vista of blue Soap Lake and the small town along the shore looked much as it did when Sam lived here. The view from Sam's farm is peaceful, inspiring, and thought-provoking.

As Sam knew so well, land is much more than a building or piece of property described in a legal deed. It embodies the history of a place and the people who lived there, who plowed fields, planted crops, enjoyed picnics, made campfires, pitched tents, and sang songs late into the night. Sam Israel's legacy, certainly, is the impressive array of properties that today are managed by the Samis Foundation and Samis Land Company. It is also the people whose lives have been touched by direct and indirect encounters

Above: Sam's farm, October 2018. Below: Sam's farm, the old "White" truck, October 2018.

with Sam's land—the teens who have received grants to travel to Israel, Jewish day school students in Seattle supported by scholarships, Jewish overnight camps, youth groups, and all of the other grantees of the Samis Foundation in Washington State and the State of Israel.

Sam and his family had left the ancestral home in Rhodes a century earlier; traveled to America; and built careers, families, and productive lives. It was their opportunity to live the American Dream like many other immigrants. And they succeeded. Although Sam had no children, he was blessed with many nieces and nephews, as well as the friendship of many Boy and Girl Scouts and other youth whom he encountered. His love for history and archaeology reflected a profound sense of his own past and respect for the people of Israel. The words in an early Samis Foundation brochure say it well: "He developed a deep sympathy for the immigrant, particularly the 'wandering Jew,' looking for a home in the Land of Israel, and his philanthropy reflects this abiding interest."

La Calle Ancha.

All of these individuals, past, present, and future, are part of the spiritual family of Sam Israel. Elie Wiesel, author and Holocaust survivor, wrote, "Hope is like peace. It is not a gift from God. It is a gift only we can give one another." Sam knew the transformative power of hope, and through his Foundation, the modest shoemaker has become a forceful catalyst for inspiring hope and enhancing the quality of Jewish life in Washington State and Israel. From Sam and past generations, we inherit a rich history and heritage of Jewish and American values that continue to remind us we are all our brother's keeper.

EPILOGUE

A Living Legacy:
The Samis Foundation

Opposite: Board members and spouses at Rhodes Fountain, 2008. From left: Victor Alhadeff, Susie Alhadeff, Dave Azose, Terry Azose, Rebecca Almo, Eli Almo, Rabbi Rob Toren (Executive Director), Al Maimon, Jeanne Maimon, and in front, Jerome O. Cohen.

Si lo que no acontece en un mundo,
acontece en un punto.

(What the world thinks impossible can happen in a moment.)

CHALLENGES IN THE AFTERMATH

In the decade after the official registration of the Samis Foundation as a nonprofit in December 1979, the organization maintained a low profile. The first trustees—Sam, Eddie Hasson, and Irwin Treiger—managed the foundation as directed by Sam. "He was careful," Eddie recalls, "to put in the actual documents that the trustees have full discretion as to what they want to donate."[1]

Sam's stroke had an immediate impact on his properties and the fledgling Samis Foundation. During the five years between Sam's stroke and his death, Samis Land Company operations were run by his nephews Eddie and David, who had been involved with Sam and his properties business for more than two decades. Eddie continued as accountant and financial adviser, as well as president of the Samis Foundation, while David managed the properties. Sam typically became more alert and interested when the three of them talked about business, but increasingly the burden of work fell on the two nephews' shoulders. After the problematic issue with Louis Leclezio erupted, Sam became paranoid about signing any documents, which made conducting business difficult for Eddie and David. When Eddie became Sam's legal guardian, things shifted, but few changes were made to properties beyond repairs and modest renovations. David Hasson notes, "When my brother and I took over after Sam had his first stroke, within the first two years we doubled the income mainly by some improvements and being more aggressive on the leasing."[2]

As Sam's health and mental acuity waned, Eddie Hasson met often with his brother David. The problem was whom to rent to. "We would look at the rent rolls," recalls Eddie Hasson, "and say, 'What should we do with this property? Should we raise the rents?' David says, 'Yeah, I wouldn't raise the rent just yet. Let's wait.'" They did have some help from one employee, an independent contractor named Jim Tresi, who acted as janitor and handyman, occasionally going into a property "to kick out bums," in Eddie's words. Later, they hired a secretary for the Samis Land Co, Trudy Angel, to work with David Hasson on managing the properties.[3]

At the time of the foundation's organization, three trustees were specified—Sam, Eddie, and Irwin Treiger—with the proviso that in the event that one became unable to fulfill the duties of trustee, the other two would elect a replacement. Following Sam's stroke in 1989, Eddie Hasson and Irwin Treiger invited Al Maimon to replace Sam as the third trustee for the Samis Foundation. Maimon, a Seattle native and a longtime friend and associate of Treiger's, was also involved in Jewish community affairs, including in the role of president of the Seattle Hebrew Academy and Sephardic Bikur Holim and vice president (of planning and allocations) of the Jewish Federation of Greater Seattle, and he was active in the Sephardic Adventure Camp and Jewish Family Service. Treiger readily saw the value of Maimon's civic connections and his professional skills as a mathematician who had a successful career in operations research and management science, and information systems design and implementation, mostly at Boeing but also as a professor at the University of Washington.[4]

With Eddie Hasson acting as president, they met twice a year to review grant applications. In 1992, the foundation made twenty-eight grants totaling $293,000, and in 1993, it made twenty-nine grants totaling $350,000. In early 1993, Eddie, in coordination with Treiger and Maimon, began to take steps that would lead to a fully functioning foundation. In February of that year, Eddie wrote to the prospective trustees identified by Sam, providing an update of recent activities and checking on their availability to become participating trustees upon Sam's passing. The foundation hired a part-time consultant, James Myers, a fundraising professional who had worked with the Jewish Federation of Greater Seattle, the United Jewish Appeal, and a

Jewish school in Australia, to assist with basic issues including a mission statement and operating policies and guidelines.[5]

A NEW PATH: THE FOUNDATION TAKES FORM

By early 1994, it was clear that the end of Sam's life was nearing. The next step taken by the three trustees, at Irwin Treiger's insistence, was formal incorporation of the Samis Foundation in May 1994, which increased tax advantages and reduced legal liabilities for the foundation. Sam's will stipulated the appointment of "at least 10 Trustees at all times" to govern the foundation upon his death. The trustees, all Jewish, were appointed for life, which is unusual, and also "must be active and knowledgeable in business affairs, preferably with respect to real estate, and in Jewish charitable activities."

During the 1980s, Sam had undertaken the work of identifying potential board members. The process was neither easy nor straightforward. Sam had lived in Soap Lake for more than two decades and had returned to Seattle only three times. He did his best to stay current with real estate matters by reading newspapers and watching TV newscasts, and he conducted most of his business by phone or mail, except for matters he handled personally with Eddie Hasson. In many ways, Sam had lost touch with the Jewish community and, to some extent, the real estate market. Trust had always come slowly to Sam, but once he trusted you, that was it. He relied on old connections, and on his Hasson nephews and his attorney. If Eddie, Robert, or Irwin recommended someone, that was a good first step. Then Sam would check them out for himself.

Mottman Building, built 1906.

So it was that by the time of Sam's death, a plan for filling the board was in place. One member had to be an Orthodox rabbi, whose role was unique: "At least one director shall be an Orthodox rabbi, and his only duties shall be to attend all meetings of the Directors and to ensure that the purposes of Samis Foundation as set forth in the Agreement are carried out." Irwin Treiger later commented, "Sam thought that a rabbi would serve as the conscience of the board, and that is exactly what did happen." Sam's choice for an Orthodox rabbi to sit on the board was Rabbi William Greenberg (1926–2007), leader of Congregation Ezra Bessaroth from 1962 to 1990, who often visited Sam at his farm over the years. Sam appointed other prominent members of the Seattle Jewish community, including an attorney, bankers, an accountant, a real estate developer, and others. Sam emphasized the role of the trustees: "For the past 2,000 years some of our devoted Hebrews have let themselves be burned alive for the preservation of our people. . . . We are our brother's keeper."[6]

In addition to the original three board members and Rabbi Greenberg, Sam asked two men who had become married relations, Michael "Mike" Israel and Dr. Alex Sytman. Mike Israel (1927–2010) was Sam's insurance agent and founder of Sprague Israel Giles Insurance Company, and was related by marriage to Sam's niece Daisy Israel.

Dr. Sytman had graduated from the University of Washington School of Medicine in 1963. He married Sam's niece Leatrice "Lucy" Israel Sytman (1939–2019), and after living in New York, Fort Lewis, and Los Angeles, they returned to Seattle in 1970.[7]

Sam reached out to some acquaintances whom he felt he could trust and who represented a broad spectrum of notable leading Jewish businesspeople. Jerome "Jerry" O. Cohen and Sam met in 1987. At the time, Jerry was president of the Jewish Day School board and president of Century Construction Company, and Sam hired his company to repair the Mercer Island house. As Sam's ideas about the foundation took form, he shared them with Jerry and asked him to serve on the board.

David Friedenberg (1934–2007) had met Sam while working as a senior vice president at Seattle First National Bank and Sam had requested "to work with a Jewish banker."

Barry Ernstoff was president of the Seattle Hebrew Academy when he received that memorable phone call from Sam that led to payment of the school's outstanding mortgage.

Eli Genauer's acquaintance with Sam dates from when he served as a vice president of the Seattle Hebrew Academy in the 1980s. At the time, Eli was president of Eilat Management Company, a property and asset management firm based in Seattle.[8]

Victor Alhadeff also became one of the original trustees. Victor got to know Sam in the late 1970s when he was actively involved with the Seattle Hebrew Academy. As founder and CEO of E&I Oil and Gas Exploration

Company, Victor advised Sam on possible drilling on his property (a firm "no" when others sought Sam's dollars for drilling), which proved sound advice, and the two men stayed in touch over the years that followed.[9]

Ernie Sherman, owner of Pacific Plumbing Supply Company, had met Sam Israel during the resolution of issues associated with the Gatewood Hotel.

Lucy Pruzan was originally suggested by Irwin Treiger. A prominent, longtime volunteer in the Jewish community and president of the Jewish Federation of Greater Seattle, Lucy had impressed Treiger, who advised Sam, "This is a modern era, and you should have a woman on the board." Although Sam did not know her personally, he replied immediately, "That's just dandy." Lucy later recalled her first meeting with Sam in 1989, noting, "Marguerite Hasson, Eddie's wife, took me to see Sam when he was at Keiro Nursing Home to introduce me." Sam appeared to be asleep, but Marguerite proceeded with the introduction. When Sam heard the name Pruzan, his eyes popped open, and he sat up. "You refused to sell me that property on Washington Street!" he blurted. Taken aback, Lucy politely corrected him, "That was not me, that was a cousin." It seemed to mollify Sam; he relaxed and lay back.[10]

Sam's typical method for sounding out candidates with whom he had relatively little contact was simple and direct—he invited them to the farm and interviewed them. As they talked about the foundation, candidates could better understand his interests, and he could better assess their commitment and willingness to abide by his wishes. Eli Almo, a Seattle businessman with a background in finance and real estate, later recalled, "Sam asked me pointed questions about the importance of Jewish education for our children. We spent a great deal of time emphasizing that the children are our future." The two men also talked about Israel, both firm believers in "the importance of making sure people travelled to Israel to experience our roots and to learn about our land through archeology."[11]

Morris Piha (1933–2013) was somewhat known to Sam. "Morrie" had married Marlene Calderon, daughter of Sam's niece Rita Israel Calderon and granddaughter of Sam's brother David. Morrie was born in Portland, Oregon, to Samuel and Vida Piha, who had immigrated from Rhodes in the early 1930s. He became a Seattle-area real estate entrepreneur in 1965 and was active in the community as a board member of the Make-A-Wish Foundation, Seattle Sephardic Brotherhood, and Foundation Bank, as well as a longtime member of Sephardic Bikur Holim Congregation. Around 1987, Eddie Hasson accompanied Morrie and his wife, Marlene, to Sam's farm. The conversation followed similar topics that Sam raised with other prospective trustees. Then Sam asked about the Jewish Community Center (JCC), which had been renamed for Seattle businessman and philanthropist Sam Stroum (1921–2001), a longtime supporter of the JCC and other community organizations: "Sam didn't like the JCC," recalls David Azose, who was Morrie's partner in Morris Piha Real Estate Services. "He called it 'a country club for rich Jews,' and complained that Stroum had let his name go on the building. 'You should be quiet about giving,' he said, 'it's just wrong to put your name on a building.'"[12]

Martin Selig was a similar case, in some ways at least. Selig had built a large and successful real estate development business in Seattle, and Sam held Selig in high regard as a savvy businessman. In June 1987, Sam invited Selig to the farm to get better acquainted and review his ideas for the foundation. Selig flew to the farm by helicopter, and they spent the afternoon discussing Sam's expectations for trustees, his philosophy of real estate and of giving, and related issues. Upon returning to Seattle, Selig wrote briefly of the visit, describing the business matters, then turning to his personal impressions of the experience. His comments are colorful and revealing:

> *It is surely interesting seeing a man of this wealth, living a very, very humble and simple life which was quite evident from the surroundings of his existing house.*
>
> *To try to describe the facilities you'd have to say the following.*
>
> *It is basically a three room shack, a bedroom, an office and a kitchen. There are probably twenty vehicles parked around the place all basically broken down. There are iceboxes spread out throughout the farm in different rows along with stoves, refrigerators, telephone poles, telephone wires, and little glass balls that are on top of telephone poles.*
>
> *The place is in a basic disarray, with all the surrounding property that is owned, which is thousands upon thousands of acres, left alone just as it is.*
>
> *You walk away with a feeling that you feel sorry, but on the other hand, who else do you know that is 88 years old who looks like a 65-year-old that has the spirit and the drive that this man has. There is something to be said for that attitude....*
>
> *It was an exceptionally interesting and pleasant day, specifically sitting next to the outdoor pool that was built specifically to clean the cattle that were supposed to be*

shipped to Israel, listening to a radio that was placed in an icebox and watching Sam sitting on a bunk bed with a pillow in the back yard listening to the rustling of the trees and the water from the water fountain nearby....

Probably one of the most interesting parts of the trip was taking this 88 year old man up in the helicopter and having him survey all of his property and having him continually say "that's my property, that's my property, two more miles here, three more miles here, go this way, go that way, why don't you go down and stop right there, I want to show this man the sign," which said, Sam Israel and the State of Washington Department of Game Welcome you to the free use of this beach front.[13]

AN ENERGETIC BEGINNING

The first gathering of the full Board of Trustees was held at the Westin in Seattle following the traditional month of mourning after Sam's death. At the meeting were the first sixteen trustees: Eddie Hasson, Irwin Treiger, Al Maimon, Jerome O. Cohen, Victor Alhadeff, Michael Israel, Rabbi William Greenberg, Eli Almo, Dr. Alex Sytman, Barry Ernstoff, Eli Genauer, Ernie Sherman, Lucy Pruzan, David Friedenberg, Morris Piha, and Martin Selig. They hoped to develop a path forward that would remain true to the basic wishes of the founder.[14]

The trustees' first task was to begin to get a grasp of the full extent of Sam's property holdings now under their management. They hired a consultant, Robert Filley, director of the University of Washington's Center for Community Development and Real Estate, who took several months to inventory the properties. In 1995, Filley submitted a report of findings and recommendations for near-term and long-term property management. The inventory identified Sam's real estate accumulation in Seattle as forty properties (totaling more than 20 acres in downtown), another sixteen properties in western Washington (an additional 357 acres), and in eastern Washington a total of eighty-seven properties in Grant and Douglas Counties, totaling more than 15,500 acres.[15] (See figure 6.)

Filley's report recommended that the foundation hire a full-time professional to manage the diverse and complex portfolio and to reposition properties with development potential. In July 1996, the trustees hired William Justen as managing director of real estate at Samis Land Company

EPILOGUE

Samis Board and staff, December 2019. From top left, Linda Sullivan (CFO), Greg Roer, Barry Ernstoff, Jerome O. Cohen, Eli Almo, Victor Alhadeff; row 2, Rabbi Ron-Ami Meyers, Al Maimon, Louis Treiger, Judy Neuman, David A. Ellenhorn, Dana Behar, Ernie Sherman; row 3, Eli Genauer, Lucy Pruzan, David Azose, Maria Erlitz, Dr. Alex Sytman, Eddie Hasson, Connie Kanter (CEO), and Adam Hasson (Director of Real Estate). Photo © Rick Dahms.

to implement the report's recommendations. Justen was a prominent figure in the Seattle real estate community and brought impressive credentials as a former executive at the Koll Company and former head of the City of Seattle's Department of Construction and Land Use. Adam Hasson, Robert's son, took over duties from David Hasson as property manager in August 1995. In November 1997, the foundation took another major step forward and hired Rob Toren as grants director, signaling a more serious and energetic commitment to philanthropy. The foundation was underway as a professional organization with a core staff and a road map for the future.[16]

Following the recommendations in Filley's report, the foundation methodically undertook a program of renovating some properties, simply maintaining others, and selling some properties that were deemed outside the core areas of real estate interest, which meant mainly properties outside downtown Seattle. Justen enthusiastically embraced his assignment to gradually maximize the long-term value of the Samis properties, which would provide a sound and sustainable financial base indefinitely for the foundation. The money available for grants was bound to grow. "We will grant out of operating income for many decades, not by selling property," Justen told the *New York Times*. "There also is enough development work in our portfolio to last a lifetime."[17]

Sam's properties in downtown Seattle attracted the most attention from real estate developers and preservationists. Many journalists and developers considered Sam a negative influence, an "absentee slumlord." Yet Sam's caretaker approach to real estate made him a de facto preservationist. Sam had refused to demolish a building and replace it with a parking lot. He let repairs at many buildings slide, but he always took care of roof repairs, even when Seattle's fire codes changed in the 1940s, 1950s, and 1960s and more extensive (and expensive) improvements were required. Sam's refusal to sell properties saved some of the city's finest historic brick buildings. The properties inherited by the foundation yielded great opportunities for revitalizing Pioneer Square and other parts of the city's Central Business District. Today the buildings are considered treasured landmarks.[18]

Under William Justen's stewardship, the foundation began participating in Pioneer Square neighborhood associations and the Downtown Seattle Association and hired a project management company to oversee building renovations. The result over time was beneficial, shifting perceptions of Samis as a hands-off owner to a hands-on property management company. Notable and profitable transactions included the Webster-Brinkley property (built to suit for the FedEx Distribution Center); the Forest Hotel (sold as a development opportunity that became the 1521 Second Avenue condominium tower); the Smith Tower (acquired, renovated, and sold); the Butler Garage (expanded from three stories to eleven stories); and renovation of four additional properties in Pioneer Square (the Washington Shoe Building, Terry Denny Building, Collins Building, and Corona Building).

The foundation's grant award priorities, following the founder's example, remained firm—to fund Jewish education, to help Jews settle in Israel, to support environmental organizations and archaeological exploration in Israel, to aid widows and orphans, and to help victims of disasters. In 1999, Samis awarded grants totaling $2.5 million, and in 2000, the foundation gave $3.5 million in grants. By the end of its first decade, the Samis Foundation had provided more than $20 million to the five Jewish day schools in the Seattle area, mostly through tuition-reduction programs.

Just a few of the notable contributions in Seattle included ones to the Northwest Yeshiva High School, the Jewish Education Council, the Seattle Hebrew Academy, the Jewish Day School, and the Sephardic Religious School. Funding to organizations in Israel included the Hebrew University of Jerusalem, Ben-Gurion University, the Society for the Protection of Nature in Israel, and the Israel Exploration Society.

The foundation launched into its second decade with a robust portfolio and a growing ability to fund projects at home and in Israel. Rob Toren, as grants director for much of the first decade, publicly marked the progress and lessons learned in an article in the fall 2005 issue of *Jewish Action*:

Many would claim that giving away money is simple. Samis has learned that it is not. In fact, after years in the business of funding Jewish education, we continue to improve through learning from our and others' experiences. And the rewards far outweigh the challenges. Samis proudly points to a few of its many accomplishments, including ... assisting in creating a K-5 day school; ... providing medical benefits for staff; assisting Seattle Hebrew Academy, which had lost the use of its building in 2001 due to earthquake damage, rebuild into one of the most beautiful state-of-the-art schools in the area and ensuring that a professionalized, fair and confidential scholarship process takes place at all the local day schools.[19]

THE EVOLVING FOUNDATION

In the decades that followed, the Samis Foundation continued to grow and mature. Issues of governance, planning, and decision-making evolved as the Board of Trustees transitioned from an informal working group to a more board-centered structure, adding working committees, hiring more professional staff, and reconfiguring the division of labor between the board and its committees and foundation staff. The culture shifted gradually from what Al Maimon describes as "a roll-up your sleeves, hands-on work group," to a more policy- and procedure-oriented organization. "An extraordinarily strong relationship with the staff helped maintain the effectiveness of the Board," says Maimon. William Justen remained as managing director of real estate through December 2010. A part-time senior program director, Amy Amiel, was hired in 2007 (she became full-time senior program officer from 2015 to 2019). Other staff changes included Rob Toren moving from grants director to executive director in 2012, where he served until retiring in 2018. Adam Hasson served as property manager until October 2012, when he was appointed director of real estate. Additional staff members include a chief financial officer (Linda Sullivan), an executive administrator (Peggy Longeway), a director of day school strategy, a program officer, a receptionist, commercial and residential property managers, an accounting manager, a property accountant, and four building engineers. In preparation for Rob Toren's retirement at the end of 2018, the board conducted an extensive yearlong search for a chief executive officer. Connie Kanter was hired in early 2019. As CEO, Connie oversees all aspects of the foundation's work, including governance, grant-making, finance, and real estate operations.[20]

Opposite Top: Butler Block (Butler Garage), built 1890. Middle: Terry Denny Building (Northern Hotel), built 1889. Bottom: Collins Building, built 1893.

Initially, the board operated with two committees: a grants committee and a property (assets) committee. Soon, a third committee was formed to manage issues related to governance and trustees. Eddie Hasson was president of the board as well as accountant and de facto finance manager; David Hasson was the property manager. Eddie's retirement as president in March 2013, plus the earlier retirements from the board of Morris Piha in 2003 and Martin Selig in 2007, prompted several changes. Al Maimon served as president from 2013 to 2016, when the term *board chair* was introduced and Jerry Cohen assumed the position. Today, new board members are appointed for a three-year term (instead of lifetime service), and there are five board standing committees: the Executive Committee, the Endowment

Schwabacher Building, built 1890.

Investment Committee, the Finance/Audit Committee, the Grants Committee, and the Trusteeship and Governance Committee.

EDUCATION AND PHILANTHROPY TODAY

Sam Israel envisioned a Jewish community in which all Jewish children have access to intensive, immersive Jewish education and experiences. Today, a quarter-century after his passing, that vision guides the foundation's grant making across the Seattle Jewish community. Since 1994, the Samis Foundation's grant giving totals nearly $100 million to support Washington State's Jewish community and Israel. Annual grants provide support to day schools, experiential Jewish education, projects in Israel, and disaster relief when crises or natural disasters hit communities across the globe. (See figures 7 and 8.)

Grants to seven Jewish day schools in Seattle provide scholarships, enabling children to access intensive and immersive education by supporting families in their choice to enroll their children in one of Seattle's Jewish day schools. The broader goal is to foster development of a Jewish community where Jews are knowledgeable about their sacred history and destiny, texts, and peoplehood, and where they feel a sense of mutual responsibility to the local and global Jewish communities, with unconditional acceptance of all Jews wherever they are. Historically, the foundation has supported organizations and programs that provide intensive, immersive, K–12 Jewish education in both formal and experiential settings. More recently, the foundation has begun to partner with organizations that provide enriched educational experiences for a wide range of Jewish teens.

To this end, the foundation collaborates with selected partners on several key initiatives. These include (1) convening lay leaders, heads of school, business managers, and advancement professionals; (2) providing professional development for capacity building of individual organizations and the community overall; (3) collaborating with the Jewish Federation of Greater Seattle to provide scholarships for overnight camps and Israel experiences; and (4) collaborating with national and international organizations and other foundations to increase opportunities for Washington State Jewish youth to participate in meaningful educational experiences.

Foundation grants lower financial barriers for families who seek a Jewish overnight camp adventure for their child. At Camp Solomon Schechter, the Sephardic Adventure Camp, and URJ Camp Kalsman, an immersive environment gives children and teens the ability to experience Jewish and Israeli culture and traditions as an essential part of everyday life. Children have an opportunity to explore what Judaism means to them, share their family's traditions with others, and deepen their learning in a dynamic, supportive environment. The traditional fun camp experiences of sports, art, dance, campfires, and tire swings are enhanced by a rich cultural context woven effortlessly into daily routines.

Since 2016, the Samis Foundation has made an increased commitment to teen engagement and to developing a meaningful connection between Seattle teens and Israel. Investments in this arena have focused on a few key areas: encouraging and supporting more teens to go to Israel on educational experiences; supporting teens to be active agents in the world, making positive change today while developing skills and values they will use throughout their lives; and creating a diverse, rich, and meaningful menu of opportunities for Jewish teens to continue their learning and social engagement regardless of background or prior Jewish educational experience. Over the last several years, the Samis Foundation has supported Jewish youth experiences in Seattle through grant pilot programs. These include the StandWithUs high school internship and teen leadership council; the Stroum Jewish Community Center Jewish Teen Funders Network Giving Initiative for Teens; Friendship Circle Jewish Action in Motion program; and the Israeli American Council Eitanim student entrepreneurship and leadership program.

Following Sam Israel's directive and his passion for the State of Israel, a vital part of the foundation's philanthropy supports Israel's people, history, and land. Over the past twenty years, the Samis Foundation has granted approximately 9 percent of its funding, totaling more than $7 million, to Israeli organizations. Two of the current foundation trustees are Israelis, and recently the foundation retained a local representative to oversee its projects in Israel. In addition, the foundation sends a group of Seattle-based staff and board members to Israel annually. The foundation supports organizations

that are making meaningful change through incubating new programs and testing new ideas.

The foundation supports those on the geographic and socioeconomic peripheries by promoting social mobility. Funding helps in the following areas: providing access to higher education through needs-based scholarships; lowering the barriers immigrants face when integrating into Israeli society, including career counseling, job placement, networking opportunities, and college preparatory programs; and supporting the vulnerable, specifically through shelters for abused women and their children, counseling services, and early childhood education.

Foundation grants support Israel's land by funding organizations engaged in wildlife conservation and education about the importance of land conservation. Samis has continued grants to the Society for the Protection of Nature in Israel (SPNI) and its work to promote education, research, and conservation. Foundation grants have been a strong support for SPNI's seventeen field study centers, which provide educational experiences for those interested in learning about the environment and tours for hundreds of students each year. Other Samis grants have helped support research on the use of barn owls as pest control agents in agriculture, as well as the implementation projects that followed, which became landmarks of international cooperative nature conservation in the Middle East.

In addition, Samis has provided grants to the Hoopoe Bird Foundation, which offers educational programs about Israel's significant migratory bird populations, and also has supported the application of science in conservation at the Samuel Israel Breeding and Veterinary Center of the Israel Aquarium. In 1999, the Samis Foundation funded the first

English edition of *Flying with the Birds*, which had been published in Hebrew in 1994. The book, which tells about the joint research project initially supported by Sam Israel in 1983, was coauthored by Yossi Leshem and Ofer Bahat and won the prestigious Yitzhak Sadeh Prize for Military Literature. In a letter to the foundation acknowledging the support, Professor Leshem, noted, "I regret that the late Sam Israel could not see the final result."[21]

Foundation grants have continued Sam Israel's support for Israel's history, especially scholarly and popular publications of significant archaeological excavations. Most notable has been Samis's funding publication of eight volumes by Professor Ehud Netzer (1934–2010) and his colleagues on research at Jericho and Herodium, as well as popular versions of his work through the Israel Exploration Society. Netzer, who had received grants beginning with Sam's first donation in 1987, became a world-renowned Israeli educator, architect, and archaeologist at the Hebrew University in Jerusalem. Netzer gained universal recognition for leading the extensive excavations at Herodium, where he unearthed the tomb of Herod the Great in 2007 and the Wadi Qelt Synagogue, the oldest synagogue yet discovered.[22]

Opposite, top: Yossi Leshem and Ofer Bahat, *Flying with the Birds*, published in Hebrew in 1994. The English version was funded by the Samis Foundation and published in 1999. Opposite, bottom: Ehud Netzer, *The Palaces of the Hasmoneans and Herod the Great*, published in 2001 with support from Samis Foundation.

At the heart of Sam Israel's legacy are the words *I am my brother's keeper*, a rephrasing of the original Hebrew, which asks, "Am I my brother's keeper?" Sam accepted the responsibility to take care of the poor Jew, the uneducated Jew, and the Jew in Israel. The Samis Foundation's original sixteen trustees and their successors have followed faithfully the basic mandates prescribed in Sam's will and funded organizations according to his preferences. Eddie Hasson notes, "It's interesting because in our Samis Foundation Board meetings, we ask the same question all the time: What would Sam think about what we're doing? Generally speaking, we feel that we're doing his wishes, and we're very cognizant of what his wishes were."[23]

EPILOGUE

Figure 6

Sam Israel Properties in 1994, Summary

REGION	NO. OF PROPERTIES	AREA (ACRES)	VALUE ($MILLION)
WESTERN WASHINGTON			
Seattle	40	21	$37.2
King County	3	15	$2.1
Western Washington timber and recreational properties	13	342	$0.9
Subtotal	56	378	$40.2
EASTERN WASHINGTON			
Soap Lake	35	2,524	$1.4
Ephrata	19	25	$1.1
Other Grant County	33	13,037	$1.3
Subtotal	87	15,586	$3.8
Total	143	15,964	$44

Figure 7

Samis Foundation Grants, 1994–2019

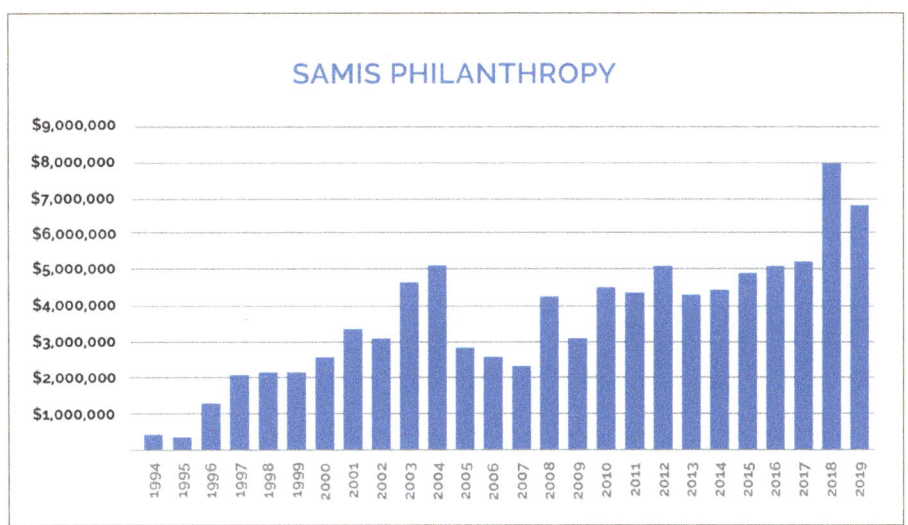

Total Grants as of December 31, 2019: $97.5 Million

Figure 8

Samis Foundation Grants by Giving Area

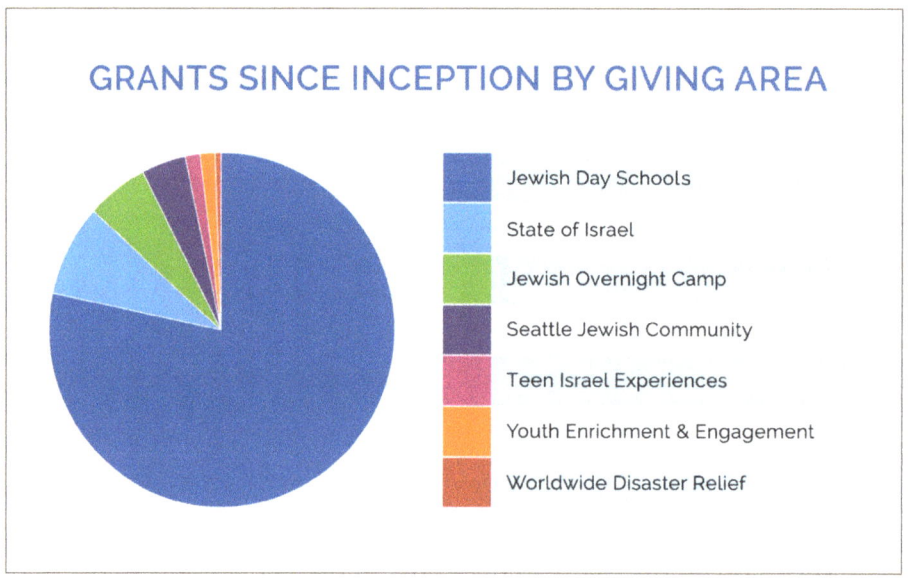

SAM ISRAEL TIMELINE

1899   March 4. The date claimed by Samuel Israel as his birthday.

April 3. The birthdate that appears on Sam's passport, issued on September 12, 1919, identifying him as an Italian citizen, born in Rhodes (then part of Italy), occupation "Calzolaio" (shoemaker).

1904   February 13. The birth date of Sam Israel as written on his Preliminary Form for Petition for Naturalization.

1906   Sam's brother David leaves Rhodes and settles in Vancouver, British Columbia.

1906–12 Sam attends the Alliance Israélite Universelle school for boys, sponsored by the Italian government, through bar mitzvah age (thirteen).

1908   Sam's brother Jack leaves Rhodes and joins David in Vancouver.

1912–17 Sam continues his apprenticeship to a Greek shoemaker.

1914   David and Jack return to Rhodes. David (age twenty-four) and Marie Franco (age seventeen) are married in Rhodes. Jack, David, Marie, and Morris leave Rhodes and settle in Seattle.

1919   September 10. Sam receives a certificate of good conduct—Certificato Penale indicating "nulla," that is, no criminal record—a prerequisite to obtaining permission to emigrate to the United States.

October 3. The SS *Patria* of the Fabre Line, carrying Sam and family friends the Rahamin Capouyas, leaves Naples and arrives in New York two weeks later.

October 28. After a weeklong train ride, Sam arrives in Seattle.

SAM ISRAEL TIMELINE

December 7. Sam's parents, Isaac and Sarah, and their youngest children, Nissim, John, and Bona, arrive in the US on the SS *Pesaro* out of Naples, Italy.

1920 January. Isaac, Sarah, Nissim, John, and Bona arrive in Seattle. They settle in the Central Area near other Sephardic Jews in a house at 167 Twentieth Avenue.

Sam and brothers Jack and David rent shop space at 224 Madison Street and begin a shoe repair business.

1923 Sam, Morris, and parents, with Nissim, John, and Bona, move to house at 1805 Spruce Street, purchased by Sam's father; Sam purchases the house in April 1939.

February 9. Sam submits his Preliminary Form for Petition for Naturalization. He lists his birthday as "Feb. 13, 1904."

1925 Rotary Shoe Repair at 224 Madison Street is opened by Sam, David, and Jack. Morris operates his own shop, Orpheum Shoe Repair Shop, at 910 Third Avenue.

1927 Rotary Shoe Repair has two locations: 215 Madison Street (managed by Jack) and 224 Madison Street.

Sam buys waterfront property at Faben Point on the north end of Mercer Island. Over the years, Sam adds adjoining parcels to total three hundred contiguous feet of waterfront.

1930 Sam opens Wingfoot Shoe Repair at 1609 Third Avenue.

1932 Sam's brother Morris initiates the first family visit to Soap Lake. Soap Lake is a favorite gathering place for Jews, Italians, Greeks, and Russians from Seattle. It becomes an annual event for the family.

1940–45 Sam receives contracts to repair shoes for the US Army during World War II.

1942 April. Sam purchases the building next door to Wingfoot Shoe Repair at 2107–2111 Third Avenue (on Third and Lenora); he names it the Army Building and sets up operations for assembly line boot repair.

1944 July 19. Sam's father, Yitzhak (Isaac) David Israel, dies at the age of ninety-two.

1946 April 9. Sam purchases original property for his farm near Soap Lake from the Northern Pacific Railway. The purchase is five lots totaling 251 acres, for $20,000.

July 1. Sam incorporates Samis Land Company.

1947 May 8. Sam's mother, Sarota (Sarah) Biton Israel, dies at age eighty-nine.

1954 January. Sam gives Wingfoot Shoe Repair to his brother John Israel.

1958 April 12. Sam purchases registered Hereford cattle for breeding stock from the W. E. Boeing estate in Falls City, Washington. The next day, Sam travels to Chehalis and adds another four head of registered Herefords. By November 1961, the Samis Hereford Ranch counts more than one hundred head, including sixteen bulls and three milk cows.

1960 c. September–December. Sam, age sixty-one, moves to his Soap Lake farm.

1967 December 16. A dispersal sale of 250 head of registered Hereford cattle by Samis Hereford Ranch is held at the Central Washington Livestock Market in Quincy. It marks the end of Sam's nine-year venture into the business of registered cattle breeding.

1973 September 20. Sam purchases airfare to Israel, with stops in Athens and Rhodes. His planned departure is October 11 with arrival in Tel Aviv the following day. Sam's trip is delayed by the Yom Kippur War. He leaves around November 1 and returns three weeks later.

1979 December 19. The Samis Foundation is registered with the Washington Secretary of State's office as a 501(c)(3) nonprofit organization.

1984 November. Sam pays off the Seattle Hebrew Academy's mortgage on the condition that the school will never again mortgage the property.

Sam promotes a Saturday bazaar for downtown Ephrata at a lot he owns on Basin Street.

1985 April. The Gatewood Hotel affair becomes widely reported in Seattle newspapers and on KING-TV, which interviews Sam.

1986 "Happy Birthday, Sam," a full-page ad, is placed in the *Grant County Journal* on February 13, 1986 by Soap Lake mayor Marina Romary.

1987 May 23–25. Sam Israel is grand marshal for the Greek Festival in Soap Lake.

1989 February 12. Sam invites Boy Scouts, Girl Scouts, and the general public from the Columbia Basin to celebrate his ninetieth birthday at the Grant County Public Utility District auditorium in Ephrata.

February 25. Jack Patrick takes Sam to Columbia Basin Hospital in Ephrata, where he is diagnosed with pneumonia. Sam is transferred to Central Washington Hospital in Wenatchee.

February 26. Sam suffers a stroke.

March 14. Sam is discharged from Central Washington Hospital in Wenatchee and transported by ambulance to Providence Hospital in Seattle.

c. April 10. Sam is moved to the Keiro Nursing Home.

c. June 10. Space becomes available for Sam at the Kline Galland Home, and he is transferred there.

1990   May. A celebration of Sam, who was chosen as "Honorary Parade Marshal," is held over Memorial Day weekend in Ephrata. Bona, Eddie, and David Hasson accompany him.

July. Eddie Hasson, via Irwin Treiger, Sam's attorney, submits a petition for guardianship to the King County Superior Court.

August 31. King County Superior Court commissioner Maurice Epstein signs documents declaring Sam Israel incompetent and appointing Eddie Hasson as Sam's legal guardian.

1991   August 18. Sam is honored for the purchase and donation of a Sefer Torah to Congregation Ezra Bessaroth.

1992   May 23–25. Sam is named honorary grand marshal of the Memorial Day weekend community parade in Soap Lake.

1994   May 31. The Samis Foundation is incorporated.

June 11 (2 Tammuz). Sam Israel dies. Funeral services are held on June 13. Sam is buried with other members of his family in the Sephardic Brotherhood Cemetery, 1230 North 167th Street, Shoreline, Washington.

SELECTED PROPERTIES DETAIL: KING COUNTY AND SNOHOMISH COUNTY

NAME	PURCHASE DATE	PAID
Duplex, 1910–1912 Spruce Street	1927	$4,000
Mercer Island, Faben Point lot	1927	$995
Mercer Island, south end lot	1927	unknown
Frame Store Building	1927	$1,400
Frame Store Building (for Cascade Market, 1935–1960; later Aurora Rex Building)	10/15/1933	$1,500
Frame Dwelling	12/28/1934	$600
Hotel Building	1/1/1935	$12,933
Frame Building	4/1/1935	$1,500
Woodland Park Store, Ninetieth Street and Aurora Avenue	3/3/1936	$12,500
Austin A. Bell Building*	6/18/1936	$2,500
Douglas Hotel	1937	$12,933
Paramount Building	11/25/1937	$42,577
Rooming House	11/25/1938	$4,000

SELECTED PROPERTIES DETAIL

NAME	PURCHASE DATE	PAID
Stoneway Garage	4/1/1939	$1,500
Old Garage Building	4/10/1939	$1,000
Residence, 1805 Spruce Street	4/10/1939	$700
Leary Way House	4/10/1939	$700
Old Factory Building	4/10/1939	$1,000
Stoneway Building	4/15/1939	$1,500
Leary Way Studio Building	4/15/1939	$3,000
Hamilton Building	10/24/1941	$5,500
Army Building*	4/1/1942	$15,950
Hartford Building**	8/23/1943	$39,500
Hardman Building	1/1/1944	$50,000
Drexel Hotel**	7/13/1944	$35,000
Yesler Building**	7/9/1945	$22,500
US Rubber Building**	12/14/1945	$82,500
Schwabacher Building**	1/2/1946	$32,500
Scientific Building**	1/3/1946	$35,000
Telephone Building*	7/1/1946	$40,000
Holyoke Building*	7/1/1946	$40,000
Beacon Hill property	9/12/1946	unknown
Webster-Brinkley Plant	1/9/1947	$114,700

SELECTED PROPERTIES DETAIL

NAME	PURCHASE DATE	PAID
Washington Shoe Building**	6/20/1947	$127,500
Frame Factory Building	8/1/1949	$45,165
Menzel Lakes properties	1950–1951	$13,750
Seventh and Seneca Parking	1954	$1,500
Packard Building	12/28/1956	$85,000
Florence Theatre/Building**	9/24/1958	$6,500
Collins Building**	9/24/1958	$129,250
Northern Hotel (Terry Denny Building)**	6/13/1960	$55,000
Seneca Building	1961 and 1966	$69,000
Fifth and Yesler Lots	9/14/1962	$23,500
Liberty Parking Lots	5/18/1966	$393,750
Mottman Building**	3/7/1967	$54,000
Atlantic Street Lot	2/1/1968	$16,500
Galland Building (Galland & Seneca Building)	1969	Property exchange for Telephone Building; $300,000 appraisal
Rainier Beach Property	10/13/1970	$850
Corona Hotel**	10/19/1970	$95,000
Army Parking Lot	9/1/1975	$83,700

SELECTED PROPERTIES DETAIL

NAME	PURCHASE DATE	PAID
Gatewood Hotel*	10/30/1975	$220,000
Broderick Building	12/12/1980	$356,000 property exchange
Stetson-Ross Plant (3 lots)	12/12/1980	$144,000 property exchange
Forest Hotel	12/12/1980	Property exchange
Butler Block (Butler Garage)**	12/17/1980	$500,000 property exchange
Second and Bell Building	2/28/1985	$225,000
Total		$3.5 million

TOTAL: 56 properties
***Seattle historic landmark**
****Pioneer Square Historic District**

SAMIS FOUNDATION BOARD OF TRUSTEES, 2019

Victor Alhadeff is one of the original sixteen trustees. He is a retired software executive.

Eli J. Almo is one of the original sixteen trustees. Eli is president and CEO of Era Living, which owns and operates independent and assisted care retirement communities.

David Azose is CEO of Azose Commercial Properties, a full-service property management, real estate leasing, and sales company. Dave joined the board in 2005 and is a great-nephew of Sam Israel.

Dana Behar is a founder of Discovery Bay Investments, which specializes in private equity investing, consulting, and real estate brokerage. Dana joined the Samis board in 2012 and is a great-nephew of Sam Israel.

Jerome O. Cohen is one of the original sixteen trustees. Jerry is a Seattle business and real estate attorney with Holmquist and Gardiner.

David Ellenhorn is a partner at Ogden Murphy Wallace, specializing in corporate and real estate law. David joined the Samis board in 2012.

Maria Erlitz is retired and was a teacher, board president, and head of school of the Jewish Day School of Metropolitan Seattle and executive coach at the Partnership for Excellence in Jewish Education. Maria joined the Samis board in 2019.

Barry Ernstoff is one of the original sixteen trustees. He is an attorney in private practice who practiced in Seattle and now does so in Israel since he made aliyah in 1985.

Eli Genauer is one of the original sixteen trustees. He is the retired president of Eilat Management Company, which provides property and asset management for privately held commercial real estate property.

Eddie Hasson is one of the original sixteen trustees. He is a CPA and retired partner of the accounting firm Hasson Laible & Company. He is a nephew of Sam Israel.

Al Maimon is one of the original sixteen trustees. He is retired from operations research and management science, and information systems design and implementation at Boeing, and was a professor at the University of Washington. He is a past president of Sephardic Bikur Holim and the Seattle Hebrew Academy and a former vice president of the Jewish Federation of Greater Seattle.

Rabbi Ron-Ami Meyers retired as the spiritual leader of Congregation Ezra Bessaroth and returned to Israel to teach. Rabbi Meyers joined the Samis board in 2013 and serves as the board rabbi.

Judy Neuman is retired and was previously CEO of the Stroum Jewish Community Center; managing partner at Centerstone Executive Search; partner at Maveron, a venture capital firm; and vice president of interactive media at Eddie Bauer. Judy joined the Samis board in 2019.

Lucy Pruzan is one of the original sixteen trustees. Lucy served as president of the Jewish Federation of Greater Seattle, among her many other volunteer activities.

Greg Roer, along with his wife, Dorothy, is the owner of Roer & Company, a CPA firm specializing in taxes and trusts. Greg joined the Samis board in 2016. He is a great-nephew of Sam Israel.

Ernie Sherman is one of the original sixteen trustees. He is owner of Pacific Plumbing Supply Company.

Dr. Alex Sytman is one of the original sixteen trustees. Dr. Sytman is a retired cardiologist and was Sam's doctor during the last months of his life. He is married to Leatrice "Lucy" Israel Sytman, a niece of Sam Israel.

Louis Treiger has a private law practice and was formerly with Herman Sarkowsky and B-Line. Louis joined the Samis board in 2019.

NOTES

PREFACE

1. Lesli Koppelman Ross, "The Importance of Remembering." https://www.myjewishlearning.com/article/the-importance-of-remembering.

INTRODUCTION

1. Sephardic proverbs quoted in this work are from Norman Amato, *Ladino Sayings My Father Taught Me* (San Bernadino, CA: Norman Amato, 2018).
2. Eddie Hasson, Sadis Filmworks Interview, September 7, 2012. All Sadis Filmworks Interviews can be found in the Samis Foundation Archives.
3. Connie Kanter, "What Does Being Jewish Mean to You?" *Jewish in Seattle*, March 21, 2018.

CHAPTER 1

1. Quoted in Marc Angel, *The Jews of Rhodes* (New York: Sepher-Hermon Press, 1978, rev. ed. 1998), 2–3. The descriptions of Sephardic Jews in Rhodes in this chapter are based on Angel, *Jews of Rhodes*; Marc Angel, ed., *Exploring Sephardic Customs and Traditions* (Brooklyn: KTAV, 2017); Marc Angel, *Foundations of Sephardic Spirituality: The Inner Life of Jews of the Ottoman Empire* (Nashville: Jewish Lights, 2006); Aron Hasson, *A Guidebook to the Jewish Quarter of Rhodes* (Los Angeles: Rhodes Jewish Historical Foundation, 2012); Esther Fintz Menascé, *A History of Jewish Rhodes* (Los Angeles: Rhodes Jewish Historical Foundation, 2014); and Charles River Editors, *Rhodes: The History and Legacy of the Greek Island from Ancient Times to Today* (no publication information available).
2. Quote from www.jewishrhodes.org.

3. Nathan Shachar, *The Lost Worlds of Rhodes: Greeks, Italians, Jews, and Turks between Tradition and Modernity* (Brighton: Sussex Academic Press, 2013), 182–85.

4. Sylvia Hasson-Berro, *The Story of a Survivor: The Memoirs of Sylvia Hasson-Berro* (privately published, 2004), 75.

5. Sam Israel quoted in "Deposition Upon Oral Examination of Samuel Israel," February 5, 1980, Columbia Pacific Industries Inc. v. Samuel Israel and Samis Land Company v. Richard L. Tall, King County Superior Court case no. 865 412, Part One, Litigation Files, Samis Foundation Archives (hereafter "Deposition of Samuel Israel").

6. There is no birth certificate for Sam Israel. The documents indicating birth dates are (1) a Declaration of Alien About to Depart for the United States form, completed by the American Vice Consul in Naples, Italy, on September 25, 1919, which indicates the birth date "3/4/1899"; (2) a Preliminary Form for Petition for Naturalization, King County Superior Court, which gives the birth date of February 13, 1904; (3) and a Certificate of Naturalization, US District Court, Western District of Washington (no. 2485627), March 27, 1927, which gives Sam's age as "23," indicating he was born in 1904. Less reliable is the US Census. The federal population count for 1920 cited Sam as "18," meaning a birth year of 1902. Some observers say that the photograph of Sam appearing on his 1919 Declaration of Alien form shows a young man closer to age fifteen than twenty. Sam Israel immigration documents, Samis Foundation Archives.

7. On the Alliance Israélite Universelle school in Rhodes, see Shachar, *Lost Worlds of Rhodes*, 78–80, 120–21, 155; Angel, *Jews of Rhodes*, 53–54, 78–83, 100–108; Angel, *Foundations*, 10, 155–59.

8. Sam Israel to Marina [Romary], May 26, 1987, Samis Foundation Archives.

9. "Deposition of Samuel Israel"; Tracy Warner, "Sam Israel Battles the Rules," *Wenatchee World*, May 16, 1977; Victor Hasson, phone interview, August 1, 2019.

10. Shachar, *Lost Worlds of Rhodes*, 98.

11. Shachar, *Lost Worlds of Rhodes*, 139.

12. Shachar, *Lost Worlds of Rhodes*, 134.

13. Rita Calderon, Sadis Filmworks Interview, September 7, 2012.

14. Daisy Israel, Sadis Filmworks Interview, September 7, 2012; Rita Calderon, Sadis Filmworks Interview, September 7, 2012.

15. "Deposition of Samuel Israel"; Devin Naar, email to the author, August 25, 2019.

16. Robert Hasson, Sadis Filmworks Interview, April 24, 2013; Sam Israel immigration documents, Samis Foundation Archives; trip log by Sam Israel handwritten in Soletreo, listing the travel itinerary from Rhodes on September 17/18 to arrival in Seattle on October 28, Samis Foundation Archives.

CHAPTER 2

1. Daisy Israel, Sadis Filmworks Interview, September 7, 2012; Eddie Hasson, author interviews, 2018; "Deposition of Samuel Israel."
2. Sam Israel immigration documents, Samis Foundation Archives; Daisy Israel, Sadis Filmworks Interview, September 7, 2012.
3. Molly Cone, Howard Droker, and Jacqueline Williams, *Family of Strangers: Building a Jewish Community in Washington State* (Seattle: Washington State Jewish Historical Society, 2003), 60–69. See also Ellen Eisenberg, Ava Kahn, and William Toll, *Jews of the Pacific Coast* (Seattle: University of Washington Press, 2010).
4. Cone, Droker, and Williams, *Family of Strangers*, 69; *The Sephardic Jews and the Pike Place Market*, directed by Stephen Sadis (Sadis Filmworks, 2001), DVD.
5. Eddie Hasson, email to the author, December 10, 2018; US Census 1920, 1930; *Polk's Seattle City Directory*, 1919–1923.
6. Daisy Israel, Sadis Filmworks Interview, September 7, 2012.
7. "Deposition of Samuel Israel."
8. Eddie Hasson, email to the author, December 10, 2018; US Census 1920, 1930; *Polk's Seattle City Directory*, 1919–1925; *Ezra Bessaroth: The Story of a Sephardic Congregation* (Seattle: Ezra Bessaroth, 2016).
9. Cone, Droker, and Williams, *Family of Strangers*, 150.
10. Eddie Hasson interview, November 15, 2000, Oral History Collection, Washington State Jewish Archives, University of Washington Libraries, Special Collections.
11. Warner, "Sam Israel Battles the Rules"; "Deposition of Samuel Israel."
12. Robert Hasson, Sadis Filmworks Interview, April 24, 2013.
13. "Deposition of Samuel Israel."
14. Sam Israel to James Horrigan, April 27, 1982, Samis Foundation Archives.
15. Eddie Hasson, author interview, October 1, 2018.

16. "Deposition of Samuel Israel"; Eddie Hasson, Sadis Filmworks Interview, September 7, 2012.
17. "Deposition of Samuel Israel."
18. Israel to Horrigan, April 27, 1982.
19. Israel to Horrigan, April 27, 1982.
20. *Polk's Seattle City Directory*, 1930.
21. *Polk's Seattle City Directory*, 1930–1936; Robert Hasson, Sadis Filmworks Interview, April 24, 2013.
22. Eddie Hasson, author interview, May 31, 2018.
23. *Polk's Seattle City Directory*, 1930–1936; Eddie Hasson, author interviews, 2018.
24. Eddie Hasson, author interview, October 1, 2018, and August 2, 2018; Victor Hasson, phone interview, August 1, 2019; Daisy Israel, comments (c. 2010) on Sam's home movie of his parents, c. 1937.
25. Eddie Hasson, author interview, August 2, 2018.
26. Eddie Hasson, author interview, September 6, 2018; Marilyn Hasson Henry, email to the author, August 31, 2019.
27. Eddie Hasson, author interview, October 1, 2018.
28. David Hasson, Sadis Filmworks Interview, April 24, 2013; Eddie Hasson, Sadis Filmworks Interview, September 7, 2012.
29. Eddie Hasson, author interview, December 4, 2018; Rob Toren, email to the author, February 13, 2019.
30. Daisy Israel, Sadis Filmworks Interview, September 7, 2012.
31. Robert Hasson, Sadis Filmworks Interview, April 24, 2013.
32. Daisy Israel, Sadis Filmworks Interview, September 7, 2012.
33. Eddie Hasson, author interview, December 4, 2018.
34. Dana Behar, phone interview, July 17, 2019.
35. David Hasson, Sadis Filmworks Interview, April 24, 2013; various letters to Sam Israel from girlfriends, nieces, and nephews, 1937–1942, Samis Foundation Archives.
36. Sam Israel to Marina [Romary], May 26, 1987, Samis Foundation Archives.
37. Daisy Israel, Sadis Filmworks Interview, September 7, 2012.
38. Daisy Israel, Sadis Filmworks Interview, September 7, 2012.
39. Mountaineers Club Records, University of Washington Libraries, Special Collections; *Seattle Daily Times*, September 27, 1925; Eddie Hasson, author interview, June 27, 2018.
40. Robert Hasson, Sadis Filmworks Interview, April 24, 2013; Rita Calderon, Sadis Filmworks Interview, September 7, 2012.
41. Eddie Hasson, author interview, September 6, 2018.

42. Daisy Israel, Sadis Filmworks Interview, September 7, 2012.
43. Eddie Hasson, author interview, August 2, 2018; Eddie Hasson, author interview, October 1, 2018.
44. The title of Julia's MA thesis was "The Ballad Sources of Los Siete Infantes de Laraand El Bastardo Mudarra." Registrar's Office, University of Washington.
45. Rita Calderon, Sadis Filmworks Interview, September 7, 2012.
46. Eddie Hasson, author interview, October 1, 2018; September 6, 2018. Not until 1948 did Morris Hanan consent to marriage for Julia. The successful suitor was attorney Edwin J. Friedman, who had graduated from law school in 1934 and a decade later became a partner in the firm of Levinson & Friedman. At the time of their marriage, Julia was twenty-five years old; Friedman was thirty-nine.
47. Rita Calderon, Sadis Filmworks Interview, September 7, 2012; Registrar's Office, University of Washington.
48. Rita Calderon, Sadis Filmworks Interview, September 7, 2012.
49. Rosie Israel to Sam Israel, February 5, 1941, Samis Foundation Archives.

CHAPTER 3

1. "Deposition of Samuel Israel"; Warner, "Sam Israel Battles the Rules"; Joe Dennis, "For Sam, the Bell Tolls," *Grant County Journal*, June 20, 1994.
2. "Deposition of Samuel Israel."
3. Sarah Israel to Sam Israel, December 28, 1940, Samis Foundation Archives.
4. Dennis, "For Sam, the Bell Tolls."
5. "3 Shoe Repair Shops Face OPA Charges," *Seattle Post-Intelligencer*, June 17, 1942.
6. Eddie Hasson, author interview, May 31, 2018; "12,000 Lbs. of Rubber Heels Turned In," *Seattle Post-Intelligencer*, June 17, 1942; *Seattle Star*, June 16, 1942.
7. Robert Hasson, Sadis Filmworks Interview, April 24, 2013.
8. Eddie Hasson, author interview, May 31, 2018; financial records, including federal income tax files, 1941–1950, Samis Foundation Archives.
9. Eddie Hasson, author interview, October 1, 2018.
10. Eddie Hasson, author interview, May 31, 2018.

11. "War-Developed Plant Is Sold," unidentified newspaper clipping, January 1947; scrapbook, Samis Foundation Archives.
12. David Hasson, Sadis Filmworks Interview, April 24, 2013.
13. David Hasson, Sadis Filmworks Interview, April 24, 2013; Adam Hasson to the author, April 29, 2019.
14. Samis Land Company Articles of Incorporation, July 1, 1946, Samis Foundation Archives.
15. Eddie Hasson, author interview, May 31, 2018; financial records, including federal income tax files, 1941–1950, Samis Foundation Archives.
16. Eddie Hasson interview, November 15, 2000, Oral History Collection.
17. Eddie Hasson, author interview, August 2, 2018.
18. Eddie Hasson, author interview, August 2, 2018; Robert Hasson, Sadis Filmworks Interview, April 24, 2013; "Deposition of Samuel Israel."
19. Eddie Hasson, author interview, August 2, 2018.
20. Eddie Hasson, author interview, August 2, 2018.
21. Eddie Hasson, author interview, August 2, 2018.
22. Eddie Hasson, Sadis Filmworks Interview, September 7, 2012.
23. Robert Hasson, Sadis Filmworks Interview, April 24, 2013.
24. Eddie Hasson, author interview, August 2, 2018.
25. Hizkia M. Franco, *The Jewish Martyrs of Rhodes and Cos.* (Zimbabwe: HarperCollins, 1994). For an inspiring story of another immigrant Rhodesli family and their survival, see Clare Barkey Flash, *A Hug from Afar*, edited and compiled by Cynthia Flash Hemphill (Bellevue, WA: Flash Media Services, 2016).
26. Angel, *Jews of Rhodes*, 152.
27. Robert Hasson, Sadis Filmworks Interview, April 24, 2013.
28. Eddie Hasson, author interview, July 12, 2018. Eddie Hasson concludes the story of his aunt: "In 1953, she did a mail order romance of another Rhodesli that she remembered as a kid, he lived in Rhodesia. They connected by mail and she went to Rhodesia and married him. Then it started all over again, they were kicked out of Rhodesia because it became Uganda. They got kicked out and moved to South Africa, and she has two children, they're all my cousins, and they raised the kids in South Africa. She never came to Seattle to visit, but her husband came once to visit, nice man, he died of course. So, then she moved to Perth, Australia with her kids. She

was in a nursing home for 10, 12 years, and she just died in 2017, 97 years old. My Auntie Sylvia."
29. Robert Hasson, Sadis Filmworks Interview, April 24, 2013.
30. Rita Calderon, Sadis Filmworks Interview, September 7, 2012. The Shema, or Shema Yisrael, which begins, "Hear, Oh Israel," is a daily morning and evening prayer that affirms the monotheistic core of the Jewish faith and is considered the most important prayer in Judaism.
31. Eddie Hasson, author interview, August 2, 2018; Robert Hasson, Sadis Filmworks Interview, April 24, 2013.
32. Robert Hasson, Sadis Filmworks Interview, April 24, 2013.
33. Eddie Hasson, author interview, August 28, 2018; Robert William (1874–1958), a British Canadian poet and writer, earned Service the label, "the Bard of the Yukon."
34. Awards and other materials in the Samis Foundation Archives; Eddie Hasson, author interview, May 31, 2018; Eddie Hasson, author interview, October 1, 2018. The photograph *Destitute* remains in the permanent collection at the Seattle Art Museum.
35. David Hasson, Sadis Filmworks Interview, April 24, 2013.
36. Rosie Israel to Sam Israel, November 10, 1940, Samis Foundation Archives; Adam Hasson, email to the author, March 25, 2019.
37. "Gift from One-Shot Sam"; Bill DeWitt, "Sam Israel Offers Lake . . . and Advice," *Wenatchee World*, April 1, 1984.
38. Robert Hasson, author interview, March 23, 2020.
39. Eddie Hasson, author interview, May 31, 2018; Robert Hasson, Sadis Filmworks Interview, April 24, 2013; "Deposition of Samuel Israel." A 1961 article by *Seattle Times* columnist Frank Lynch, "Civic Need—A Statue of Henry Yesler," mentions Grace McWhirter and can be found in the Samis Foundation Archives.
40. Undated newspaper clippings titled "Brick Building Slows Viaduct," "Owners Won't Move Building," "Court Rules against City," and "Sum to Move Building Too Low, Says Firm," scrapbook, Samis Foundation Archives.
41. Ibid.
42. "Sum to Move Building Too Low, Says Firm," scrapbook, Samis Foundation Archives. The building, later called the Catholic Seamen's Center, was sold in 2015 and the Center moved to a building south of downtown near Harbor Island. Internal Revenue Service to Sam Israel, April 15, 1954, and August 21, 1958, Samis

Foundation Archives; Robert Hasson, Sadis Filmworks Interview, April 24, 2013.
43. David Hasson, Sadis Filmworks Interview, April 24, 2013.
44. Contracts and Warranty Deeds, Grant County Auditor, General Index, 1946–1955, Washington State Archives, Central Regional Branch.
45. "Basin Festival Queen Named," *Wenatchee World*, May 12, 1952.
46. Eddie Hasson, author interview, September 6, 2018; Bonnie Holt Morehouse, email to the author, July 10, 2020.
47. "Record," Samis Foundation Archives.

CHAPTER 4

1. Eddie Hasson, author interview, August 28, 2018.
2. Eddie Hasson, author interview, August 28, 2018; Dana Behar, phone interview, July 17, 2019.
3. Eddie Hasson, author interview, August 28, 2018.
4. Jack Patrick, Sadis Filmworks Interview, June 13, 2012.
5. Dana Behar, phone interview, July 17, 2019.
6. Candace Dempsey, "The Howard Hughes of Washington State," July 1982 newspaper clipping, Samis Foundation Archives.
7. Victor Hasson, Sadis Filmworks Interview, April 4, 2012; Victor Hasson, phone interview, August 1, 2019.
8. David Hasson, Sadis Filmworks Interview, April 24, 2013; Eddie Hasson, author interview, September 6, 2018.
9. Duane Scheib, Sadis Filmworks Interview, June 13, 2012.
10. Duane Scheib, Sadis Filmworks Interview, June 13, 2012.
11. "Record," Samis Foundation Archives; "Samis Ranch Buys Registered Herefords," source unknown, [c. April 14, 1958].
12. Eddie Hasson, author interview, August 2, 2018.
13. Gideon Saguy to Sam Israel, November 2, 1966, Samis Foundation Archives; C. K. Wilson, DVM, to Sam Israel, August 7, 1967, Samis Foundation Archives.
14. Eddie Hasson, author interview, August 2, 2018; Robert Hasson, Sadis Filmworks Interview, April 24, 2013; Samis Land Company tax return, 1967, Samis Foundation Archives.
15. "Deposition of Samuel Israel."
16. David Azose, phone interview, July 29, 2019.

17. Eddie Hasson, author interview, February 5, 2018; Frank Lynch, "Seattle Scene: The Shattered Dream of a Mighty Hunter," *Seattle Post-Intelligencer*, no date; 1961. The photograph is displayed at the Samis Foundation.
18. Eddie Hasson, author interview, August 28, 2018.
19. Eddie Hasson, author interview, August 2, 2018.
20. Dana Behar, phone interview, July 17, 2019.
21. Robert Hasson, phone interview, March 23, 2020.
22. Adam Hasson, email to the author, March 25, 2019; Dana Behar, phone interview, July 17, 2019.
23. David Hasson, Sadis Filmworks Interview, April 24, 2013.
24. Victor Hasson, Sadis Filmworks Interview, April 4, 2012.
25. Eddie Hasson, author interviews, June 27, 2018; September 6, 2018; and October 1, 2018; and Eddie Hasson, Sadis Filmworks Interview, September 7, 2012.
26. Robert Hasson, Sadis Filmworks Interview, April 24, 2013.
27. Robert Hasson, Sadis Filmworks Interview, April 24, 2013.
28. Louise Hasson, *Poems*, publisher unknown, 2011.
29. Dana Behar, phone interview, July 17, 2019.
30. Sam Israel to Yair Mundlak, June 8, 1972; Mundlak to Sam Israel, September 20, 1972, Samis Foundation Archives.
31. Eddie Hasson, author interview, July 12, 2018; Victor Hasson, Sadis Filmworks Interview, April 4, 2012. See also related correspondence to Sam in Samis Foundation Archives.
32. Victor Hasson, Sadis Filmworks Interview, April 4, 2012.
33. Hasson, *Guidebook to the Jewish Quarter of Rhodes*, 4–19; Victor Hasson, phone interview, August 1, 2019.
34. Rita Calderon, Sadis Filmworks Interview, September 7, 2012.
35. Eddie Hasson, author interviews, July 12, 2018, and August 2, 2018; William Hensleigh (Soap Lake High School) to Sam Israel, May 31, 1983, Samis Foundation Archives.
36. Eddie Hasson, author interview, July 12, 2018.
37. Eddie Hasson, author interview, August 2, 2018.

CHAPTER 5

1. Victor Hasson, Sadis Filmworks Interview, April 5, 2012. The Mourner's Kaddish is the prayer traditionally recited in memory of the dead, although it makes no mention of death. *Minyan* is a

quorum of ten men over the age of thirteen required for certain religious observances.

2. Joel Benoliel to Eliyahu Honig (Hebrew University of Jerusalem), November 15, 1976, Samis Foundation Archives.

3. Israel to Horrigan, April 27, 1982. Sam wrote to Horrigan, "For the last five years I have been writing wills and establishing a charitable foundation."

4. Sam Israel, "Rough Draft, Distribution of Funds to Charities," Samis Foundation Archives.

5. Eddie Hasson, author interview, October 1, 2018; Irwin Treiger, Sadis Filmworks Interview, April 24, 2013; Samis Foundation Articles of Incorporation, 1979, Samis Foundation Archives.

6. Eddie Hasson interview, November 15, 2000, Oral History Collection.

7. Receipts for donations are randomly filed in various files, Samis Foundation Archives; "Home for Aged Honors Sam Israel," *Grant County Journal*, June 5, 1972.

8. Jim Whittaker to Sam Israel, December 16, 1974, Samis Foundation Archives. The 1975 K2 expedition failed to reach the summit, but Whittaker's team was successful on the second attempt in 1978.

9. Eddie Hasson interview, November 15, 2000, Oral History Collection.

10. Barry Ernstoff, email to the author, February 11, 2019.

11. Eddie Hasson, author interview August 2, 2018.

12. Daisy Israel, Sadis Filmworks Interview, September 7, 2012.

13. The anecdotes are related by Rob Toren, email to the author, February 13, 2019.

14. Eugene Normand, "Sam Israel Story," email to the author, March 2, 2020.

15. Carey Quan Gelernter, "Samuel Israel, Soap Lake Recluse Has Place in Seattle's Future," *Seattle Times*, July 13, 1981.

16. "He's Tops in State Property Holdings," July 14, 1981, newspaper clipping in Samis Foundation Archives; David Hasson, Sadis Filmworks Interview, April 24, 2013.

17. Gelernter, "Landlord Sam, a Prince of Parcels," *Seattle Times*, July 13, 1981; Carey Quan Gelernter, "Samuel Israel, Eccentric and a Loner; His Holdings Make Him an Important Man Here," *Seattle Times*, July 13, 1981; Gelernter, "Samuel Israel, Soap Lake Recluse"; Carey Quan Gelernter, "Who 'Owns' Seattle? A Soap Lake Recluse with Old World Notions Hangs On to Much of It," *Seattle Times*,

July 13, 1981; "He's Tops in State Property Holdings," July 14, 1981, newspaper clipping, Samis Foundation Archives; Richard Seven, "The Collector—For Decades Sam Israel Bought Cheap and Never Sold; Today His Legacy Means Change for Seattle," *Seattle Times Magazine*, April 11, 1999.

18. Dennis, "For Sam, the Bell Tolls"; "Samis Foundation Property Business Plan," University of Washington, Center for Community Development and Real Estate, November 27, 1995, revised January 25, 1996, Samis Foundation Archives; Gelernter, "Samuel Israel, Soap Lake Recluse."
19. Dempsey, "The Howard Hughes of Washington State," July 1982 newspaper clipping. Eddie Hasson recalls that Sam kept cash in a toolbox in his bedroom. When Sam died, Robert found the box and was stunned to discover it contained more than $100,000. Sam kept a separate bank account for his Social Security checks, with Bona as a co-signer, and at the time of Sam's death, she inherited the money.
20. Gelernter, "Samuel Israel, Soap Lake Recluse."
21. Eddie Hasson, author interview, June 27, 2018; Eddie Hasson, Sadis Filmworks Interview, September 7, 2012.
22. Marilyn Hasson Henry, email to the author, August 31, 2019; Adam Hasson, email to the author, October 4, 2019.
23. David Hasson, Sadis Filmworks Interview, April 24, 2013; Eddie Hasson, author interview, August 2, 2018.
24. David Hasson, Sadis Filmworks Interview, April 24, 2013.
25. "Deposition of Samuel Israel."
26. "Deposition of Samuel Israel."
27. Hasson, Sadis Filmworks Interview, April 24, 2013.
28. Dempsey, "The Howard Hughes of Washington State," July 1982 newspaper clipping.
29. George E. Benson to Sam Israel, April 29, 1982, Samis Foundation Archives.
30. Eddie Hasson, Sadis Filmworks Interview, September 7, 2012.
31. Greg Kucera, phone interview, October 5, 2019.
32. Greg Kucera, phone interview, October 5, 2019. See also https://gregkucera.com.
33. "Home for Aged Honors Sam Israel," *Grant County Journal*, June 5, 1972.
34. Victor Alhadeff, phone interview, July 14, 2019.
35. Victor Alhadeff, phone interview, July 14, 2019.
36. "Deposition of Samuel Israel."

37. Eddie Hasson, author interview, August 28, 2018.
38. Rick Anderson, "Low-Rent Sam," *Seattle Weekly*, July 6, 1994.
39. Gelernter, "Landlord Sam"; Gelernter, "Samuel Israel, Eccentric and a Loner"; Gelernter, "Samuel Israel, Soap Lake Recluse"; Gelernter, "Who 'Owns' Seattle?"
40. Gelernter, "Landlord Sam"; Gelernter, "Samuel Israel, Eccentric and a Loner"; Gelernter, "Samuel Israel, Soap Lake Recluse"; Gelernter, "Who 'Owns' Seattle?"
41. Dempsey, "The Howard Hughes of Washington State," July 1982 newspaper clipping, Samis Foundation Archives.
42. Eddie Hasson, author interview, September 6, 2018.
43. Dick Clever, "First Avenue Hotel Caught in Open-Shut Tug of War," *Seattle Times*, April 13, 1985; Eddie Hasson, author interview, September 6, 2018.
44. Jack Hamann, phone interview, September 30, 2019; "KING-5 TV, interview 1985," DVD, Samis Foundation Archives (includes the documentary *Shelter from the Storm*, copyright 1986 by KING Broadcasting Company).
45. Jack Hamann, phone interview, September 30, 2019.
46. Eddie Hasson, author interview, May 31, 2018; Ernie Sherman, email to the author, February 11, 2019.
47. Michael Carroll, "Mr. Israel Very Cooperative in Working Out the Details," undated newspaper clipping, Samis Foundation Archives.
48. Maude Scott, "Israel vs. Seattle; Israel Beats City Tax," *Seattle Daily Journal of Commerce*, February 12, 1988.
49. David Hasson, Sadis Filmworks Interview, April 24, 2013; Jack Patrick, Sadis Filmworks Interview, June 13, 2012.
50. "Samis Foundation Property Business Plan," University of Washington, Center for Community Development and Real Estate, November 27, 1995, revised January 25, 1996, Samis Foundation Archives.
51. Case file, Litigation files, Samis Land Company.
52. Dick Moody, "Siphon Project Now Official!" *Columbia Daily Herald*, August 27, 1976; Art Johnson, "Sam Israel; Fight's Not Over," *Columbia Basin Daily Herald*, May 4, 1977; Warner, "Sam Israel Battles the Rules"; Tracy Warner, "Israel Land Withdrawal from Basin Denied," *Wenatchee World*, [c. 1977].
53. "Why Pollution? Who Am I Fighting?" *Grant County Journal*, March 25, 1971; Ephrata City Council Meeting Minutes, March 25, 1971, Washington State Archives, Central Regional Branch, plus several

newspaper articles from March 11 to April 13, 1971, appear on the website http://www.bigbendrailroadhistory.com/search/label/Purdy; Eddie Hasson, author interview, September 6, 2018.

54. "Sam Israel Says State Can Use His Basin Land," *Columbia Basin Herald* (Moses Lake), August 25, 1982; DeWitt, "Sam Israel Offers Lake."
55. Warner, "Sam Israel Battles the Rules."
56. Nancy Wolf, "Basin Photos Capture History," *Columbia Basin Herald*, March 2, 1981.
57. Dennis, "For Sam, the Bell Tolls"; Bill DeWitt, "Sam Israel Donates Bell as Token of Good Will," *Wenatchee World*, September 28, 1983.
58. Bonnie Holt Morehouse, email to the author, July 10, 2020.
59. Marina Romary, Sadis Filmworks Interview, June 13, 2012; Jack Patrick, Sadis Filmworks Interview, June 13, 2012; Eddie Hasson, author interview, August 2, 2018.
60. Kathy Nopson to Sam Israel, October 12, 1980, Samis Foundation Archives.
61. Eddie Hasson, author interview, August 2, 2018.
62. Dempsey, "The Howard Hughes of Washington State," July 1982 newspaper clipping; Eddie Hasson, author interview, August 2, 2018; Robert Hasson, Sadis Filmworks Interview, April 24, 2013; Duane Scheib, Sadis Filmworks Interview, June 13, 2012.
63. Robert Siler, "Making a Million, Israel Style," *Wenatchee World*, February 1989.
64. Eddie Hasson, author interview, August 28, 2018.
65. "Istanbul It's Not, but Bazaar Hopes to Grow," *Wenatchee World*, May 6, 1984; "Sam Israel Promoting Saturday Bazaar for Downtown Ephrata," *Columbia Basin Herald*, 1984.
66. Joe Dennis, "City, Israel Are Headed to Court Over Fire," *Grant County Journal*, March 20, 1986; Joe Dennis, "Homestead Barricades May Come Down Soon," *Grant County Journal*, October 26, 1987.
67. Eddie Hasson, author interview, August 28, 2018; Tracy Warner, "Walls Stay Up, Ephrata Drops Suit Against Sam Israel," *Wenatchee World*, February 5, 1988.
68. Unknown publication, August 8, 1958; Christian J. Miss et al., *The Smokian and Sam Israel Sites: Archaeological investigations in the Lower Grand Coulee* (Seattle: Northwest Archaeological Associates, 1997).
69. Ehud Netzer to Sam Israel, August 17, 1987, Samis Foundation Archives; Ehud Netzer, *Hasmonean and Herodian Palaces at Jericho*;

Final Reports of the 1973 Excavations (Jerusalem: Israel Exploration Society, Yad Ben-Zvi Press, 2013); Ehud Netzer *The Palaces of the Hasmoneans and Herod the Great* (Jerusalem: Israel Exploration Society, Yad Ben-Zvi Press, 2001).

70. Dr. Yossi Leshem, "Migrating Birds Know No Boundaries," email to the author, July 3, 2019.
71. Dr. Yossi Leshem, "Migrating Birds Know No Boundaries," email to the author, July 3, 2019.
72. Robert Hasson, Sadis Filmworks Interview, April 24, 2013.
73. ". . . Challenge for Scouts," source unknown, May 21, 1987; "Camp Israel," DVD, [1989?], Samis Foundation Archives; "Israel Invites Girls Too," *Wenatchee World*, February 10, 1989.
74. David Hasson, Sadis Filmworks Interview, April 24, 2013.
75. The ad appeared in the *Grant County Journal* on February 13, 1986.
76. Marina Romary, Sadis Filmworks Interview, June 13, 2012.
77. Marina Romary, Sadis Filmworks Interview, June 13, 2012; *Grant County Journal*, c. May 25 or 26, 1987.
78. Robert Siler, "Making a Million, Israel Style," *Wenatchee World*, February 1989; Stephen Maher, "Soap Lake Legacy," *Wenatchee World*, December 7, 1997.
79. "Scouts to Honor Sam Israel," *Grant County Journal*, February 6, 1989; "Israel Invites Girls Too," *Wenatchee World*, February 10, 1989; Robert Siler, "Sam Israel to Celebrate Birth by Giving Cash to Basin Scouts," *Wenatchee World*, February 9, 1989; Robert Siler, "Making a Million, Israel Style," *Wenatchee World*, February 1989.
80. Soap Lake School District 156 to Sam Israel, March 2, 1989, Samis Foundation Archives.

CHAPTER 6

1. Sam Israel to E. Michael Graham, MD, March 29, 1987, Samis Foundation Archives; Dr. Alex Sytman, email to the author, January 11, 2019.
2. Eddie Hasson, author interview, April 24, 2019.
3. Irwin Treiger to Sam Israel, August 1, 1988, Samis Foundation Archives; Sam Israel to Irwin Treiger, August 7, 1988, Samis Foundation Archives; Samis Land Company v. Municipality of Metropolitan Seattle, April 4, 1988; Samis Foundation Archives.

4. Eddie Hasson, author interview, September 6, 2018; Eddie Hasson, emails to the author; "Israel Hospitalized," *Columbia Basin Daily Herald*, [c. March 14, 1989].
5. Dr. Alex Sytman, email to the author, January 10, 2019.
6. Victor Hasson, Sadis Filmworks Interview, April 4, 2012; Samis Foundation draft Articles of Incorporation, Samis Foundation Archives.
7. Eddie Hasson, author interview, September 6, 2018, and October 1, 2018.
8. Victor Hasson, Sadis Filmworks Interview, April 4, 2012.
9. Eddie Hasson, author interview, October 1, 2018.
10. Eddie Hasson, Sadis Filmworks Interview, September 7, 2012; Jerome Cohen, email to the author, February 19, 2019.
11. Eddie Hasson, Sadis Filmworks Interview, September 7, 2012; Robert Hasson, author interview, March 23, 2020.
12. Eddie Hasson, author interview, September 6, 2018.
13. Eddie Hasson, author interview, September 6, 2018; Dana Behar, phone interview, July 17, 2019; Marilyn Hasson Henry, email to the author, August 31, 2019.
14. Eddie Hasson, author interview, October 1, 2018.
15. Eddie Hasson, author interview, October 1, 2018.
16. Eddie Hasson, author interview, December 12, 2018.
17. Eddie Hasson, author interview, December 12, 2018.
18. Report of Guardian Ad Litem, King County Superior Court, no. 90-4-032-30-0, August 23, 1990, Samis Foundation Archives.
19. Report of Guardian Ad Litem.
20. Julie Emery, "Well-Known, Rich Eccentric Ruled Incompetent; Guardian Appointed," *Seattle Times*, August 31, 1990.
21. Eddie Hasson, email to the author, January 24, 2019; Anderson, "Low-Rent Sam"; Louis Leclezio and Wendy L. Leclezio, husband and wife, Plaintiffs, v. Eddie Hasson, Guardian for Samuel Israel, No. 90-2-12620-0, July 5, 1991, Samis Foundation Archives.
22. Eddie Hasson, author interviews, 2018.
23. Eddie Hasson, Sadis Filmworks Interview, September 7, 2012; Eddie Hasson, author interviews, 2018.
24. *Clarion*, September 1991, Congregation Ezra Bessaroth Records, University of Washington Libraries, Special Collections; Eddie Hasson, author interview, May 31, 2018; "Dedication of the New Sefer Torah to Congregation Ezra Bessaroth by Mr. Sam Israel, Sunday, August 18, 1991, Elul 8, 5751," pamphlet, Samis Foundation

Archives; Isaac (Ike) Azose, phone interview and emails, August 22, 2019.

25. "Greek Festival," [1989], DVD, Samis Foundation Archives; "Flagpole Dedication," *Grant County Journal*, May 11, 1992.
26. Eddie Hasson, author interview, October 1, 2018; "Perspective in the Journal . . . People Watching at the Panayiri," *Grant County Journal*, May 28, 1992.
27. Victor Hasson, phone interview, August 1, 2019; Victor Hasson, Sadis Filmworks Interview, April 4, 2012.
28. Eddie Hasson, author interview, May 31, 2018; Cathy Reiner, "Sam Israel, 95, Owner of Many Seattle Buildings, Dies," *Seattle Times*, June 13, 1994.
29. Daisy Israel, Sadis Filmworks Interview, September 7, 2012.
30. Norman B. Rice to Bona Hasson, June 14, 1994, Samis Foundation Archives.
31. Reiner, "Sam Israel"; Sylvia Wieland Nogaki, "Israel's Empire to Remain Intact," *Seattle Times*, June 20, 1994; Craig Degginger, "Sam Israel Remembered as Shrewd Businessman, Community Benefactor," *Jewish Transcript*, June 24, 1994; Anderson, "Low-Rent Sam"; Craig Degginger, "Sam Israel's Legacy: The Samis Foundation," *Jewish Transcript*, June 24, 1994.
32. Eddie Hasson, author interview, September 6, 2018. The author extends appreciation to Rabbi Rob Toren for translation of the Hebrew text.
33. Eddie Hasson, Sadis Filmworks Interview, September 7, 2012.
34. Rita Calderon, Sadis Filmworks Interview, September 7, 2012; Irwin Treiger, Sadis Filmworks Interview, April 24, 2013; Rabbi Solomon Maimon, Sadis Filmworks Interview, June 23, 2014; Robert Hasson, Sadis Filmworks Interview, April 24, 2013.
35. Eddie Hasson, Sadis Filmworks Interview, September 7, 2012.
36. David Hasson, Sadis Filmworks Interview, April 24, 2013.

CHAPTER 7

1. Victor Hasson, phone interview, August 1, 2019.
2. Hazan Isaac (Ike) Azose, phone interview, August 6, 2019; Victor Hasson, phone interview, August 1, 2019.

EPILOGUE

1. Eddie Hasson, Sadis Filmworks Interview, September 7, 2012.
2. David Hasson, Sadis Filmworks Interview, April 24, 2013.
3. Eddie Hasson, author interview, May 31, 2018.
4. Al Maimon, email to the author, July 28, 2019.
5. Eddie Hasson to Jerome O. Cohen, February 17, 1993, and June 28, 1993, copies provided by Mr. Cohen.
6. Sam Israel's last will and testament, 1988, Samis Foundation Archives; Irwin Treiger, Sadis Filmworks Interview, April 24, 2013.
7. Eddie Hasson, email to the author, March 26, 2019; Eddie Hasson, author interview, September 6, 2018.
8. Jerome Cohen, email to the author, February 19, 2019; Barry Ernstoff, email to the author, February 11, 2019; Eli Genauer, email to the author, February 11, 2019; Victor Alhadeff, email to the author, February 18, 2019; Ernie Sherman, email to the author, February 11, 2019.
9. Victor Alhadeff, phone interview, July 14, 2019.
10. Eddie Hasson, email to the author, March 26, 2019; Eddie Hasson, author interview, September 6, 2018; Lucy Pruzan to the author, June 13, 2019.
11. Eli Almo, email to the author, February 18, 2019.
12. "Morris Piha," obituary, *Seattle Times*, May 15, 2013; David Azose, phone interview, July 29, 2019.
13. Memorandum, Martin Selig to File, June 28, 1987, courtesy of Mr. Selig.
14. Eddie Hasson, author interview, October 9, 2018.
15. "Samis Foundation Property Business Plan," University of Washington, Center for Community Development and Real Estate, November 27, 1995, revised January 25, 1996, Samis Foundation Archives.
16. Justen remained in the post through December 2010. Adam Hasson served as property manager until October 2012, when he was appointed director of real estate. Rob Toren served as grants director from 1997 to 2012, when he became executive director of the foundation.
17. Eddie Hasson, author interview, May 31, 2018; Harriet King, "In Seattle a Cobbler's Legacy Is Being Repaired," *New York Times*, August 13, 2000; Craig Degginger, "Samis Foundation Trustees Warn of Three-Year Wait before Money Flows," *Jewish Transcript*,

November 11, 1994; "CBD Market Enjoys Surge in Leasing," *Seattle Daily Journal of Commerce*, July 1, 1994; Randy Bracht, "Soap Lake Ponders Land Acquisition," *Grant County Journal*, October 10, 1994.

18. Mildred Tanner Andrews, ed., *Pioneer Square: Seattle's Oldest Neighborhood* (Seattle: Pioneer Square Community Association, 2005), 197–99.
19. Rob Toren, "Thoughts on Giving," *Jewish Action*, Fall 5766/2005, 27.
20. Al Maimon, phone interview, July 28, 2019. Information on the Samis Foundation today is compiled from various interviews, emails, and other data provided by the foundation.
21. Dr. Yossi Leshem, "Migrating Birds Know No Boundaries," email to the author, July 3, 2019; Yossi Leshem to Rob Toren, July 5, 1999, Samis Foundation Archives. Today, Dr. Leshem is professor emeritus of life sciences at Tel Aviv University, and he continues his five-decades-long involvement in bird conservation.
22. See Netzer, *Palaces of the Hasmoneans and Herod the Great*; and Netzer, *Hasmonean and Herodian Palaces*.
23. Eddie Hasson interview, November 15, 2000, Oral History Collection.

PHOTO CREDITS

All photos courtesy of Samis Foundation, except those listed below.
Dahms, Rick: viii, 186, © Rick Dahms.
Grant County Journal: 108, 136, 147.
Hasson, Aron: 177.
Hobbs, Richard S.: 170, 175, 176.
Israel, Samuel: 42, 66, 69 (top), 93, 94 (top-right), 96, 102, 106, 137, 141, 142, 145.
Naval History and Heritage Command: 18.
Puget Sound Regional Archives: 55, 59, 118 (bottom), 120, 125, 181.
Rhodes Jewish Historical Foundation: 10, 12, 16.
Scheib, Theresa Bennett: 138, courtesy of Theresa Bennett Scheib.
Schmidt, Micah: 167.
Seattle Times: 5.
Sytman, Dr. Alex: xiii
Washington State Jewish Historical Society: 165.

BIBLIOGRAPHY

ARCHIVES AND SPECIAL COLLECTIONS

Interviews, Emails, and Miscellaneous
    Alhadeff, Victor
    Almo, Eli
    Azose, David
    Azose, Isaac (Ike)
    Behar, Dana
    Cohen, Jerome O.
    Ernstoff, Barry
    Genauer, Eli
    Hamann, Jack
    Hasson, Adam
    Hasson, Aron
    Hasson, Eddie
    Hasson, Robert
    Hasson, Victor
    Henry, Marilyn Hasson
    Kucera, Greg
    Leshem, Yossi
    Maimon, Al
    Naar, Devin
    Normand, Eugene
    Pruzan, Lucy
    Roer, Greg
    Selig, Martin
    Sherman, Ernie
    Sytman, Alex
    Toren, Rob
    Treiger, Karen

Sadis Filmworks Interviews:
    Calderon, Rita
    Hasson, David
    Hasson, Eddie
    Hasson, Robert
    Hasson, Victor
    Israel, Daisy
    Maimon, Rabbi Solomon
    Patrick, Jack
    Romary, Marina
    Scheib, Duane
    Treiger, Irwin

Broderick, Henry. Papers. University of Washington Libraries, Special Collections.
Congregation Ezra Bessaroth Records. University of Washington Libraries, Special Collections.
Mountaineers Club Records. University of Washington Libraries, Special Collections.

Oral History Collection. Washington State Jewish Archives. University of Washington Libraries, Special Collections.
Samis Foundation Archives. Seattle, Washington.
Washington State Archives. Central Regional Branch. Central Washington University.

BOOKS AND OTHER PUBLISHED WORKS

Amato, Norman. *Ladino Sayings My Father Taught Me.* San Bernadino, CA: Norman Amato, 2018.
Andrews, Mildred Tanner, ed. *Pioneer Square: Seattle's Oldest Neighborhood.* Seattle: Pioneer Square Community Association, 2005.
Angel, Rabbi Marc, ed. *Exploring Sephardic Customs and Traditions.* Brooklyn: KTAV, 2017.
———. *Foundations of Sephardic Spirituality: The Inner Life of Jews of the Ottoman Empire.* Nashville: Jewish Lights, 2006.
———. *The Jews of Rhodes.* New York: Sepher-Hermon Press, 1978, rev. ed. 1998.
Broderick, Henry. *The HB Story: Henry Broderick Relates Seattle's Yesterdays, with Some Other Thoughts by the Way.* Seattle: F. McCaffrey, 1969.
Charles River Editors. *Rhodes: The History and Legacy of the Greek Island from Ancient Times to Today.* [No publication information available.]
Cone, Molly, Howard Droker, and Jacqueline Williams. *Family of Strangers: Building a Jewish Community in Washington State.* Seattle: Washington State Jewish Historical Society, 2003.
Danz, Carolee, with David Wilma. *Shards of Light: Seattle's Jewish Family Service, 1892–2012.* Bothell, WA: Book Publishers Network, 2015.
Eisenberg, Ellen, Ava Kahn, and William Toll. *Jews of the Pacific Coast.* Seattle: University of Washington Press, 2010.
Evans, Mike. *Christopher Columbus, Secret Jew.* Phoenix: TimeWorthy Books, 2014.
Ezra Bessaroth: The Story of a Sephardic Congregation. Seattle: Ezra Bessaroth, 2016.
Flash, Clare Barkey. *A Hug from Afar.* Edited and compiled by Cynthia Flash Hemphill. Bellevue, WA: Flash Media Services, 2016.
Franco, Hizkia M. *The Jewish Martyrs of Rhodes and Cos.* Zimbabwe: HarperCollins, 1994.
Frankl, Victor E. *Man's Search for Meaning.* Boston: Beacon Press, 1959; 2006.

Hasson, Aron. *A Guidebook to the Jewish Quarter of Rhodes.* Los Angeles: Rhodes Jewish Historical Foundation, 2012.

Hasson, Louise. *Poems.* Publisher unknown, 2011.

Hasson-Berro, Sylvia. *The Story of a Survivor: The Memoirs of Sylvia Hasson-Berro.* Privately published, 2004.

Menascé, Esther Fintz. *A History of Jewish Rhodes.* Los Angeles: Rhodes Jewish Historical Foundation, 2014.

Miss, Christian J., et al. *The Smokian and Sam Israel Sites: Archaeological Investigations in the Lower Grand Coulee.* Seattle: Northwest Archaeological Associates, 1997.

Netzer, Ehud. *Hasmonean and Herodian Palaces at Jericho; Final Reports of the 1973 Excavations.* Jerusalem: Israel Exploration Society, Yad Ben-Zvi Press, 2013.

———. *The Palaces of the Hasmoneans and Herod the Great.* Jerusalem: Israel Exploration Society, Yad Ben-Zvi Press, 2001.

Polk's Seattle City Directory.

Sadis, Stephen, dir. *The Sephardic Jews and the Pike Place Market.* Sadis Filmworks, 2001. DVD.

Shachar, Nathan. *The Lost Worlds of Rhodes: Greeks, Italians, Jews, and Turks between Tradition and Modernity.* Brighton: Sussex Academic Press, 2013.

Sono, Masayuki. "The Second Transformation: Intervention to the Drexel Hotel—The Last Pre-fire Building in Downtown Seattle." Master's thesis, University of Washington, Seattle, 1996.

Treiger, Karen I. *My Soul Is Filled with Joy: A Holocaust Story.* Seattle: Stare Lipki Press, 2018.

Wiesenthal, Simon. *Sails of Hope; The Secret Mission of Christopher Columbus.* Translated by Richard and Clara Winston. New York: Macmillan, 1973.

ARTICLES

Angel, Marc. "Progress—Seattle's Sephardic Monthly, 1934–1935." *American Sephardi* 5 (1971): 90–95.

———. "The Sephardim of the United States; An Exploratory Study." *American Jewish Yearbook* 74 (1973): 77–138.

Alhadeff, Emily K. "The Legend of Sam Israel." *Jewish in Seattle Magazine*, August 1, 2016.

Anderson, Rick. "Low-Rent Sam." *Seattle Weekly*, July 6, 1994.

Anderson, Ross. "Awash in Hope—Decades Ago Soap Lake Attracted Believers Who Thought Its Soft, Salty Waters Were Therapeutic. Can the Town Now Lure Crowds of Aging Boomers?" *Seattle Times*, November 9, 1997.

"Basin Boy Scouts Gather for Camporee." [unknown publication; no date].

Bond, Jeff. "Sam Israel's Legacy." *Washington CEO*, November 1997.

Boyer, Tom. "From Vice to Nice." *Seattle Times*, January 19, 2006.

Bracht, Randy. "Soap Lake Ponders Land Acquisition." *Grant County Journal*, October 10, 1994.

Broberg, Brad. "Developing Character." *Puget Sound Business Journal*, December 6–12, 2002.

Cantwell, Brian J. "Go for the Mud (and More) at Soap Lake." *Seattle Times*, August 17, 2013.

Carroll, Michael. "Gatewood Hotel; Mr. Israel Very Cooperative in Working out the Details." [unknown publication; no date].

". . . Challenge for Scouts." [unknown publication], May 21, 1987.

Clever, Dick. "First Avenue Hotel Caught in Open-Shut Tug of War." *Seattle Times*, April 13, 1985.

Cohen, Todd. "No Verdict Yet in Trespass Trial of 16 Over Gatewood Occupation." *Seattle Times*, July 17, 1988.

Columbia Basin Daily Herald. "Israel Hospitalized." [c. March 14, 1989].

———. "Millionaire Sam Israel." N.d.

———. "Sam Israel Promoting Saturday Bazaar for Downtown Ephrata." 1984.

Columbia Basin Herald (Moses Lake, WA). "Sam Israel Says State Can Use His Basin Land." August 25, 1982.

Conklin, Ellis. "The Local Soaps; In Search of the Cure at Soap Lake." *Puget Sound Journey*, May–June 1998.

Degginger, Craig. "Samis Foundation Trustees Warn of Three-Year Wait before Money Flows." *Jewish Transcript*, November 11, 1994.

———. "Sam Israel Remembered as Shrewd Businessman, Community Benefactor." *Jewish Transcript*, June 24, 1994.

———. "Sam Israel's Legacy: The Samis Foundation." *Jewish Transcript*, June 24, 1994.

Dennis, Joe. "City, Israel Are Headed to Court Over Fire." *Grant County Journal*, March 20, 1986.

———. "For Sam, the Bell Tolls," *Grant County Journal*, June 20, 1994.

———. "Homestead Barricades May Come Down Soon." *Grant County Journal*, October 26, 1987.

DeWitt, Bill. "Sam Israel Donates Bell as Token of Good Will." *Wenatchee World*, September 28, 1983.

———. "Sam Israel Offers Lake . . . and Advice." *Wenatchee World*, April 1, 1984.

Dorpat, Paul. "An Art-full Restoration." *Seattle Times Magazine*, January 26, 2003.

———. "Highs and Lows of the Butler." *Pacific NW Magazine*, n.d.

Emery, Julie. "Well-Known, Rich Eccentric Ruled Incompetent; Guardian Appointed." *Seattle Times*, August 31, 1990.

Emery, Julie, and Richard Seven. "Court Ruling Leaves Millionaire's Property in Limbo." *Seattle Times*, September 1, 1990.

Enlow, Clair. "Gatewood Hotel to House the Homeless." *Seattle Daily Journal of Commerce*, April 22, [1991?].

Epes, James. "Smith Tower May Be Sold to Big Pioneer Square Landlord." *Puget Sound Business Journal*, October 18–24, 1996.

Farbiarz, Rachel. "Becoming Every Brother's Keeper." https://www.myjewishlearning.com/article/becoming-every-brothers-keeper/.

———. "Sam Israel to Celebrate Birth by Giving Cash to Basin Scouts." *Wenatchee World*, n.d.

Gavin, Robert, and Jim Carlton. "Prosperity Planning Helped Save Seattle." *Wall Street Journal*, March 2, 2001.

Gelernter, Carey Quan. "Landlord Sam, a Prince of Parcels." *Seattle Times*, July 13, 1981.

———. "Samuel Israel, Eccentric and a Loner; His Holdings Make Him an Important Man Here." *Seattle Times*, July 13, 1981.

———. "Samuel Israel, Soap Lake Recluse Has Place in Seattle's Future." *Seattle Times*, July 13, 1981.

———. "Who 'Owns' Seattle? A Soap Lake Recluse with Old World Notions Hangs On to Much of It." *Seattle Times*, July 13, 1981.

Godes, Kerry. "Nephews Take Over Sam Israel Empire." *Seattle Post-Intelligencer*, n.d.

Grant County Journal. "Flagpole Dedication." May 11, 1992.

———. "Home for Aged Honors Sam Israel." June 5, 1972.

———. "Perspective in the Journal . . . People Watching at the Panayiri." May 28, 1992.

———. "Scouts to Honor Sam Israel." February 6, 1989.

———. "Why Pollution? Who Am I Fighting?" March 25, 1971.

"Greek Festival . . ." [unknown publication], 1987.

Hasson, A. "The Sephardic Jews of Rhodes in Los Angeles." *Western States Jewish Historical Quarterly*, 1974.

Henry, Mary T. "Israel, Samuel (1899–1994)." HistoryLink.org, February 5, 2010. https://www.historylink.org/File/9307.

Higgins, Mark. "From Smith Tower to Lesser Lights, Samis Plans to Upgrade Its Buildings." *Seattle PI.com*, [June 25, 2000?].

Jago, Jill. "Renovations Bring Boom Times Back to Pioneer Square." *Seattle Daily Journal of Commerce*, October 12, 2000.

Johnson, Art. "Sam Israel; Fight's Not Over." *Columbia Basin Daily Herald*, May 4, 1977.

Kanter, Connie. "What Does Being Jewish Mean to You?" *Jewish in Seattle*, March 21, 2018.

Kaufman, Jonathan. "Finding Center: Many of American's Jews Are Reasserting Their Faith." *Wall Street Journal*, August 10, 2000.

Keene, Linda. "Death Did Its Part." *Seattle Times*, July 14, 1996.

———. "Stubborn Land Mogul's Legacy: A Nicer Downtown." *Seattle Times*, July 3, 1996.

Kerr, Charles. "Basin Land Inclusion Protested." *Wenatchee World*, n.d.

King, Harriet. "In Seattle a Cobbler's Legacy Is Being Repaired." *New York Times*, August 13, 2000.

"Late Tycoon's Land Might Revive Soap Lake Resort Town." *Eastside Journal*, December 9, 1997.

Lear, Jason. "Column of Many Orders . . . Renewal a la Samis . . ." [unknown publication; no date].

Lynch, Frank. "Seattle Scene: The Shattered Dream of a Mighty Hunter." *Seattle Post-Intelligencer*, 1961.

Maher, Stephen. "Soap Lake Legacy." *Wenatchee World*, December 7, 1997.

Moody, Dick. "More to Sam Israel Than Meets the Ear." *Columbia Daily Herald*, n.d.

———. "Siphon Project Now Official!" *Columbia Daily Herald*, August 27, 1976.

Nabbefeld, Joe. "Sam Israel's Once Seedy Empire Is Going Upscale." *Puget Sound Business Journal*, n.d.

Nogaki, Sylvia W. "Israel's Empire to Remain Intact." *Seattle Times*, June 20, 1994.

Oregonian. "Trustee for Land Mogul Envisions Grand Upgrades." July 6, 1996.

Pacific NW Magazine. "Immigrant's Dream." *Seattle Times*, April 11, 1999.

Pike, Rose. "Blocks That Blight." *Seattle Weekly*, September 26, 1990.

Puget Sound Business Journal. "Heard & Overheard . . . Towering View." November 5–11, 1999.

———. "Newsmakers of 1997 . . . William Justen." December 26, 1997–January 1, 1998.

Pulkkinen, Levi. "What You Didn't Know about Seattle's Pioneer Square: 23 Strange Stories from the City's Oldest Neighborhood." *Seattle Post-Intelligencer*, December 12, 2017.

Reiner, Cathy. "Sam Israel, 95, Owner of Many Seattle Buildings, Dies." *Seattle Times*, June 13, 1994.

Ross, Lesli Koppelman. "The Importance of Remembering." https://www.myjewishlearning.com/article/the-importance-of-remembering/.

"Samis Acquires Smith Tower as Part of Pioneer Square Redevelopment." [unknown publication], November 8, 1996.

"Samis Ranch Buys Registered Herefords." [unknown publication], c. April 14, 1958.

Savelle, Jon. "Justen to Manage Samis Land." *Seattle Daily Journal of Commerce*, n.d.

———. "Samis to Rehab All of Its Properties." *Seattle Daily Journal of Commerce*, October 29, 1996.

Scott, Maude. "County May Buy Smith Tower." *Seattle Daily Journal of Commerce*, October 21, 1996.

———. "Israel vs. Seattle; Israel Beats City Tax." *Seattle Daily Journal of Commerce*, February 12, 1988.

———. "It's a New Day for the Samis Foundation." *Seattle Daily Journal of Commerce*, February 28, 1997.

"Scouting Relays." [unknown publication; no date].

"Scouts Gather." [unknown publication; no date].

Seattle Daily Journal of Commerce. "CBD Market Enjoys Surge in Leasing." July 1, 1994.

———. "Samis." February 22, 2001.

Seattle Post-Intelligencer. "3 Shoe Repair Shops Face OPA Charges." June 17, 1942.

———. "12,000 Lbs. of Rubber Heels Turned In." June 17, 1942.

———. "City Sues to Reopen Low-Income Hotel." September 30, 1986.

———. "Court Testimony Gives Rare View of Real Estate King." May 28, 1987.

———. "Nephews Take Over Sam Israel Empire." September 1, 1990.

———. "Protesters Tussle Over Helping the Homeless." January 4, 1988.

———. "Resort May Rise from Soap Lake Ranch." December 12, 1997.

———. "Sam Israel Colorful Landowner Dies." June 14, 1994.

———. "Tunnel Tax Idea Hits 3 Big Snags." June 27, 1987.

Seattle Times. "Besieged Building Is Target of Lawsuit; City Acted 16 Months before Homeless Did." January 5, 1988.

———. "First Ave. Hotel Caught in Open-Shut Tug of War." April 13, 1985.

Seattle Times Magazine. "It's the Water." November 9, 1997.

Seattle Weekly. "Bleak Houses; Callous Landlords and Poorly Enforced Laws Make Life Miserable for Many Tenants in Seattle's Low-Income Housing; Here's How 6 Landlords Play Ball." November 9, 1988.

———. "Slumlord or Savior? The Death Last Month of Sam Israel, Seattle's Least-Understood Landlord, Opens New Possibilities for the Future of Downtown." July 6, 1994.

———. "Stranded Again; A Guerilla in the Homeless Cause, but Bob Willmott and His Strand Helpers Never Give Up Their Mobile Mission." January 13, 1988.

Seven, Richard. "The Collector—For Decades Sam Israel Bought Cheap and Never Sold; Today His Legacy Means Change for Seattle." *Seattle Times Magazine*, April 11, 1999.

Shapiro, Nina. "Samis' Sweetheart." *Seattle Weekly*, May 10, 2000.

Siler, Robert. "Sam Israel to Celebrate Birth by Giving Cash to Basin Scouts." *Wenatchee World*, February 9, 1989.

———. "Making a Million, Israel Style." *Wenatchee World*, February 1989.

Spokesman Review. "Millionaire 91 Now Has Guardian." September 1, 1980.

Toren, Rob. "Thoughts on Giving." *Jewish Action*, Fall 5766/2005, pp. 24–27.

Warner, Tracy. "Israel Land Withdrawal from Basin Is Denied." *Wenatchee World*, [c. 1977].

———. "Sam Israel Battles the Rules." *Wenatchee World*, May 16, 1977.

———. "Walls Stay Up, Ephrata Drops Suit against Sam Israel." *Wenatchee World*, February 5, 1988.

Watson, Emmett. "Sam Israel Can't Take It with Him; There's Simply Too Much." *Seattle Times*, June 22, 1989.

Wenatchee World. "Basin Festival Queen Named." May 12, 1952.

———. "Israel Invites Girls Too." February 10, 1989.

———. "Istanbul It's Not, but Bazaar Hopes to Grow." May 6, 1984.

Wolf, Nancy. "Basin Photos Capture History." *Columbia Basin Herald*, March 2, 1981.

WEBSITES

Congregation Ezra Bessaroth, http://www.ezrabessaroth.net.
Rhodes Jewish Museum, http://www.rhodesjewishmuseum.org.
Samis Foundation, http://samisfoundation.org.

INDEX

Page numbers in *italics* indicate illustrations.

Acropolis, 84–85, 101
Agnew, Henry, 72
Alaskan Way Viaduct, 35, 71–72
Alhadeff, David, 73
Alhadeff, Nessim, 28
Alhadeff, Sarah Israel (niece), 24, 38, *41*, 48, 56, 60, 72–73
Alhadeff, Susie, *178*
Alhadeff, Victor, *viii*, 121–23, *178*, 182–83, 185, *186*, 206
Alliance Israélite Universelle, *16*, 16–17, 102
Almo, Eli, *viii*, *178*, 183, 185, *186*, 206
Almo, Rebecca, *178*
Amiel, Amy, 189
Amiel, Sam, 174
Anderson, Ralph, 117
Anderson, Rick, 167
Angel, Rabbi Marc, 65
Angel, Trudy, 180
anti-Semitism and persecution, 3, 11, 33, 64, 112, 129, 139
archaeology, x, 143–45, 177, *192*, 193
Armistead, Ray, 128
Army Building, *55*, 55–56, 59, 76, 199, 203
Aronson, Henry M., 125
Audley, Henry R., 33
Auschwitz, 64–66
Austin A. Bell Building, 35, *35*, 50, 202
Azose, David, *viii*, *178*, 184, *186*, 206
Azose, Isaac "Ike," 164, *164*, 174
Azose, Sarah (great-niece), *94*
Azose, Terry, *178*

Bahat, Ofer, *192*, 193
Banks, Gail H., 160, 161
Behar, Dana (great-nephew), 39, 84, 92, 95, 99, 158, *186*, 206
Behar, David J., 44
Behar, Norman, *164*
Benaroya, Jack, 62
Benaroya Hall, 109, 122
Benezra, Joe, *42*
Benezra, Mr. & Mrs. Sam, *42*
Benson, George E., 117
Bensussen, Esther, 24
Beverly, Washington, 133
Bikur Cholim-Machzikay Hadath, 163

bird conservation, 144–45, 192–93
Biton, Jacob (grandfather), 15, 24
Biton, Rabbi, 163
Blue and White Building, Ephrata, *142*, 142–43
Blumenthal Building (Scientific Building), 59, *59*, 76, 203
Bogle & Gates, 107, 124–25
Bontius, I. C., 73
Bontius Building, 73
Boy Scouts, *xi*, 5, *70*, *145*, 145–46, *146*, *148*, 149, 177
Brindley, Ralph, 127
Broderick, Henry "HB," 33–34, 59, 60, 113
Broderick Building, 124–25, *125*, 150, 205
Burgett, George, 32
Butler Block, 124–25, 151, *188*, 205
Butler Garage, 118, 151, 187, *188*, 205

Calderon, Jack, 48–49
Calderon, Marlene, 183–84
Calderon, Rita Israel (niece), 20–21, 24, *41*, 43, 48–49, 66, 102, 168, 183
Calvo, Solomon, 28
Camp Israel, 146, *146*
Cannon, Linda, 121
Capeluto, Jewel, *164*
Capeluto, Morrie, *164*
Capouya, Rahamin family, 7, 22, 27
Capuano, Mazaltov (grandmother), 15, 24
Caroline Kline Galland Home. *See* Kline Galland Home
Carroll, Michael, 133
Cascade Market, *xiii*, 35–36, 50, 61, 63, 202
Catholic Seamen's Club, 72, 214n42
Chin, Que, 68
Cohen, Jerome "Jerry" O., *viii*, *164*, *178*, 182, 185, *186*, 189, 206
Collins Building, 77, 187, *188*, 204
Columbia Basin Water Festival, 73
Columbia Pacific Industries, 124–25
Columbus, Christopher, 103
concentration camps, 64, 65
Congregation Ezra Bessaroth
    Greenberg as rabbi, 99, 182
    Isaac Azose as hazan, 174
    Ladies Auxiliary, 63
    Sam Israel's donations, 108
    Sefer Torah, 161–64, *162*, *164*
    Sephardic Adventure Camp, 110

synagogue building, 30
weddings, 40, *42*, 44
Corona Hotel, *118,* 118–19, 150, 187, 204

Dane, John, 33
Dempsey, Candace, 127
Destitute (Sam Israel photograph), 68–69, *69,* 78, 79, 214n34
Diamond, Joe, 71, 72
Doldrums (Sam Israel photograph), 78
Douglas County, 113, 185
Douglas Hotel, 35, 50, 202
Drexel Hotel, 59, 76, 203
Drittenbas, Harry, 136
Ducks Unlimited, 137

Ellenhorn, David A., *186,* 206
environmental concerns, 5, 135–38, *136, 192,* 192–93
Ephrata, 3, 5, 133-34, 138-39, 141-43, 148-49, 164-65, 194
Epstein, Maurice, 161
Erlitz, Maria, *186,* 206
Ernstoff, Barry, *viii,* 109, 182, 185, *186,* 206
Evergreen Camera Club, 68, 79

Fetterman, Paul, 113
Filley, Robert, 185
Flying with the Birds (Leshem and Bahat), *192,* 193
Forest Hotel, 124–25, 151, 187, 205
Fox, Norman E., sketch by, *35*
Franco, Marie, 7–8, 20–21, 24, 27–29, *41*
Friedenberg, David, *viii,* 182, 185
Friedman, Edwin J., 212n46

Galante, Reina, 24, *41*
Galland Building, 77, *120,* 121–23, 204
Gallery Frames, 120
Gatewood Hotel, *126,* 126–33, 150, 156, 183, 205
Gelernter, Carey Quan, 127
Genauer, Eli, *viii,* 185, *186,* 206
Girl Scouts, 5, 146, 148, 177
Gold, Anna, *166*
Gortler, Josh, 110
Graham, E. Michael, 153
Grand Coulee Cavalcade, 73
Grant County, 4, 5, 73, 86, 90, 102, 127, 134–40, *136,* 142, 194. *See also* Ephrata; Soap Lake
Grant County Historical Museum, 157
Great Depression, 34–35, 48, 53–54
Greek Festival, Soap Lake, 146, *147,* 147–48, *148,* 165, *165*
Greenberg, Rabbi William H., *viii,* 99, 182, 185

Greg Kucera Gallery, 118–20
Guy F. Atkinson Construction, 135

Haggadah, 64, 166
Hamann, Jack, 128–32
Hanan, Julia, 47–48, *49,* 72, 159, 212n46
Hanan, Leatrice, 48
Hanan, Matilda, 47, 48
Hanan, Morris, 47, 48, 212n46
Hartford Building, 76, 118, *118,* 203
Hasson, Adam (great-nephew), 60, 92, *93,* 95, *95,* 115, 166, 186, *186,* 189, 224n16
Hasson, Albert, 12, *44,* 65, *93, 104*
 background, 37
 Cascade Market, 35, 63
 death, 105–6
 marriage and children, 25, 43, 61–62, *63*
 Seattle homes, 34, 43, 61–62
 Soap Lake farm, 83, *83,* 92, 100
Hasson, Albie (great-nephew), 92, *93, 97*
Hasson, Bona. *See* Israel, Bulisa "Bona"
Hasson, Bonnie (great-niece), 92, *96*
Hasson, David (nephew), *169*
 childhood homes, 62
 family, 25
 property management, 115, 117, 119, 133, 179–80, 186, 189
 Sam Israel, 40, 60, 69, 72, 85, 113, 117, 146, 168
 Sam Israel's headstone, 167
 Sam Israel's later life, 158, 160, 161, 165, *173,* 179–80
 Samis Foundation, 189
 Soap Lake farm visits, 95, *96*
Hasson, Eddie (nephew), *169*
 anti-Semitism, 139
 arranged marriages, 43
 Aunt Sylvia, 65–66, 213n28
 Blue and White Building, 143
 Cascade Market, 36
 childhood homes, 62, 154
 Dick Tall affair, 125
 Ephrata Saturday Bazar, 141, *141*
 family, 25
 family relations, 38, 66, 92, 114
 family's religious observance, 3, 38–39, 63, 64
 Gatewood Hotel, 127–28, 132, 133
 grandparents, 36, 37, 62
 interviews, xii
 Mercer Island house, 45, 47, 63
 mother as violin teacher, 62–63
 Sam Israel as man about town, 40
 Sam Israel's correspondence, xii
 Sam Israel's finances, 4, 31, 58, 140, 218n19
 Sam Israel's guardian, 133, 180
 Sam Israel's headstone, 167–68

INDEX

Sam Israel's hobbies and interests, 42, 67, 90, 102, 103, 156
Sam Israel's immigration, 27, 31
Sam Israel's Jewish cemetery plans, 155–56
Sam Israel's later life, 140, 154–60, 164, *164*, 165, 179–80
Sam Israel's legacy, 168
Sam Israel's philanthropy, 5, 109, 126
Sam Israel's property holdings, 32–34, 59, 61, 71, 115, 117–18, 160
Sam Israel's relationship with Julia Hanan, 47, 48
Samis Foundation, *viii*, 107, 108, 179–81, 183–85, *186*, 189, 193, 207
Samis Land Company, 179–80
Soap Lake farm, 74, 82, 83, 84, 86–87
Soap Lake farm visits, 92, *93*, 95, 97, 140, *157*, 174–75, *175*
State Department of Fish and Game property, *137*
Hasson, Joey (great-nephew), 92, *93*, *97*, *141*
Hasson, Louise, 92, 98–99
Hasson, Marguerite, 92, *93*, *97*, 141, *141*, *152*, *166*, 183
Hasson, Marilyn (niece). *See* Henry, Marilyn Hasson
Hasson, Michele, 92, *96*
Hasson, Randy (great-nephew), 92, *93*, *97*, *164*, *166*
Hasson, Robert (nephew), *169*
  Boy Scouts, *70*, 145–46
  childhood homes, 62
  family, 25
  family relations, 38, 66
  Grace McWhirter, 71
  grandparents, 62, 66
  Holocaust, 65
  in Israel, 100
  relationship with Sam Israel, 38
  Sam Israel's fear of enemies, 140
  Sam Israel's finances, 58, 72, 218n19
  Sam Israel's girlfriends, 67
  Sam Israel's hunting philosophy, 69–70
  Sam Israel's later life, 155, 156–58, *164*, 165, 166, *173*
  Sam Israel's legacy, 168
  Sam Israel's Mercer Island house, 45, 70, *70*
  Sam Israel's musicianship, 43
  Sam Israel's shoemaking career, 31
  Samis Foundation, 181
  Samis Hereford Ranch, 87–88
  Soap Lake farm visits, 92, 95, *95*, 97–98
  as violinist, 62–64
Hasson, Sara (great-niece), 92, *95*
Hasson, Tama (great-niece), 92, *96*

Hasson, Victor (nephew), *169*
  childhood homes, 62
  family, 25
  father's death, 105–6
  grandparents, 36
  in Israel, 91, 100
  Rhodes visit, 173–74
  Sam Israel, 18, 85, 144, 155, 156
  Sam Israel's later life, 165–66
  Sefer Torah, 161, 163, 164
  Soap Lake farm visits, 92, 95, 97, 106, *106*
Hasson-Berro, Sylvia, 12, 65–66, 213n28
Hebrew University of Jerusalem, *80*, 100, 103, 106, 144, 188, 193
Henry, Bobby, *166*
Henry, Marilyn Hasson (niece), 25, 37, 62, 92, *94*, 115, 158
Henry, Mira, (great-niece) *166*
Henry, Risha,(great-niece) *166*
Henry Broderick Inc., 33–34
Herodium, 144, 193
historic preservation, 1, 117, 187
Holocaust, xi, 12, 64–66, 102, 174, 177
homeless, 126, 127–28
Homestead Building. *See* Blue and White Building
Horrigan, James, 33–34, 113, 217n3
hunting, *137*, 137–38, 156

Internal Revenue Service (IRS), 72, 124
Israel
  archaeology, 144, *192*, 193
  bird conservation, 144–45, *192*, 192–93
  Sam Israel's love of, 3, 4, 102–3
  Sam Israel's philanthropy, 87, 100, 106
  Sam Israel's trip to, 99–103, *101*
  Samis Foundation grants, 191–93
Israel, Asher "John" (brother)
  birth and childhood, *6*, *14*, 15, 25
  character traits, 115
  death, 25, 153
  education and language skills, 36
  emigration to US, 8, 28
  family gatherings, *41*, *104*
  marriage and children, 25, 44
  property management, 114–15
  relationship with Sam Israel, 114–15
  Samis Land Company, 60
  Seattle homes, 29
  shoe repair business, *26*, 34, 35, 36, 61, 114
  Soap Lake farm visits, 92, *93*
Israel, Beverly (niece), 25
Israel, Bulisa "Bona" (sister)
  Albert and Sam, *44*
  birth and childhood, *6*, *14*, 15, 25
  death, 25

INDEX

education and language skills, 36
emigration to US, 8, 28
Ephrata Saturday Bazar, 141, *141*
family gatherings, *41, 42, 104, 166*
husband (*see* Hasson, Albert)
marriage and children, 25, 43, 61–63
relationship with Sam Israel, 38, 61–64, 83, 92, 95, 97, 106, *152*, 153–55, 158, *164*, 165, 218n19
Rhodesli traditions, 63
Sam Israel's death, 167
Seattle homes, 29, 34, 43, 61–62
Soap Lake farm, 83, *83*, 92, *93*, 95, *96*, 100
US citizenship, 62
as violinist, 43, 62–63
war effort, 63
widowhood, 106
Israel, Bulisa (grandmother), 15, 24
Israel, Daisy (niece)
family, 25
family relations, 38
grandparents, 36, 44
immigration, 21
Israel family home, 29
marriage, 182
Sam Israel, 27, 40, 109, 166–67
Soap Lake Farm visits, *94*
Israel, David (brother)
birth, 15, 24
character traits, 38
death, 24, 105
emigration to US, 7–8, 20–21, 27
family gatherings, *41*
marriage and children, 7, 20–21, 24
patriotism, 39
Sam Israel's immigration, 28
Seattle employment, 31
Seattle home, 29
shoe repair business, 32, 34, 35, 36
Israel, David (grandfather), 24
Israel, Emily (niece), 24
Israel, Gentil, (Gentil Levy) 25, 40, *41, 42*, 66, *104*
Israel, Grace (niece), 24
Israel, Irving (nephew), 25, 87–88
Israel, Isaac (nephew), 24, 29, *41*
Israel, Jack (nephew), 24, 38
Israel, Jacob "Jack" (brother)
birth, 15, 24
character traits, 38
death, 24, 92
emigration to US, 7–8, 20–21, 27
family gatherings, *41*
marriage and children, 24
Sam Israel's immigration, 28
Seattle employment, 31
Seattle homes, 29

shoe repair business, 32, 34, 35
Israel, Juliette, (Juliette Levy) 25, 44, *105*, 115
Israel, Leon (nephew), 25
Israel, Lucille (niece), 25
Israel, Marie Franco, 7–8, 20–21, 24, 27, 28, 29, *41*
Israel, Michael "Mike," *viii, 94*, 182, 185
Israel, Nissim (brother)
birth and childhood, *6, 14*, 15, 25
Cascade Market, 35–36, 61
character traits, 38
death, 25, 105
emigration to US, 8, 28
family gatherings, *41, 104*
marriage and children, 25, 44
Morris and Gentil's wedding, *42*
relationship with mother, 66
Seattle employment, 32
Seattle homes, 29
Soap Lake farm visits, 92, *93*
Israel, Rachel (niece), 24
Israel, Raye, (niece) 24, *41*
Israel, Robert (nephew), 25, *41*, 48
Israel, Rose Lee (niece), 25
Israel, Rosie (friend), 69
Israel, Sallie (niece), 25
Israel, Samuel "Sam," *xvi, xviii*
awards and accolades, *108*, 121, *146*, 146–48, *147*, 149, 164–65
birth and childhood, 2, *6*, 9–19, *14, 20*, 91–92
birth date, 13, 15, 21–22, 24, 92, 209n6
birthday celebrations, *xi*, 5, *146*, 146–47, *148*, 148–49, *173*
Boy Scouts, *xi*, 5, *70, 145*, 145–46, *146, 148*
brother's keeper, 32, 35–36, 38, 139
as cantankerous and difficult, xii, 1, 3, 4, 115–17, 122–23
clothing and appearance, *iv*, 4, *29*, 40, 91–92
controlling, 38, 64, 92, 97–99, 110, 114, 122–23
death, 3, 24, 166–68, *167*
devotion to family, 2, 4–5
documents and letters, xii, *xvii*, 217n3
dogs, 38, 73, *73, 83*, 90, 127, 157
education, 16, 48
emigration to US, 2, *2, 5*, 7–8, *8, 21*, 21–22, *22, 23*, 27–28
in Ephrata, *138*, 139
family and relations in Seattle, 27–30, 36–39, *41, 44*, 61–62, 63–64, 66, *104*
family background, 2, 24–25
finances, 4, 5, 113, 140, 218n19
generosity, 3, 4–5, 55, *57*, 57–58

INDEX

health concerns, 105–6, 133, 153–55, 158–61, 165
hobbies, 12, 40, 42, 43, *43*, 62, 67, 69, 71
honesty, 3, 4, 123, 133
hunting, 69–70, *89*, 89–90, *90*
language skills, 11, 36
later life, *104*, 140, 149, *152*, 152–66, *166*, 172, 183–85
leaving home, 19–23
legacy, 167, 168, 173, 175, 177
love life, 47–49, 67, 127, 159, 172
love of Israel, 3, 4
as man about town, 39–44
nicknames and appellations, 1, 3, 89
patriotism, 3, 55, *57*, 57–58
personal safety concerns, 140
philanthropy, 103, 108–11
relationship with his brothers, 92, 114–15
relationship with his mother, 66
relationship with nephews and nieces, 48–49, 63, *70*, 95, 97
religious observance, 3, 39–40, 64, 69–70, 89, 95, 106
Samis Foundation, x, 2, 5, 179, 181, 182, 183–85
in San Francisco, *30*
seasons of his life, 171–73
Seattle homes, 29, 61, 154
solitary nature, 1, 3, 73, 117
timeline, 197–201
US citizenship, 39, 43, *44*
Israel, Sarah (niece, David's daughter), 24, 29, 38, *41*, 48, 56, 60, 72–73
Israel, Sarah (niece, Jack's daughter), 24, *41*
Israel, Sarota (Sarah) Biton (mother), *37*
brother's keeper, 35–36
birth, 15
character traits, 36
children, 15, 24–25
as *curandera*, 37
death, 66
emigration to US, 8, 28, 31
family background, 15
family portraits, *6*, *14*, *41*
language skills, 36–37
later life, 62, 66, *66*
Seattle homes, 29, 61
Soap Lake, 44
Israel, Shirley (niece), 25
Israel, Solomon (nephew), 24
Israel, Violet (Violet Hasson), 25, *42*, 44, *104*
Israel, Yecoutiel/Morris (brother)
birth and childhood, *6*, 13, *14*, 15, 25, 92
death date, 25
emigration to US, 8, 21, 27
family gatherings, *41*, *104*
marriage and children, 25, 40, *41*, *42*

Orpheum Shoe Repair Shop, 32, 34, 35
religious observance, 39–40
Sam Israel's immigration, 28
Seattle employment, 31
Soap Lake, 43–44, 66, 92, *93*
Israel, Yitzhak (Isaac) (father), *37*
brother's keeper, 32
character traits, 36
children, 15, 24–25
death, 62
emigration to US, 8, 28, 31
finances, 112
Israel Brothers Shoe Repair, 32
later life, 62
life in Rhodes, *6*, 12–13, *14*, 19
Seattle homes, 29–30, 61
Israel, Yitzhak (nephew), 25
Israel Brothers Shoe Repair (Rotary Shoe Repair), 32–33, 34, 36
Israeli Air Force (IAF), 144–45

Jericho, 144, 193
Jewish Action, 188
Jewish Television Institute, 103
Jonas Brothers Taxidermy, 156
Jones, Mrs., 154
Justen, William, 185–86, 187, 189, 224n16

K2 expedition, 108–9, 217n8
kaddish, 106, 216n1
Kahal Kadosh Shalom Synagogue, Rhodes, Greece, 11, 101, 174, *174*
Kanter, Connie, 5, *186*, 189
King County, 71–72, 194, 202–5
Kline Galland Home, 108, *108*, 110, 121, 155, 158–60, 163
Kucera, Greg, 118–20

Lake Lenore, 138
Leary Way House, 51, 203
Leclezio, Louis, 159–61, 179
Leshem, Yossi, 144–45, *192*, 193, 225n21
Levy, Hortense, *42*
Levy, Ike, *30*
Levy, Isaac, *42*
Levy, Sarah, *42*
Levy, Rabbi Yamin, 163, 164
Lipson, Joanne, *166*
litigation
Blue and White Building, 143
Dick Tall affair, 123–25
eastern Washington, 134–35
Gatewood Hotel, 126–33
property holdings, 71–72
Seattle Metro, 154

Little, Shannon (Michele Hasson's daughter), 92, *96*
Longeway, Peggy, 189

Maimon, Al, *viii, 178,* 179, 185, *186,* 189, 207
Maimon, Jeanne, *178*
Maimon, Rabbi Solomon, 110, 163, 167, 168
Mariuch (dog), 38, 73, *73, 83,* 129
Marlowe, Wendy B., 160
Marta, James, 149
McAllister, Lynn, 121
McNamara, Caleb, *148*
McNamara, Tim, 146, *148*
McWhirter, Grace, 71
memory, ix, x, xi, 174
Menzel Lake, 71, 76, 204
Mercer Island
    Dick Tall affair, 123–25
    Leclezio affair, 159–61
    Sam Israel's house, *45,* 45–47, *46,* 50, 53, 67, 156
    Sam Israel's property purchases, 34, 202
Meyers, Rabbi Ron-Ami, *186,* 207
Michel, Cliff, 121
Morehouse, Bonnie Holt, 139
Morehouse, Keith, 139
Moses Lake, 133, 134
Mottman Building, *181,* 204
Muckleston, J. M., 160
Mundlak, Yair, 100
Mussolini, Benito, 64
Myers, James, 180–81

Netzer, Ehud, 144, *192,* 193
Neuman, Judy, *186,* 207
Nopson, Kathy, 139–40
Normand, Eugene, 110–12

Orpheum Shoe Repair Shop, 32, 34
our brother's keeper
    headstone, *167,* 167–68
    Robert Hasson on, 38
    Sam Israel as, 172–73, 193
    Sam Israel on, 139, 168, 182
    Samis Foundation, 182, 193
    Sarota (Sarah) Israel on, 35–36
    Yitzhak (Isaac) Israel on, 32

Pacific Northwest Magazine, *5*
Pappas, John, 139
Paramount Building, 35, *35,* 50, 61, 71–72, 202
Paramount Pictures Distributing Company, 35
Parrot, Del and Sheryl, 157
Passover, 38, 95
Patria, SS, *18,* 27
Patrick, Jack, 84, 133–34, 139, 155, 165
Pesach, 64, 165–66, 168

Pesaro, SS, 28
Photographic Society of America, 69, 79
photography (Sam Israel's)
    Destitute, 68–69, *69,* 79, 214n34
    Doldrums, 78
    equipment, 4, 68, 156
    exhibitions, *63, 68,* 68–69, *69,* 78–79
    Grant County, 139
    Israel, 100
    Morris and Gentil's wedding, 40, *42*
    Rhodes, 101, 102
    Second Bacon Siphon and Tunnel, 134–35
    Soap Lake, 89
    studio, 67–68
    Trawler's Nest, 79
    Western, 68, 79
    White Russian, 79
Piha, Morris "Morrie," *viii,* 132, 183–84, 185, 189
Piha, Samuel and Vida, 183
Pike Place Market, 28, 132
Pike Place Market Preservation and Development Authority, 133
Pinnacle Peak, 42
Pioneer Square Preservation District, 76–77
Pioneer Square (Skid Road), 60, 113, 117–21, 187
Plymouth Congregational Church, 132–33
Policar, Jacob, 28
Pollock, Scott, 158
property holdings
    1919–1940 acquisitions, 50–51
    1941–1947 acquisitions, *59,* 59–60
    1941–1960 acquisitions, 76–77
    1950s, 70–72
    1961–1994 acquisitions, 150–51
    1994 summary, 194
    absentee landlord, 1, 128–29, 187
    eastern Washington, 133–35, 194
    Great Depression, 35
    historic preservation, 1, 117, 187
    inventory, 185
    litigation 71–72
    number of, 1, 134
    philosophy and practice, 32–33, 60, 112–23, 129
    real estate brokers, 33–34, 133–34
    Samis Land Company, 60–61
    Seattle, 2, 112, 150–51, 187, 194
    tax liability, 72
    value, 1, 59, 134
    Washington State, 2, 112–13
Pruzan, Lucy, *viii,* 183, 185, *186,* 207
Purdy Company, 135–37, 140

Qualtrics Tower, 122
Quincy-Columbia Basin Irrigation Project, 134–35

Rainier, Mount, xii, 42
real estate. *See* property holdings
remembering, ix, x, xi, 174
Rhodes, Greece, 6–23
    Acropolis, 85, 101
    anti-Semitism and persecution, 11, 64
    emigration, 7–8, 19–23
    family and growing up, 2, *6*, 9–19
    Holocaust, 64–66, 102, 174
    Italian rule, 13, 18–19, 64
    Sam Israel's visit, 100, 101–2, *102*
    Sephardim, 8–12, *10, 12*, 15, 19–20
    Victor Hasson's visit, 173–74
Rice, Constance, 167
Rice, Norm, 167
Roer, Greg, *186,* 207
Romary, Marina, 139, 146–48, 165, *165*
Roosevelt, Franklin D., 53, 54
Ross, Lesli Koppelman, xi
Rotary Shoe Repair (Israel Brothers Shoe Repair), 32–33, 34, 36

Sadis, Stephen, xii
Sahalie Ski Club, 43
Sails of Hope (Wiesenthal), 103
Samis Foundation, 178–93
    archaeology projects, 144
    archives, xii
    Board of Trustees, vii–viii, *viii,* 99, 121, *178,* 179, 180, 181–85, *186,* 189, 206–7
    brochure, 177
    committees, 189–90
    creation, 2, 5, 102, 107
    early years, 179–81, 185-88
    evolution, 189–90
    focus areas and priorities, 2, 107, 112, 155, 187–88, 190–93, 196
    funding of, 108, 187
    Galland Building, 122
    Gatewood Hotel, 132
    grants awarded, 187–88, 195–96
    incorporation, 181
    Kahal Shalom Synagogue prayer books, 174, *174*
    Mercer Island property, 161
    philanthropy dollars, ix
    praise for, 168
    property management, 185, 186–87
    Sam Israel's vision for, 106–8
    Seattle Metro litigation, 154
    staff, 185–86, *186,* 189
Samis Hereford Ranch, 86–89, *87, 88*
Samis Land Company, xii, 60-61, 71–72, 113, 124-25, 179-80, 185–86
Scheib, Duane, 85–86, 140
Schwabacher Building, *190,* 203

Scientific Building, 59, *59*, 76, 203
Seattle
    historic preservation, 1, 117
    Jewish cemetery (proposed), 155–56
    Sam Israel's philanthropy, 108–11
    Sam Israel's property holdings, 1, 2, 150–51, 194
    Samis Foundation grants, 190–91
    Sephardic community, 21, 27–30
    shoemaking, *26,* 26–49
Seattle Art Museum, 69, 78, 214n34
Seattle Center Pavilion, 165, *165*
Seattle Hebrew Academy (SHA), 108, 109, 166–67, 180, 182, 188
Seattle International Exhibition of Photography, *68,* 68–69, 78
Seattle Photographic Society, 68, 78
Seattle Youth Symphony Orchestra, 63
Second Bacon Siphon and Tunnel, 134–35
Sefer Torah, 161–64, *162, 164*
Selig, Martin, *viii,* 184–85, 189
Sephardic Adventure Camp (SAC), 110–12, 180, 191
Sephardic Bikur Holim (SBH), 110–12, 180, 183
Sephardic Brotherhood Cemetery, 166
Sephardim
    Rhodes, 8–12, *10, 12,* 15, 19–20
    Seattle, 21, 27–30
Service, Robert W., 67, 214n33
Shelter from the Storm (documentary film), 128–32
Sherman, Ernie, *viii,* 132, 183, *186,* 207
shoemaking
    apprenticeship, 17–18
    quality control, 56
    in Seattle, *26,* 31–36, *34,* 58, 61
    US Army contract, 2, 34, 49, 54–61
Skanska USA, 122
Skid Road. *See* Pioneer Square
Smith Tower, 187
Snohomish County property holdings, 202–5
Soap Lake
    Camp Israel, 146, *146*
    Grand Coulee Cavalcade, 73
    Greek Festival, *147,* 147–48, *148,* 165, *165*
    healing waters, 12, 43–44, 81–82
    public opinion about Sam Israel, 3, 138–40
    Sam Israel on beach, *48*
    Sam Israel's Acropolis, 84–85
    Sam Israel's philanthropy, 5, 73
    Sam Israel's photography, 89
    Sam Israel's property acquisitions, 61, 73, 133, 134, 194
Soap Lake farm, 72–75, *91, 92, 170*
    Acropolis, 84–85

animals, 74–75, 82
archaeology, 143–44
bunkhouse, 82–83, *175*, 184
disposition of goods, 156–58
Hasson home, 83, *83*
hunting, 70
improvements, 74–75, 82
irrigation issues, 134–35
ledger, 74–75, *75*
move to, 2, 74, 75
Samis Hereford Ranch, 86–89, *87, 88*
vehicles and equipment, 83–84, *176*
visitors, 84, 91–99, *93, 94, 95, 96, 97*
workers, 74–75, 85–86
Soap Lake High School, 149
Society for the Protection of Nature in Israel (SPNI), 144–45, 188, 192
Stetson-Ross Plant, 124–25, 151, 205
Stoneway Garage, 50, 203
Stroum, Sam, 184
Stroum Jewish Community Center (JCC), 184, 191
Sullivan, Linda, *186*, 189
Sytman, Alex, *viii*, 154, 155, 182, *186*, 207
Sytman, Leatrice "Lucy" Israel, *xiii*, 182
Sytman, Nissim, xiii

Tall, Leonard, 123
Tall, Richard "Dick," 123–25
Tarshis, Sam, *108*
taxes, xii, 2, 72, 126–27
Telephone Building, 67–68, 76, 121, 150, 203
television interview, 128–32
Terry Denny Building, 77, 187, *188*, 204
Toobert, Michael, 159, 160, 163, *164*, 165, *166*
Toren, Rabbi Rob, *178*, 186, 188, 189, 224n16
Trawler's Nest (Sam Israel photograph), 79
Treiger, Irwin
  Leclezio affair, 160
  Sam Israel, 108, 168
  Samis Foundation, *viii*, 107, 179, 181–82, 183, 185, 207
  Samis Land Company, 124–25, 154
Treiger, Louis, *186*
Tresi, Jim, 180
2+U complex, 122

Union Trust Building, 117
United Jewish Appeal, 103, 180
United Methodist Church, 139
United Shoe Repairing Machines Company, 34, 61
US Bureau of Reclamation, 134–35
US Rubber Building, 59, *59*, 76, 203

Victoria International Salon of Photography, *63*, 78

Wadi Qelt Synagogue, 193
Warner, Tracy, 138
Warshal, Sam, 43
Washington Mutual Bank, 121–22
Washington Shoe Building, 76, 114, *114*, 187, 204
Washington State Department of Fish and Game, *137*, 137–38, 185
Waterfront Streetcar, 117
Webster-Brinkley plant, 59–60, 76, 187, 203
Western Life Insurance Company, 71–72
Western (Sam Israel photograph), *68*, 79
wetlands preservation, 137–38
White Russian (Sam Israel photograph), 79
Whittaker, Jim, 109, 217n8
Wiesel, Elie, x, 177
Wiesenthal, Simon, 103
wildlife philanthropy, 143–45
Wilmar, Diana, 128
Wingfoot Shoe Repair, *26, 34, 34,* 36, 58, 61, 114
Wolf, Hank, *108*
Wolf, Nancy, 139
World War II
  Bona Hasson's war effort, 63
  boot repair contract, 2, 34, 49, 54–61
  Holocaust, xi, 64–66, 102, 174
  preparedness, 49, 53–54
Wright Runstad & Company, 121–22

Yesler Building, *52*, 76, 203
YMCA, xii, 42
Yocom, Larry, 120

Zoberblatt, Benjamin, 32

ABOUT THE AUTHOR

Richard S. Hobbs is Senior Consulting Archivist and Historian with The Winthrop Group, Inc. He is based in the Seattle area and brings to clients more than twenty years of experience as a historian, archivist, and records/information manager. He has created digital archives and provided archives and records management services to corporations, family-owned businesses, nonprofits, state and local governments, the University of Washington, and the Government of Bahrain. Among his publications are magazine and newspaper articles, poetry, and six history books, including *The Cayton Legacy: An African American Family*; *The Broughtons of Dayton: Family & Business in the Northwest Heartland*; *Charles J. Broughton: Letters to Family, 1873-1919* (ed.); *Frontier Bank: The First 25 Years* (with Robert J. Dickson); *Catastrophe to Triumph: Bridges of the Tacoma Narrows*; and *Spanning Washington: Historic Highway Bridges of the Evergreen State* (with Craig Holstine). The website he wrote on the Tacoma Narrows Bridges history for Washington State's Department of Transportation won awards in 2004 and 2005. Richard Hobbs holds a Certificate in Archives & Records Administration from Western Washington University, an MA in History from Washington State University, and a PhD in History from the University of Washington.

CPSIA information can be obtained
at www.ICGtesting.com
Printed in the USA
LVHW071535060222
710401LV00005B/32